THE
transforming
HABITS OF A
growing
CHRISTIAN

THE
transforming
HABITS OF A
growing
CHRISTIAN

WILLIAM D. WATKINS

BETHANYHOUSE
Minneapolis, Minnesota

Published by Bethany House Publishers
11400 Hampshire Avenue South
Bloomington, Minnesota 55438
www.bethanyhouse.com

Bethany House Publishers is a Division of
Baker Book House Company, Grand Rapids, Michigan.

Printed in the United States of America

Library of Congress Cataloging-in-Publication Data

Watkins, William D.
    The transforming habits of a growing Christian : a compelling call to spiritual growth / by William D. Watkins.
        p.   cm.
    Includes bibliographical references.
    ISBN 0-7642-2635-5 (pbk.)
    1. Spiritual life—Christianity. I. Title.

    BV4501.3.W38   2004
    248.4—dc22   2004005569

To my mom,
who loved God before I did,
and whose love of him and of me
played a critical role in leading me
to embrace the One who loved me
even before she did.

WILLIAM D. WATKINS has written dozens of articles and essays as well as several Bible study guides and books, including *The New Absolutes*. A conference speaker nationwide, he teaches world history, logic, and Christian discipleship at Rocky Mountain Christian Academy. Bill has taught Sunday school since the mid-1970s and served as a mini-pastor and deacon. He has degrees in philosophy (California State University at Fresno) and theology (Dallas Theological Seminary). Bill and his wife, Donna Rae, make their home in Colorado.

Acknowledgments

No book is the product of one solitary mind, no matter how creative the author may be. Writers have support from family, friends, other writers, editors, publishers, past and present teachers, and a host of others who have built into their lives as well as encouraged and sharpened their craft. I am no exception, so here I would like to single out those who especially supported me during the writing of this book.

First, to Donna Rae, who loves me well, and who urged me on gently, gave me many useful suggestions for improving the text, heard my passion for this book, and kept me focused so I could complete it.

Second, to Rick Ebbers, who gave me his friendship, his prayers, and his assessment of numerous chapters, even in the midst of handling his own demanding schedule.

Third, to Steve Laube, my friend and first editor at Bethany House, who initially believed in this project and never stopped believing in it, even when the deadline had to be stretched to accommodate a huge paradigm shift that came to me in the midst of the writing.

Fourth, to Julie Smith and Christopher Soderstrom, the editors of this work, who stepped in on the editorial side and did a fine job improving the book.

Fifth, to all the fine people at Bethany House, who have been this author's dream team.

Sixth, to the other reviewers of this book—Brian and Tonia Manzanares, as well as Kim and Robb Novak, Todd Borger, and Jim Mitchell—who offered me their comments and thereby enriched the book you now hold in your hands.

Seventh, and most important, to the God who pursued me and never fails to love me. May he bless this written effort in all the ways only he can.

Contents

PART I

THE *most* EXCELLENT WAY

1. The *Most* Important Answer

What would you say is the essence of the Christian life? By that I mean, if you took away all the extras that get attached to it, what necessary thing would remain? What is this life's heart and soul?

Since my conversion many years ago, few questions have been harder for me to answer. Nevertheless, how can we live the Christian life unless we know what it really is? We cannot live what we do not know. *What, then, is the ultimate meaning of the Christian life?*

Obeying the commands of Christ?

Sharing the gospel of Christ?

Relating personally with God through Christ?

Meeting the needs of others on behalf of Christ?

Attending church in worship of Christ?

Giving money to further the work of Christ?

Reading the Bible to learn about Christ?

Honoring leaders in deference to Christ?

Your answer will markedly shape and define your life.

If your answer is "obedience," you will focus on God's commands, ordering your life around them, legalistically judging yourself and others according to how proficiently or how poorly the life of obedience is being lived.

If your answer is "evangelism," you might spend your days and nights telling everyone the salvation message while probably neglecting the deeper truths and applications of the faith.

If your answer is "my personal relationship with God," it will be difficult for you either to reach out to the unsaved or to use your spiritual gifts to equip and encourage the body of Christ. After all, you will tend to see Christianity as essentially about *your* relationship with God, not as much about someone else's connection with him.

If your answer is "serving the needs of others," you are likely to expend your own resources to the point of collapsing from exhaustion, crushed under the weight of doing good, instead of becoming good.

All of the above answers run into similar problems. They are not big enough, rich enough, or full enough to capture the heart and soul of the Christian life. Something much more comprehensive, something far grander is required.

Fortunately, we do not have to guess at the answer: The ultimate meaning is found in the life of Jesus himself, for he lived it out and gave it to us during his earthly ministry. The answer is simple and straight, yet profound and boundless: *Love.* Jesus explained this to his twelve closest disciples:

> Just as the Father has loved Me, I have also loved you; abide in My love. If you keep My commandments, you will abide in My love; just as I have kept My Father's commandments and abide in His love. . . . This is My commandment, that you love one another, just as I have loved you. (John 15:9–10, 12 NASB)

The Father's love comes to us through the Son, and it's the Son who calls on us to receive his love and pass it along to others. In short, *the essence of the life to which Christians are called through Jesus Christ is the life of love.*

This answer, love, is the "most excellent way" described by the apostle Paul (1 Cor. 12:31ff.). It is the only answer with sufficient vastness to encapsulate our calling. In fact, this answer is so enormous that it describes God himself. As we'll see, this answer is also the key to understanding and applying the habits that the Spirit uses to conform us to Christ and to transform us into his likeness.

In fact, love is the most important answer, the most comprehensive answer, to the most significant questions asked by both believers and unbelievers:

Why are we here? Love.

How did we get here? Love.

What are we supposed to do here? Love.

Why do we have significance? Love.

Love—true love—is absolutely necessary to *all* life.

Accordingly, this book is about the Christian life as a life of love: what it is, what it looks like, where it comes from, how it can be obtained and cultivated, and how it can change us and those around us forever.

LIVING THE LIFE OF LOVE

But *how* does love bring about remarkable and all-encompassing change in our lives?

Seeking the answer to that question has revolutionized my life. It's an answer that has taken me much of my Christian life to discover, understand, and embrace. It's an answer that has simplified my life as it has liberated and empowered it. It's an answer that involves truths grounded in the Bible and worked out in the church's experience with the Lord. At the same time, the answer includes a different understanding of what's traditionally known as the spiritual disciplines—disciplines such as prayer, study, meditation, service, and the like.

What I discovered is that the spiritual disciplines are more than a training program for running the spiritual race . . . more than preparations for fighting the spiritual war . . . more than activities we should do out of faithful obedience to God's commands. While these understandings are biblical and worthwhile, they fail to capture the fullness of the disciplines and the life they are to help bring about. Rather, I have come to see that the spiritual disciplines are best understood through the grander vision of love. Love is the paradigm of paradigms, the very essence of the Christian life. And the spiritual disciplines, when seen through love, are the habits believing lovers should foster to help deepen and enrich their love relationship with God.

The spiritual disciplines are the habits of love. As we'll see, they even have parallels to the ways we develop relationships with our human loves. Through those habits, the Divine Lover works within us to make us into the beloveds he created us to be.

This is not some mushy, mystical approach to the Christian life. Far from it. I've found that it is as realistic as it is rewarding, as challenging as it is comforting, as humanly impossible as it is divinely prescribed and co-accomplished. It is nothing less than the fullness of Christ's life lived in and through us.

To see this, we must begin where love does—with God. He is love itself, and the life he calls us to live begins and ends with his love for us. This is the life that the apostle Paul calls "the most excellent way" (1 Cor. 12:31).

2. The *Supreme* Source

God is love.

These are not the words of some hopeless romantic, wide-eyed poet, syrupy lyricist, or liberal theologian. These words are found in Holy Writ, penned by John, the disciple beloved by Jesus.[1] In his first letter, John tells us that "God is love" (4:8) and that "love comes from God" (4:7).

John should know. He saw deity clothed in human flesh. He walked the roads of the Holy Land with the Son of God. He shared meals with the Messiah. He heard Jesus teach, watched him heal the sick and demon-possessed. He witnessed the restoration of Peter's mother-in-law and the resurrection of Jairus's daughter.

John saw Jesus transfigured and declared by God the Father to be his beloved Son. He listened as Jesus predicted the destruction of Jerusalem. He was sent to help Peter prepare for the last Passover celebration of the First Coming. He was there for Jesus' prayerful agony in Gethsemane, his treacherous betrayal by Judas, and his interrogation before the Sanhedrin.

John was the only disciple present at the Crucifixion, where Jesus appointed him to care for his mother, Mary. He was one of the first disciples to hear about the empty tomb and the first to check it out for himself; he identified Jesus in his resurrected state. He knew firsthand that Jesus was God incarnate, the divine Word who took on a human nature "and made his dwelling among us" (John 1:14). If anyone knew God's nature, John did, and he said that God is love and love comes from God.

But what does it mean that God is love? What is love, anyway?

LOVE, LOVE, LOVE

Scripture never gives a definition of love; it never tells us exactly what love is. Not even the famous 1 Corinthians 13 *defines love*. Instead, Paul and the rest of the biblical writers *describe what love does*. We're told how love behaves, what it looks like through its activities. What we learn from the descriptions is that love is the strongest force before, in, and after the universe.

Not just any kind of love is this powerful. In koine ("common") Greek, the language of the New Testament, there were four words for *love*. However, the New Testament writers used just two of these words to describe *divine* love, and among these two, only one of them is supernatural through and through. Before we consider that supernatural love in detail, we'll work up to it by briefly looking at the other three, all of which are natural loves—that is, we routinely find them in us and around us.

The Greek word *stergō* means to "feel affection." This term and its derivatives cover any kind of *feeling* love: the affection expressed between parents and children, the love people have for a political leader, the love a dog has for his master, the affection a child has for her favorite doll or blanket. This word for *love* never appears in the New Testament, except in the negative compound *astorgos,* meaning "heartless" or "without natural affection," and in the positive compound *philostorgos,* which means "brotherly love" or "loving dearly."[2]

The second Greek term is *phileō;* its basic meaning is "the attraction of people to one another who are close together both inside and outside the family; it includes concern, care, and hospitality, also love for things in the sense of being fond of." Words that come from *phileō* show this primary meaning: *philos,* "a friend"; *philēma,* "a kiss"; and compound words such as *philosophia,* "love of knowledge," and *philadelphia,* "brotherly love."[3] *Phileō* and its derivatives commonly appear in the New Testament, often in regard to friendship, including when Jesus calls the disciples his friends.[4] The word is also used to describe the Father's love for his Son and our love for the Lord.[5]

The third Greek term, *erōs,* refers to the sensual or sexual love between the genders, including marital sexual love. *Erōs* "embraces longing, craving and desire." While the ancient Greeks had a god named Eros, this word never appears in the New Testament, not even in any compound form.[6]

The fourth Greek term will command our greatest attention—this is the word for *love* most frequently found in the New Testament. The root (noun) is *agapē,* which speaks of divine love and how we're to apply it to the totality of life. This word originally meant "to honor or welcome"; it was actually the most generic word for *love* in the Greek language. When the New Testament writers used *agapē,* however, it became pregnant with reference to the highest form of love—the love that God is by nature, the love shared within the Trinity, the love God gives to us, and the love we are to have for him and for all else he loves. This is the supernatural love that Paul describes and praises in 1 Corinthians 13. We cannot whip it up on our own; *this love comes from God alone.* Consider what Paul says about *agapē.*

Patient

"Love is patient" (v. 4). The Greek word translated *patient* means long-suffering, "slow to anger, slow to take offense or to inflict punishment," the opposite of being quick- or short-tempered.[7]

Undoubtedly, the most patient figure in Scripture is God. Over and over he reaches out to the Hebrews, even though they consistently complain, disobey, and run after false gods. At one point Moses even refers to them as "a stiff-necked people" (Deut. 9:6). Centuries later the Lord would say, "All day long I have held out my hands to an obstinate people, who walk in ways not good, pursuing their own imaginations—a people who continually provoke me to my very face" (Isa. 65:2–3). In Paul's day, Jesus, overlooking the Holy City, would lament, "O Jerusalem, Jerusalem, you who kill the prophets and stone those sent to you, how often I have longed to gather your children together, as a hen gathers her chicks under her wings, but you were not willing" (Matt. 23:37).

God endures human rebellion, patiently loving those who shake a fist in his face, despising and defying him. Why? The apostle Peter tells us: "He is patient with you, not wanting anyone to perish, but everyone to come to repentance" (2 Peter 3:9). The Lord wants all of us to know and enjoy his *agapē* forever, so he endures our sin and woos us with the gracious offer of complete forgiveness and full redemption through faith in his Son, Jesus Christ:

> For God so loved the world that he gave his one and only Son, that whoever believes in him shall not perish but have eternal life. For God did not send his Son into the world to condemn the world [even though that's all we deserved], but to save the world through him. (John 3:16–17)

Now, *that* is longsuffering love.

I received my first tangible awareness of the power of patient love while growing up. My Christian parents exercised tremendous patience toward me, helping me with schoolwork assignments, drilling me daily on math, preparing me for exams, and teaching me how to write reports of all kinds. They suffered through countless hours of trombone and percussion practice, putting up with grating squeaks and missed notes, with clanging cymbals and vibrating drumheads. When I'd get frustrated with slow progress and stomp off in anger, I'd find consoling arms and words of support. Even when I was ready to give up on myself, they never would, and they refused to let me experience defeat at my own hand. What they so consistently showed me was a wonderful foretaste of the longsuffering love I finally came to know in my heavenly Father.

Kind

"Love is kind," reveals Paul (1 Cor. 13:4). *Agapē* does what is good, and when it comes to God, that goodness is superabundant, as the Psalms say: "His lovingkindness is great toward us" (117:2 NASB), and "as high as the heavens are above the earth, so great is His lovingkindness toward those who fear Him" (103:11 NASB). While those who love God receive the blessings of his kindness without measure, the Lord pours out kindness on believers and unbelievers alike: "He has shown kindness by giving you rain from heaven and crops in their seasons; he provides you with plenty of food and fills your hearts with joy" (Acts 14:17). I like the way Phillip Keller described God's kindness and the ways he experienced it in his own life:

> It is the kindness of God expressed in Christ and revealed to us by His Spirit that supplies my salvation. His kindness makes provision for my pardon from sins and selfishness at the cost of His own laid-down life. It is His kindness that forgives my faults and accepts me into His

family as His dearly beloved child. His kindness enables me to stand acquitted of my wrongdoing, justified freely in His presence. God's kindness removes my guilt, and I am at one with Him and others in peace. It is the kindness of God that enables Him to share Himself with me in the inner sanctuary of my spirit, soul, and body. His kindness enables me to be remade, refashioned, reformed gently into His likeness. His kindness gives enormous meaning and dignity to this life and endless delight in the life yet to come.[8]

God's goodness is showered upon us in countless ways, even when we're "ungrateful and wicked" (Luke 6:35). Yes, love is kind.

Not Envious

After revealing two positive behaviors of *agapē,* Paul begins to tell us what love does *not* do. Envy is the first negative (1 Cor. 13:4).

Envy is sorrow over another person's good—a spouse, a church, a well-behaved or successful child, a job promotion, a new car, even an answered prayer. Whatever the good may be, envy says, "I hate you for having that in your life." Envy looks down on others for having something it lacks yet wants.

God has no envy and cannot be envious; no one has any good that God lacks. In fact, he is the Source of all the goodness we enjoy. We need him, while he doesn't need us. Paul makes this crystal clear:

> The God who made the world and everything in it is the Lord of heaven and earth and does not live in temples built by hands. And he is not served by human hands, as if he needed anything, because he himself gives all men life and breath and everything else. . . . "For in him we live and move and have our being" (Acts 17:24–25, 28).

As for what God has, he does not hoard but freely and profusely shares with us. He shares his creative abilities by giving us the power to procreate and to invent. He shares his sovereignty by giving us the authority to exercise limited control over the earth. He created us as his image-bearers, giving us finite versions of certain divine attributes (e.g., reason, free will, virtue) and a social structure as male and female that reflects his unity as Father, Son, and Spirit.[9] He sets us in a world fine-tuned for the enjoyment of optimal life.[10] God is not the Cosmic Hoarder but the Boundless Giver. From his infinite goodness he pours out his love, even sacrificing the Son's life for our benefit. "God demonstrates his own love for us in this: While we were still sinners, Christ died for us" (Rom. 5:8).

Agapē is definitely not envious. Just the opposite, in fact, for *agapē* needs nothing. Its very nature is to give itself away.

Not Boastful

Agapē "does not boast" (1 Cor. 13:4). Love doesn't seek admiration, attention, and applause from others. It doesn't point to itself and say, "Hey, look at me! Aren't I wonderful?" Love simply goes about doing good for others.[11]

The contrast between boasting and loving is clearly seen in Christ's teaching about the differences between hypocritical routine and authentic devotion. The boastful practice their "'acts of righteousness' before men, to be seen by them," grandly announcing their giving so they will be "honored by men." They love to pray in front of others to be noticed and admired; their actions are all for show, to win praise for their false piety. *Agapē*, though, gives without recognition from the public eye. *Agapē* fervently prays without any display. Boasters receive an earthly reward without eternal blessing, while lovers are rewarded from the hands of their heavenly Father.[12] Lovers reflect God; boasters radiate sinfulness.

Not Proud

Love does not engage in pride (1 Cor. 13:4). Pride, the greatest evil, the root of all others, was Lucifer's original sin.[13] Pride is *self*-exaltation over *God*-exaltation. Pride says, "I want it my way" rather than "I want it God's way." Pride puts self above everyone and everything else. Pride declares that the greatest commandment is to love one's self (not God) with all one's heart, soul, strength, and mind. "Pride," as Peter Kreeft tells us, "is willful arrogance, arrogating to yourself what is really God's. . . . Pride is essentially a lust for power,"[14] a competition over what does not belong to the one claiming it.

God's love is not prideful. God is unlimited in all that he is;[15] he lacks nothing good, and everything he is, he is infinitely. Thus he has no need to lust after anything, since he lacks nothing of any value (including power), and he competes for nothing because he is the only God.[16] We may foolishly strive to become gods, but God has no need to become human. God the Son chose to take on a human nature not for his sake but for ours.[17] We needed the Son to become like us, which he did out of his love for us and for his Father. God lavishes himself on us because he loves us and we need him.

In fact, the opposite of pride is *humility*. Where pride seeks to exalt self over others, humility seeks to serve others over self. Pride is self-obsessed; humility is other-focused. Pride plays power games to enrich self; humility surrenders power to enrich others. Pride is delusional, fantasizing that self is greater than it really is; humility is realistic, seeing self accurately. Pride thinks of self rather than others; humility thinks less about self, clearing the way to better serve others. Satan is pride incarnate; Christ is humility incarnate. Satan is bent on serving himself at the expense of everyone else, whereas Christ came to serve others at his own expense. God's *agapē* is humble love, and he sent us his Son, who came "not . . . to be served, but to serve, and to give his life as a ransom for many" (Matt. 20:28).

As clear as this message is in the New Testament, I'm amazed at how many people see God as the Cosmic Dictator determined to force us into submission. The first time I encountered this perspective was many years ago when I spoke with a teenager who claimed he had numerous intellectual objections against Christianity. I asked him if he was open to discussing them, and he agreed.

"All right then," I replied. "Give me your first objection, and I'll try to answer it. Once I've answered it to your satisfaction, we'll move on to your next objection and deal with it until you voice your satisfaction with my answer. We'll keep going until we've worked through all your objections. Okay?"

"Yeah, that sounds fine." He seemed skeptical and nervous. As for skepticism, he'd posed his objections to many Christians and usually received superficial answers; perhaps he pridefully thought I'd be no different. On the other hand, his nervousness seemed to indicate doubt as to what he'd do if I did manage to answer his objections, which was my determined intention.

He tossed out the first one; I answered, and he said my response satisfied him. So we moved on to the second objection, then the third and the fourth. The process continued through thirteen objections; however, after he accepted my answer to that final criticism, he jumped back to his very first objection and posed it as if we hadn't already examined it.

"Wait a minute," I countered. "I answered that almost two hours ago, and you said you were happy with my answer. What's going on? Why are you bringing it up again?"

He looked down at the floor, not saying a word for a minute or so. When he finally met my eyes again, his face was the most defiant I'd seen during our entire discussion. "I'll tell you why," he began. "I don't want to accept Christ as my Savior or as my anything else. I know that when I do, he'll want control over my life, and I don't want anyone controlling my life except me." As his eyes bore into me, I saw anger, fear, pride, and determination.

"So you want to be the captain of your own soul?" I asked.

"I *am* the captain—and the whole crew. I run my life, and no one else, not even God, will run it for me." His eyes burned as he spoke.

He believed that once he was in God's grip, he would be ruled with an iron fist, and he was adamant that he would not give in to such a tyrant—he would fight to the bitter end.

"You have God all wrong," I replied. "He doesn't want to run your life for you. He wants to change your life, to give you every good thing to overflowing. He wants to serve you, to empower you to become all he created you to be."

"I don't buy it." His wall of defense was high and defiant.

After some silence on my end, I spoke up one more time. "You've convinced yourself that God is out to control you, to force you to do what he wants you to do, which isn't true. But so be it. Just do me one favor." I paused, waiting for him to answer.

"What's that?" he finally ventured.

"Don't tell people you reject Christianity because you have intellectual objections against it. I gave you good answers to your objections, and you accepted every one of them. So from now on, be intellectually honest and tell people the truth. Tell them that you won't accept Christ because you want to be in complete control of your life. Okay?"

"Sure, I'll do that."

———

Three years after our talk, I received a phone call from his mother. It had been about two years since I'd seen her (I'd moved to another state), but I had not forgotten about her son. After we got caught up with each other, she told me that he had recently accepted Christ as his Savior.

"Really? How did it happen? What changed his mind?" (I was stunned.)

"Well, he told me that the conversation you'd had with him that night kept dogging him. He couldn't get it out of his mind no matter how hard he tried. And no matter how hard he tried to control his own life, it kept spiraling more and more out of control. He was miserable. So he finally decided that he couldn't run his own life. He needed help. That's when he turned his life over to Christ. Bill, I haven't seen him this happy since he was a little boy. He's in love with God, and he knows God loves him too."

Divine love is not proud; instead, it's humble enough to reach out to us, even in the midst of our prideful pursuit for complete control. Love will pick us up from our lowest debasement and raise us up into its waiting arms.

Not Rude

Love "is not rude," says Paul (1 Cor. 13:5). *Agapē* never behaves shamefully or in an unbecoming way. Love has manners. It's respectful and observes appropriate decorum.

Lewis Smedes points out that rudeness is a form of arrogance.

> The rude person is the one who is so hell-bent on staying upright that in his anxiety he cuts and bruises anyone who threatens him, even as he uses anyone who can help him. . . . Arrogance drives us to be rude to people who have nothing to offer us, nothing to help us look good, while we use the devious tactics of boasting on those who have something to offer. . . . What I can get out of you determines what I will give you. If you have nothing to offer, I can be rude to you.[18]

God's love is never rude; *agapē* does good to others for their sake alone. Because God lacks nothing, he can give and give and give, then give some more, without requiring anything from us to help him look good or to fill up some need of his own. And God gives respectfully—he honors us as persons, letting us use our divinely bestowed freedom to choose how we will respond to him. Of course, God is free to respond to our choices as he sees fit, which is always in accordance with his all-good nature. Out of *agapē*, he suffers our rudeness without responding in kind. He endures our bad choices as he patiently waits for us to come to our senses and return to him. When we do, rather than hearing "I told you so," we'll hear him call for a celebration because we are no longer lost but found, no longer dead but alive.[19]

Love is respectful and courteous, not rude or inconsiderate.

Not Self-Seeking

Agapē is other-centered, not self-centered (1 Cor. 13:5). Jesus said, "I am among you as the one who serves" (Luke 22:27). Serving others is loving others. Putting others first is love's way.

Now, this does not mean loving oneself is bad, for Jesus also said that the second greatest commandment was to "love your neighbor *as yourself*" (Matt. 22:39, emphasis added). Because God created us as his image-bearers, we have intrinsic worth; we have been made lovable. God does not create worthless junk, throwaways that should be used up and then despised. He loves his creation—he declared it "very good" (Gen. 1:31)—so for us to love ourselves, as long as our love for God comes first, is good and right. And, as Jesus observed, our self-love provides part of the basis for our love of others. When I understand and act on my intrinsic value as God's image-bearer, I have the understanding I need to love my fellow human beings as image-bearers too.

What all this tells us is that *agapē* is unselfish and uncontainable. God's love overflows to the creative work of his hands, especially to humans, upon whom he has placed his special divine imprint. Like our Creator, the One in whose likeness we're made, we are to give our love away: to love our Creator and all he loves. As love spreads, love multiplies:

> The more we love, the more we are loved, and the more we are loved, the more we love. There is no necessary limit to this process. . . . There is no upper limit, no wall, to love. And there is no drag, no gravity built into love. When love wears down, that is due to external friction, not internal friction: love itself has no tendency to wear down, only to increase.[20]

In short, love seeks one to love: a beloved. The triune nature of God demonstrates this truth as an eternal reality. God is three divine persons—Father, Son, and Spirit—existing in perfect unity and harmony within the same divine nature. This nature is characterized by love, revealed through the loving relationships between the three Persons. The Father is the Lover who loves the Son;[21] the Son is the Beloved, as Jesus well knew;[22] and the Holy Spirit is the Act (or Bond) of Love between the Father and the Son. Love brings unity; it's the Spirit who brings about the fruit of love and therefore is the primary bringer of unity, including unity in the church:[23] "For we were all baptized by one Spirit into one body—whether Jews or Greeks, slave or free" (1 Cor. 12:13); "Make every effort to keep the unity of the Spirit through the bond of peace. There is one body and one Spirit" (Eph. 4:3–4).

So God is the fullness of love, being and experiencing *agapē* within himself perfectly and unendingly. While he needs no one other than himself to love, out of his love he chose to create others to love. Again, though God does not need us, he clearly desires us. And what is better—to be "loved" out of need or to be loved out of want? The former uses loved ones to meet its own needs for its *own* sake; the latter seeks to meet the needs of loved ones for *their* sakes. *Agapē* is not self-seeking because it doesn't need to seek its own; it already is all that it needs. Since Divine Love has no needs of its own, it can wrap its arms around us and fully give us what we need. *Agapē*, then, is not self-centered but other-centered, not selfish but selfless, not egotistic but altruistic, not exhaustible but unlimited, not confinable but free-flowing.

As true as all this is, do not conclude from it that *agapē* means giving 100 percent without expecting anything in return. I bought into this false belief early in my first marriage. I learned to give and give and give and give, even when my love was rarely returned, frequently spurned, and almost unilaterally taken for granted. I sank my love into a bottomless pit of another's demands, and in the process I eventually teetered on the edge of losing myself. I finally came to my senses when I realized that as incredibly giving as God is, he requires everything we are and have in return. Jesus told us that the greatest commandment is to "love the Lord your God with *all* your heart and with *all* your soul and with *all* your mind" (Matt. 22:37, emphasis added). God gives us his infinite abundance; the way we receive it is by giving him our finite all. The exchange is far from equal, but it's an exchange, nonetheless.

A love *relationship,* whether it is with another person or with God himself, is not a relationship when the loving goes one way. The existence of a loving *relationship* requires three elements: (1) a lover, (2) a loved one, and (3) a bond of love between them.

In heaven, believers will forever experience the completed fullness of the love relationship they've begun with God here on earth. Hell's boarders, on the other hand, will discover the absolute horror of their earthly refusal to embrace the love God longed to give them. *Agapē* cannot be forced on anyone, not on earth or in hell or even in heaven.

If we want all that God has for us, we must choose him by faith, then love him with our all. There is no other way, for this is the very nature of love.

Not Easily Angered

Furthermore, *agapē* has a long fuse (1 Cor. 13:5). Love can become angry, but it will not do so quickly or irrationally. The Bible reveals many instances where God displays his anger, yet the record also displays his anger as an outgrowth of his love, not a sign of its breakdown or defeat. He rebukes us, disciplines us, punishes us, and endures us—*all because he loves us.* The writer of Hebrews makes this clear:

"My son, do not make light of the Lord's discipline, and do not lose heart when he rebukes you, because the Lord disciplines those he loves, and he punishes everyone he accepts as a son."

God disciplines us for our good, that we may share in his holiness. No discipline seems pleasant at the time, but painful. Later on, however, it produces a harvest of righteousness and peace for those who have been trained by it.[24]

God loves us so much that like a loving parent, he doesn't want us to remain as we are. He's determined to see that we get the opportunities—even the painful ones—to become as good as we can be. Part of this entails purging us of our sin so we can become truly holy. As Paul explains,

> Christ loved the church and gave himself up for her to make her holy, cleansing her by the washing with water through the word, and to present her to himself as a radiant church, without stain or wrinkle or any other blemish, but holy and blameless. (Eph. 5:25–27)

Remarking on this truth, C. S. Lewis said,

> Love, in its own nature, demands the perfecting of the beloved. . . . When we fall in love with a woman, do we cease to care whether she is clean or dirty, fair or foul? Do we not rather then first begin to care? Does any woman regard it as a sign of love in a man that he neither knows nor cares how she is looking? Love may, indeed, love the beloved when her beauty is lost: but not because it is lost. Love may forgive all infirmities and love still in spite of them: but Love cannot cease to will their removal. Love is more sensitive than hatred itself to every blemish in the beloved.[25]

Our Divine Lover, then, seeks our perfection. And when we've chosen to accept his love, he works to make us perfect, promising that one day we will indeed be perfect.[26] But this task is not one-sided. The Lord respects our freedom and works alongside us to bring about our complete transformation through our obedience. And he works patiently with us through this process, as loving parents do with their children. At times, however, gentleness and kindness make for too soft an approach. We need a stronger hand, a disciplinary action, even a punishing stance from our heavenly Father. This he gives us for our highest good.

Love is not easily angered, but it can become angry over our persistence in hurting others or ourselves, as well as over our attempts to thwart love's best instead of receiving and cooperating with it. Just as parents grow angry with a child who constantly disobeys their directive not to play in the street because of its traffic, so God loves us too much to abandon us to our destructive ways. He too will express his anger, not to cause us hurt but to attempt to rescue us from our own foolishness, even if that loving anger brings us temporary pain.

Keeps No Record of Wrongs

God is all-knowing: "Nothing in all creation is hidden from God's sight," including "the thoughts and attitudes of the heart. . . . Everything is uncovered and laid bare before the eyes of him to whom we must give account" (Heb. 4:12–13). Even so, God does not desire to judge us but to save us: "God our Savior . . . wants all men to be saved and to come to a knowledge of the truth" (1 Tim. 2:3–4). The Lord's love reaches out to us to wipe clean our record. He hungers to forgive us, not to condemn us. He's not a Cosmic Prosecutor seeking whomever he may accuse, arrest, and arraign. Rather, he's the greatest Lover of all, sacrificing even his own Son so we could find in him complete forgiveness, full reconciliation, and everlasting transformation into his all-good, all-perfect image.

This Lover forgives all our wrongdoing through his Son, Jesus Christ.

> Once you were alienated from God and were enemies in your minds because of your evil behavior. But now he [God the Father] has reconciled you by Christ's physical body through death to present you holy in his sight, without blemish and free from accusation. (Col. 1:21–22)

The Father has "rescued us from the dominion of darkness and brought us into the kingdom of the Son he loves, in whom we have redemption, the forgiveness of sins" (vv. 13–14). "Therefore," Paul concludes in another letter, "there is now no condemnation for those who are in Christ Jesus" (Rom. 8:1). When we put our ultimate trust in the Son to be our Savior, his Father forgives all our sin. He erases every trace of iniquity from our record.

When a friend of mine is asked, "How are you doing?" his regular response is, "Better than I deserve." So it is in our relationship with the Divine Lover. He treats us infinitely better than we deserve, including forever removing our record of evil when we embrace him through his beloved Son.

Does Not Delight in Evil

Love springs from good, not evil. The One who is all-loving is likewise all-good, and his Word draws the connection between his goodness and his love. Psalm 136 is the most obvious example: The psalmist opens with the call,

"Give thanks to the LORD, for he is good. *His love endures forever*" (v. 1, emphasis added). Then after each of the next twenty-five reasons to give thanks, he adds, "*His love endures forever.*" The goodness of God is seen through the love of God, and his love is eternal.

Because God is infinitely good and loving, he cannot endorse or ignore evil, much less participate in it. "Your eyes are too pure to approve evil," Habakkuk says, "and You can not look on wickedness with favor" (Hab. 1:13 NASB). Indeed, to the misguided who would try to blame evil on God, the apostle James warns,

> Let no one say when he is tempted, "I am being tempted by God"; for God cannot be tempted by evil, and He Himself does not tempt anyone. . . . Do not be deceived, my beloved brethren. Every good thing given and every perfect gift is from above, coming down from the Father of lights, with whom there is no variation or shifting shadow. (James 1:13, 16–17 NASB)

Evil is opposed to God, and God is opposed to evil. As love, he finds no delight in corruption (1 Cor. 13:6). How could it be otherwise? Love is selfless; evil is selfish. Love is creative; evil is destructive. Love flows from goodness; evil comes from sin. Love is patient and kind; evil is impatient and cruel. Love forgives, unifies, and restores; evil shames, divides, and demolishes. Love is heavenly; evil is hellish.

Love and evil do not and cannot mix. They are as opposite and far removed from each other as the east is from the west.

Rejoices With the Truth

In 1 Corinthians 13:6, when Paul says that *agapē* "rejoices with the truth," he's not talking about propositional truth but moral truth; he's contrasting the unrighteousness of evil with the righteousness of good. While love does not revel in wrong, it does delight in good. Love's joy is over *what's right.*

About four centuries before Christ, Malachi revealed that many of God's people had "wearied the LORD" with their claim that "all who do evil are good in the eyes of the LORD, and [that] he is pleased with them" (Mal. 2:17). Of course, nothing could be farther from the truth. Good is not evil, and evil is not good.[27] The all-good God celebrates goodness as beautiful and highly treasured. One day he'll replace this evil-ridden world, creating "a new heaven and a new earth, the home of righteousness" (2 Peter 3:13), a world forever free from evil and its consequences.[28] In this new world only goodness will be; in this, Love will rejoice all the more.

Always Protects

Now Paul gives a series of four "always" statements about love.

The first is that *agapē* "always protects" (1 Cor. 13:7). The Greek word that the NIV translates *protects* (*stégei*) could mean "protects" or "covers," for it's related to another term that means "roof."[29] If Paul is conveying this meaning, then he's indicating that love protects the good as well as the bad, the selfless and the selfish. This is not a foreign idea in Scripture; we have noted, for example, that God sends sunshine and rain to both the righteous and the evil.[30] *He seeks to save all, no matter how good they think they are or how bad they know they are.* While on earth, the Son called on the Father to forgive his executioners, thereby protecting them from the Father's punishing hand.[31] Christ also told his followers to love and pray for their enemies, not just for those who love them already, for God is "kind to the ungrateful and wicked" (Luke 6:27–28, 35). Peter even tells us that "love covers over a multitude of sins" (1 Peter 4:8). In other words, love reaches out to all, seeks to save all, and has compassion on all.

> Christian love is not blind to sin, but [is] interested in the genuine welfare of others. . . . It refuses to deliberately expose the sins it encounters to the gaze of all; it prefers to refrain from and discourage all needless talk about them. . . . The gracious action of true love promotes the peace and harmony of the brotherhood, and is the very opposite of hatred that deliberately exposes sin in order to humiliate and injure.[32]

On the other hand, Love will sometimes publicly expose sin for the good of the sinner and sin's other victims.

> There are some hidden evils that cannot be undone unless they are publicized. To undo evils that hurt people[,] love drives us to expose them. . . . Wherever secret evil in centers of power inflicts injustice on people, love will drive us to ferret it out. Love exposes for the same reason it covers—the good of persons.[33]

Because God is all-knowing and all-good, he knows when and how love should either cover or expose sin.

In 1 Corinthians 13:7, Paul may also have another meaning in mind for *stégei*. Rather than "protects" or "covers," the term can also mean "supports."

If so, then Paul is affirming that love is all-supporting: love seeks to lift up instead of tear down; love is a sustaining (not destructive) force. We certainly see this in our Divine Lover. In Christ, "all things hold together" (Col. 1:17). He sustains the entire universe in existence by his loving, upholding power; our every movement and breath is totally dependent, moment by moment, on God's sustaining activity.

We are like the flame in a gas-powered fireplace. As long as the divinely supplied fuel keeps pouring into us, we will burn brightly. But if that fuel supply were cut off, our life-flame would extinguish—we would cease to exist in body and soul. It is God who "gives all men life and breath and everything else" (Acts 17:25). He sustains all; *nothing* is outside his power.

Whichever meaning we see in Paul's use of *stégei*—whether "protects"/ "covers" or "supports"—*both* present precious truths about the God who loves us.[34]

Always Trusts

In the statement love "always trusts" (1 Cor. 13:7), the term for *trusts* is usually translated "faith" or "believes." "Faith loves and love believes," Smedes observes, and "love is a believing power."[35]

You see, God believes in us. Yes, he knows we fail, and yes, he knows how faithless we can be. But he also knows how great humanity was before our first parents rebelled against him, and he knows how great is our potential to once again become the awesome creatures he made us to be. He even tells us that he will one day call upon us to judge the angels, an indication of the authority and glory we will eventually have.[36] He also promises those of us in Christ that he will make us immortal, imperishable, sinless, and perfect in every way that is possible for human beings.[37] This perfect state is nothing less than the glorified fullness of Christ's image.[38] One day we will be as perfect as Christ is in his transformed human nature. This is the incredible potential the Lord sees in each of us—in you and me. *He believes in us.*

As if this were not astounding enough, the Bible also tells us that God trusts us. The incarnate Son, after a full night of prayer to the Father, chose twelve men from all of his disciples to walk closely with him. He taught them, modeled perfection before them, encouraged them, and commissioned them, giving them authority to carry out the ministry he established. In other words, Jesus placed his trust—at the Father's command—in these men to carry on his work. His faith came from his Father's love for him and for them.[39]

We also know that the disciples often misunderstood Jesus and failed him.

One of them, Peter, even denied Jesus during his darkest hour. Another, Judas, violated Jesus' trust so heinously that it led to his brutal crucifixion. Still, God's love reached out to all twelve, and eleven responded in renewed faith—all except Judas. Rather than confessing his sin and finding reconciliation with God, Judas chose his own solution, a grief-stricken suicide. Judas gave up on himself, the result of bowing to a false deity, the fallen angel Lucifer, also known as Satan. God, however, never gave up on this disciple. The Son was offering forgiveness even while suffering horrible agony.[40] Judas could have received this forgiveness if he had only been willing, but he was not.

Faith loves even faithless and traitorous disciples. Love believes that even the worst of us can one day become the best—clothed with a splendor that if we saw it now, we "would be strongly tempted to worship."[41]

Always Hopes

Love desires and works toward the betterment of others, no matter how bleak and desperate that goal may appear. In other words, *agapē* "always hopes" for the best (1 Cor. 13:7).

God knows that not all people will trust in him and thereby find salvation, but he still seeks to save all, and at the highest cost imaginable—the sacrifice of his own Son.

God knows that the ones who love him will sometimes grieve him, even rebel against him, yet he remains faithful to them, continuing his work to bring them to perfection.

The Father sent his Son into the world, knowing that the world would reject him and crucify him, but the Father refused to give up on the world, seeking those people in it who would turn back to him by faith in the Son.

The Spirit knows that not all of us will repent of our sins, yet he still carries out his mission to "convict the world of guilt in regard to sin and righteousness and judgment" (John 16:8).

The Son knew that not all the people to whom he presented the kingdom of God would accept his message, but he presented his case before all comers, even those who criticized, tried to trap, and plotted to kill him.[42]

Love always hopes for the best, even when it knows that the best will not be achieved because the objects of Love's affections will not receive all that Love offers. Only the willing get all of Love's best. The unwilling do not because Love must be welcomed—forced love is not love but assault. Real love will not impose itself. Love will woo, persuade, challenge, and even allow its objects to experience the consequences of its rejection. But Love will not coerce anyone, because he desires and works for their best, even despite their rebellion against his overtures.

I know firsthand that this is true. Despite all the love I received from God through my parents and the churches of my youth, I turned away and followed the way of an atheist for two years. I lived on my terms, thinking I could create a better way and a better life than the one Christianity had to offer.

God never gave up on me. He kept loving and pursuing me, all the while showing me how futile my life had become. Although I'd become faithless, God remained faithful. He never left me, even though I left him. And when I finally turned and invited him into my life, he filled me with his love. Love saved me from myself, and in the process gave me a new self, a better self, a self free to love itself and others through the greatest Lover of all.

Agapē "always hopes."

Always Perseveres

The last "always" declaration Paul makes about *agapē* is that it "always perseveres" (1 Cor. 13:7). The Greek word translated *perseveres* is a military term that carries the idea of bearing up under or enduring "the assaults of suffering or persecution."[43] The same word is used in Hebrews 12:2 in reference to Jesus enduring the torturous death of crucifixion for our sake.

Isaiah, more than seven hundred years before Jesus' birth, predicted what the Messiah would endure for us. Here's some of what he saw, all of which was fulfilled in Jesus Christ:

> He was despised and rejected by men, a man of sorrows, and familiar with suffering. Like one from whom men hide their faces he was despised, and we esteemed him not.
>
> Surely he took up our infirmities and carried our sorrows, yet we considered him stricken by God, smitten by him, and afflicted. But he was pierced for our transgressions, he was crushed for our iniquities; the punishment that brought us peace was upon him, and by his wounds we are healed. We all, like sheep, have gone astray, each of us has turned to his own way; and the LORD has laid on him the iniquity of us all.
>
> He was oppressed and afflicted, yet he did not open his mouth; he was led like a lamb to the slaughter, and as a sheep before her shearers is silent, so he did not open his mouth. By oppression and judgment he was taken away. . . . For he was cut off from the land of the living; for the transgression of my people he was stricken. He was assigned a grave

with the wicked, and with the rich in his death, though he had done no violence, nor was any deceit in his mouth. . . .

He poured out his life unto death, and was numbered with the transgressors. For he bore the sin of many, and made intercession for the transgressors. (Isa. 53:3–9, 12)

Love suffers what it does not deserve for the good of others. Love is not a masochist, seeking the infliction of pain upon itself; however, Love will endure humiliation, insult, shame, agony, anger, contempt, and even death if such sacrifice will pave the way for the healing of others. This is what God the Son did for us two thousand years ago, and his painful perseverance has transformed hundreds of millions of lives, giving hope that many millions more can find the Divine Lover who gives everlasting life to the undeserving—a class that includes all human beings throughout time regardless of color, culture, nationality, religion, gender, financial status, or political persuasion. Only Jesus Christ is not a member of this undeserving class, never having sinned and thus pleasing the Father in every way.[44] Jesus required no redemption: It was out of his love (and that of the Father and the Spirit) that Jesus gave us redemption through his sacrificial death. By his wounds, we can find healing love, the love only the triune God can give.

Never Fails

Of all the descriptions of *agapē* Paul provides, the one about love never failing (1 Cor. 13:8) has been troublesome to me. After all, even the God who *is* love can be rejected. Lucifer and the other once-good angels who rebelled with him have forever turned away from their Creator. They are at war with him and with anyone who follows him.[45] Likewise, humans can spurn God all the way into hell, forever refusing the love he longs to give them.[46] Then there are the countless prodigal sons and daughters and spouses who never return to their families. The depressed and despairing people who give up on life and commit suicide, or who live in a never-ending cycle of numbing their brokenness through painkillers of choice, only to die from their addictions without ever possessing the love that could have been theirs. Are these not cases of love failing? Do these not prove that love can be defeated?

If Paul were saying that love could never be rejected, he'd be wrong—there's no doubt that it can. If love must be accepted freely, it can also be rejected freely. History is full of examples of both.

However, Paul is not claiming that love is impossible to reject; he's saying that love always abides. Love never ceases. *Love is permanent and eternal.* Because God is *agapē*, the Beginning and the End, the First and the Last, so is love.[47] Love has always been, is now, and will ever be. Nothing can cause *agapē* to die. Love can be turned away, but love never ceases giving itself away. Love could be compared to Niagara Falls: a perpetual outpouring, whether or not anyone chooses to put a bucket under it and receive of its bounty. God's love is unending, and those who open their lives to it will be filled, while those who choose not to will go away empty. This is not Love's fault but the fault of those who refuse its boundless gifts.

So while Love can be forever spurned, Love's fountain can never be turned off. *Agapē* is as enduring as its Source, who is literally timeless, immortal, and indestructible. Love cannot be stopped.

Those who open their arms and receive Love are forever blessed. They will inherit Paradise—everlasting bliss and perfect union with the One who is love. They will become like the Divine Lover himself—not like him in the sense of being gods, but like him in the sense of becoming restored and transformed image-bearers of the Father's beloved Son.[48] Lovers of God will forever share his bountiful love in an unhindered state. They will not only receive his love, they will become love-bearers themselves. Love's imperfect recipients will become perfect lovers.

LOVE'S HEART

Given these incredible descriptions of Love's actions, can we say what *agapē* is? What is the heart of love? In the most complete sense, because God is love, *love is all God is.* God is all-powerful, all-knowing, and all-good. So is his love. God is perfect, eternal, and immortal. So is his love. God is unchanging, personal, and holy. So is his love. All that God is, his love is also.[49]

However, getting to the heart of all God tells us about *agapē* in his Word, we come to something along these lines: *Love is desiring and doing what is truly good for the beloved.* This is the nature, the essence, the heart of love. And because the essence of God is love, love is the ultimate virtue—greater than hope or faith, gentleness or self-control, courage or wisdom, compassion or justice, patience or kindness. *Agapē* is the greatest good, the all-enduring good, the all-fulfilling good. In love, all the other virtues find their utter fulfillment and sublime expression, including the three other kinds of love. Peter Kreeft explains this truth, beginning with the virtue of patience:

How can we become patient? By praying, "God, give me patience and do it right now!"? No, despite our good intentions, despite our sincerity, despite our need, we find ourselves continually losing patience even with those we love most. The natural loves [*stergō, phileō,* and *erōs*], valuable as they are, are not enough. They are like a garden . . . but they need a gardener with rake and hoe. That is the role of *agape;* it cultivates and perfects the other loves. When we have *agape* toward someone, it becomes not only possible but natural to have patience toward them, for "*agape* is patient." . . .

Agape is the catalyst not only for other virtues, like patience, but also for other loves like affection or liking. When we have *agape,* we find that we can begin liking the people we used to dislike. Once you truly love someone, you no longer rely on liking them, and the surprising result is that you end up liking them more, not less. . . .

Agape is even a catalyst for the perfection of erotic married love. Selfish sex is not even good sex in the erotic sense. Lust spoils sex just as addiction spoils alcohol. Winos can't appreciate wine, which God invented "to gladden the heart of man" (Ps. 104:15). Just so, sex addicts can't appreciate sex, which God also invented for that same reason, among others. They lack the self-forgetfulness needed for true joy. The only way to total sex is total love of the beloved.[50]

As all the virtues flow from *agapē,* so do all the other loves in their best expressions.

Moreover, apart from *agapē,* nothing we do or become has any eternal value. In fact, a life without love at best amounts to noise and at worst comes to nothing.[51] This is why Paul calls a life infused with *agapē* "the most excellent way" (1 Cor. 12:31).

But *agapē* is not found in nature, nor is it naturally resident in us. *Agapē* has but one source—the triune God. So, if we want an *agapē* kind of life, we must go to the One who is *agapē* and follow his way in obtaining it. How we do this is not a restricted secret; God has made the way clear so that all of us can have *agapē*-filled lives.

What is this way? It's what we'll discover next.

3. The *Way*

Two thousand years ago Jesus told his disciples, "I am the way" (John 14:6), and in this context he meant that to get to the Father they had to go through him. Indeed, he is the One who revealed the Father; placing your faith in him is tantamount to trusting in the Father, which leads to the Spirit-empowerment Jesus promised.[1] In other words, following his way is supposed to lead to the Christian life. But what is his way?

Soon after I became a believer, at the age of nineteen, I was told that Christ's way consisted of three foundational actions: (1) having a daily "quiet time," including prayer and Bible study; (2) attending church regularly and putting money in the offering plate each Sunday; and (3) sharing the faith with everyone possible. Of course, there was talk about other aspects of "the way of Christ," but these three activities were at the core.

I accepted this approach, and I followed it most of the time. Though I sensed something was missing, I couldn't tell what it was; I simply didn't know enough about the Bible or the church's practices through the centuries to conclude anything else. Yet I somehow knew that these efforts were inadequate to lead a person into Christian maturity; there had to be more.

I later discovered what was missing. Through my study of Scripture and church history, I came across this well-trodden path: the practice of the truth. I found that the Spirit of God had kept Christ's promise: He had been guiding his church "into all truth" (John 16:13), and not only the *knowledge* of the truth, but also the *practice and experience* of the truth. Furthermore, the Spirit's guiding work had not ended with the completion of the New Testament or with the death of the last of the twelve apostles. The Spirit of Truth had been maturing the church in the truth for two millennia; the church had learned a great deal in the process, and now I was discovering these lessons also. As the Spirit had used them in times past to reshape and transform believers, so he was using them to do the same in me.

Moreover, with these ancient yet newfound practices in mind, I returned to the Bible to see if they were there. And they were, now obvious for me to see. In fact, I found them commonplace among Jesus and his early followers. The way of truth had been revealed and practiced since the time of Christ and even long before. His way was indescribably more effective and richly satisfying than the spiritual fundamentals I'd first been taught. The ancient way included those basics, but it went much further: The way of our Divine Lover, the way to him and all his love has to offer us, begins in relationship, grows in relationship, and finds its complete fulfillment in relationship. Throughout this relational process, a number of critical factors are at work, all of which we need to understand in order to grow as God intends.

FAITH TO FAITH

One of these critical factors is *faith*. We cannot begin to grow in our relationship to God until the relationship itself is established. God desires to lavish us with his love, but he will not force himself on us. He doesn't break down the door of our lives and steal in like a thief; he wants to be invited in. Jesus says, "I stand at the door and knock. If anyone hears my voice and opens the door, I will come in and eat with him, and he with me" (Rev. 3:20). The barrier is not with him, but us. We keep the door locked and refuse to answer the Christ who seeks entry. The way to him starts when we accept his invitation to open our lives for his personal, intimate presence. This acceptance is an act of trust, a choice of faith.

I first trusted Christ and invited him into my life in April 1972. This was an act of faith that embraced him as the fullness of *life*. It took longer to see that I also had to trust him as the fullness of *truth*, and through that I began to find that he was also the fullness of the *way*. I finally saw what Paul proclaimed long ago, that a right relationship with Christ is "by faith from first to last" (Rom. 1:17). The Christian life starts by faith, continues by faith, and finds its everlasting completion at the end of faith. Through it all, love abides. Christ's loving way is begun and carried along by our faith in him.

Since faith is essential in our relationship with God, we must understand what faith is. Basically, *faith is a whole-person response of trust to the only One fully worthy of that trust.* Faith involves our mind, emotions, and will. These characteristics are the defining traits of personhood: Persons think, feel, and choose. Rocks and trees do not, because they are impersonal. Humans, like God, are personal; each human being is a person, and the one God is tri-personal (Father, Son, and Spirit). You and I each have a personal center that thinks, feels, and acts, whereas God has three personal centers, *each* of which think, feel, and act. Our personhood reflects his, though his is perfectly harmonious and infinitely loving, while ours is imperfect, frequently in conflict within itself, and too often unloving. In other words, there is a qualitative difference between God's personhood and ours, yet both are still personal: God and humans possess the personal essentials of mind, emotions, and will.

Again, faith encompasses all we are as persons. Consider first the *intellectual* aspect of our personhood: Faith is an act of the mind to believe in the truth. When Paul says that there is "one faith" (Eph. 4:5), he's referring to the truths Christianity reveals and teaches, the beliefs that all authentic Christians embrace. The one faith is the body of teaching "that was once for all entrusted to the saints" (Jude 3), what Paul in another letter calls "sound doctrine" (Titus 1:9). Faith involves an intellectual assent to the truth of Christ, revealed in creation and Scripture and affirmed and passed down through the centuries by the church. The exercise of faith requires a mental choice of trust.

Faith also involves the *emotional* side of our personhood. Faith is a feeling of assurance and trust in the personal God. It's the kind of confidence that led a Roman centurion to believe Jesus could heal his paralyzed servant from a distance. "Just say the word," he urged, "and my servant will be healed. For I myself am a man under authority, with soldiers under me. I tell this one, 'Go,' and he goes; and that one, 'Come,' and he comes. I say to my servant, 'Do this,' and he does it."

Jesus was astonished, saying to his followers, "I tell you the truth, I have not found anyone in Israel with such great faith." Then he told the soldier, "Go! It will be done just as you believed it would" (Matt. 8:8–10, 13).

"Faith is the assurance of things hoped for, the conviction of things not seen" (Heb. 11:1 NASB). This is the faith the Roman officer had. His assurance in Christ's ability resulted in his servant's healing.

There is likewise a *volitional* aspect to our faith: Along with our mind and emotions, faith requires our will. We must choose to receive what God has for us and to obey him in what we do. A saving faith is a working faith—it brings results, it bears fruit, as did the faith of the Old Testament heroes:

> By faith Noah, when warned about things not yet seen, in holy fear built an ark to save his family. By his faith he condemned the world and became heir of the righteousness that comes by faith. (Heb. 11:7)
>
> By faith Abraham, when God tested him, offered Isaac as a sacrifice. He who had received the promises was about to sacrifice his one and only son, even though God had said to him, "It is through Isaac that your offspring will be reckoned." Abraham reasoned that God could raise the dead, and figuratively speaking, he did receive Isaac back from death. (11:17–19)

Faith enjoins the will to receive good from God and to do good on God's behalf. Faith performs what God asks. Faith obeys its Lover—no matter what.

Is this unreasonable or untenable? No. Look at the One in whom we're to put our total trust: Is he not completely trustworthy? His power cannot fail us because he's all-powerful. His knowledge cannot let us down because he knows everything—past, present, and future. His goodness is beyond reproach, and his undying love for us has been demonstrated repeatedly throughout history, especially through the death, resurrection, and ascension of his Son. God is eternal love, infinite *agapē*. He will never deceive us or deny us. Even when "we are faithless" with him, "he will remain faithful, for he cannot disown himself" (2 Tim. 2:13). God always delivers on his promises because he must act in accord with his own nature, which is truth. All he asks us to do is trust him—completely, without reservation, with full abandon, from our initial act of faith until we behold him in heaven. And even when we can't give him our all, he'll accept from us the faith of a mustard seed, the tiniest act of faith,[2] because he loves us so much and knows how weak we are. How can we go wrong trusting him?

Throughout my Christian life, I've had times when my faith was full-bodied, when I served my Lover with all I had. But I've also been frail and confused, sometimes hurt and angry. At those points my faith has been anorexic; its exercise has been feeble, even racked with doubt. However, every time I've turned over to God whatever little faith I had, he has taken it and multiplied its effectiveness. His faithful work in my life has grown my faithfulness to him. He can do the same for you, but the process begins with exercising faith in him each day, regardless of how faltering your trust occasionally might be.

Indeed, all relationships require some level of faith. Friendships cannot form, marriages cannot endure, parents cannot let children out of their sight, ministers cannot nurture Christians . . . unless a bond of trust exists. Our relationship with God, like all the other relationships, must be centered on trust in order to begin and grow. *Unlike* all other trust unions, though, our relationship with the Lord deserves our full faith, for *only* he will never abandon us. "Never will I leave you," he assures, "never will I forsake you" (Heb. 13:5). We can take him at his Word.

PROCESS VS. PERFECTION

Another critical factor is understanding that the Christian life is a *process,* not perfection. Once we initially trust God and as we keep trusting him, our relationship with him gradually grows. We do not start out fully mature, nor do we immediately become fully mature.

When we are spiritually reborn through faith in Christ, we not only *have* a new life but we *are* a new life. If "anyone is in Christ," writes Paul, "he is a new creation; the old has gone, the new has come! All this is from God" (2 Cor. 5:17–18). God takes us, his fallen, marred image-bearers, and begins the inner renewal process. Over time he restores our brokenness, gradually overcoming the damage and restoring the completeness of the divine image in us. Our new redeemed self is "being renewed in knowledge in the image of its Creator" (Col. 3:10), who is none other than the Son of God through whom "all things were created" (1:16). Through the work of the Holy Spirit in our lives, we are "being transformed into his [Christ's] likeness with ever-increasing glory" (2 Cor. 3:18). The Spirit grows our new life—Christ's life in us—making us more and more like him instead of our being weighed down by sin's power.

But this process of new creation is not complete upon our initial exercise of faith in Christ, any more than a human baby's departure from the womb immediately makes her a grownup. Our spiritual formation begins in infancy, with the goal that it will pass through the childhood years, grow through adolescence, and mature into adulthood. Our new life in Christ increasingly becomes more Christlike as we keep growing in the faith.

This teaching is found throughout the New Testament, even in reference to Jesus. In his humanity, Jesus began as a supernaturally fertilized ovum in the Virgin Mary's womb, growing until he was ready to be born. Under the tutelage of Mary and her husband, Joseph, as well as through the enlightening and empowering work of the Spirit, the boy Jesus "grew constantly in wisdom and in body, and in favor with God and man."[3] "Although he was a son," Hebrews says, Jesus "learned obedience from what he suffered and, once made perfect, he became the source of eternal salvation for all who obey him" (5:8–9). Jesus never sinned, but as a real finite man he still had to grow and learn until he became perfect and thereby could become the perfect sacrifice for us.

Like our loving Savior, we are to grow up spiritually too. We begin in our relationship with God as "newborn babes" (1 Peter 2:2), mere children in the faith. In this condition we're immature, undiscerning, and fragile. We can only feed on milk—what Hebrews calls "the elementary truths of God's word" and "the elementary teachings about Christ" (5:12; 6:1). We need to learn the basics of the faith and how to apply them; mature Christians must come alongside us and tenderly care for our needs, feeding us what we can handle and no more. In time, we will be able to take in more than spiritual milk: We'll graduate from faith's basics to its meatier matters, passing from the childhood stage of *complete dependence* to the adolescent stage of *mistaken independence.*

In our spiritual teen years, we're likely to think we can make the rest of the journey alone. We tend to challenge traditional teachings, methods, and institutions. We question tried-and-true wisdom, foolishly thinking our way is the best way because it's ours and it's "new." We try on different doctrinal clothes to see how they'll fit, and we gravitate to just about any mode of worship that seems more contemporary, more "with it," than what we've known before. While some insights about self, God, and life can come out of this tumultuous period of spiritual growth, the lessons learned tend to be more negative than positive: We learn more what *not* to believe and do than what to believe and do.

The third stage of spiritual growth is adulthood. Here we realize the myth of independence and grow increasingly accepting of our interdependence upon God, his church, and his created order. We see that we're co-laborers with Christ and our fellow believers.[4] We need each other "so that the body of Christ may be built up until we all reach unity in the faith and in the knowledge of the Son of God and become mature, attaining to the whole measure of the fullness of Christ" (Eph. 4:12–13). Spiritual adulthood, a process that has no end on this side of heaven, is a continual "progressing toward maturity."[5] We will not be completely Christlike—the ultimate goal of the Christian life—until we stand before him in our bodily resurrected and fully transformed state. Only then will we be immortal, imperishable, faultless, and holy. Only then will we be entirely reflective of Jesus. Only then will God's work in us be fulfilled.

Tragically, far too many Christians get the message that the spiritual life is one of perfection in the here and now. This is the message I first received.

In my early years of faith, the focus of pastors and teachers and authors was more on *what we do as believers* than on *who we are in Christ*. These folks certainly talked about how to become a Christian and about the ultimate centrality of Christ. But after the initial step of faith, the emphasis shifted from becoming a Christian to doing "Christianly" things. It was on the doing side that prayer, Bible study, church attendance, giving, evangelism, and the like were placed. By *doing* these things, we were *being* Christians, showing the reality of our confession of Jesus in the deeds we did for him. And we were being obedient to what these leaders said the Bible taught us to do.

The more sermons and lessons I heard on this approach, the more my guilt level rose. Books on the Christian life only added to my shame. I worked harder and harder to do all the right and expected things, but I kept falling short of that "perfect Christian doer" all these leaders talked about. The perfect Christian prayed and studied his Bible every day (preferably in the morning). He shared his faith with everyone who crossed his path. He went to church every Sunday and was always involved in service projects, whether teaching, singing in the choir, serving on a board, writing to missionaries, and/or a host of other ministry-minded and officially recognized activities. He gave at least a tenth of his income and pledged additional funds to every capital campaign. He was unfailingly kind and caring, honest and gracious. It was best if he was married, had well-managed children, and never contemplated (much less initiated) divorce. *The perfect Christian lived a perfect life with perfect relationships while attending a perfect church with other perfect Christians.*

I was not a perfect Christian. I did not and could not measure up. I struggled with some deep-seated sins. I was married to a professing believer who wrestled with her own demons. I was sometimes impatient with my children, who clearly had a mind and will of their own that didn't always conform to what I wanted. I was in a church where miscommunication, backbiting, and personal agendas arose in ways that threatened our unity. For about five years I was so financially poor that I had little or nothing to put in the offering plate, so I gave more of my time to the church . . . which occasionally took time away from my family, which needed it even more. I was sometimes fearless in witnessing, while at other times I was frightened into silence. I often doubted certain aspects of what some Christians taught as truth; sometimes I decisively rejected and ridiculed it.

My life was far from perfect. However, like many believers, I justified my beliefs and behavior the best I could, convincing myself—or so I thought— that I was living out what Christ intended for us.

Then I left the environments of my local church and secular university, moving from California to Texas to attend a theologically conservative semi- nary. I went there to seek out answers to my many questions about the faith and to deepen my understanding and application of Scripture. After I arrived, I learned that all first-year students had to take a battery of psychological tests. I'd never done this before, so I had no idea what to expect. I initially perceived that the process was painless and benign . . . but then I was called into the counselor's office to receive the results.

Gently yet forcefully, he looked across his large desk and said, "You carry around a lot of false guilt, don't you?"

I just sat there, staring at him, not knowing what to say. *False guilt? I thought. Guilt? What do I have to feel guilty about? I'm living the Christian life. What more am I supposed to do?*

For the next hour or so he pinpointed my perceptions about myself and my relationships, including my bond with Christ and his church. He helped me see things about myself that had been invisible to me. Within hours of his "revealing me to me," I knew this counselor had accurately assessed my con- dition. I was bearing an overwhelming load of guilt—false guilt. I was blaming myself for not being the perfect Christian, for not having the perfect Christian life. Somehow I had to stop the self-blame.

So I took what many around me thought was a radical step: I stopped reading anything that had to do with Christian living, and, instead, I turned my full focus to exploring Christian doctrines, especially those about God and the life of Christ as revealed in the Gospels. I figured that since Christian prac- tice followed from Christian belief, the more I understood the theology of the faith, the more clearly I would see how that faith should be lived out. Since the first and only perfect believer was Jesus Christ, I would primarily look to him for direction on what life is really all about and how it should be lived.

I began this approach in early 1979; it wasn't until the mid–1990s that I returned to reading other books on the practice of the Christian life. During those intervening years, I not only purged practically all of my false guilt, but I was also liberated from the false model of the perfect Christian. I finally saw that our life is a process of growth that involves risk and change, failure and success. Sometimes we choose foolishly, sometimes wisely. At times we embrace holiness, while at other times we gravitate toward sin. As we keep growing, though, we become wiser and holier Christians until, in the final fulfillment, God completes the work in us that he began when we first accepted Christ by faith.

NEVER ALONE

Yet another critical factor is *community*. God never intended that we grow up in Christ by ourselves. The notion that the Christian life is "Just you and me, Lord" is American individualism disguised in religious language.

God does not redeem us merely to have us live one-on-one with him. As we have seen, God himself is a community of persons—Father, Son, and Spirit—who eternally love each other, serve each other, and work together in complete harmony to accomplish their united wills. They are the Divine Family, and they save us into an earthly family of their creation. *This created family is the church.* We are "God's children," and our spiritual Father is none other than the first person of the Trinity, whom we can now call *'Abbā,* our Father (Rom. 8:15–16). As children of God, we are thereby brothers and sisters. We share the same eternal Father, his eternal Son, and their eternal Spirit, through whom the Father and Son gradually work to purify us.

This Spirit works in us both individually and corporately. His work in me is not for my sake alone; he wants to reshape me in ways that will help his reshaping work in you as well. God is family-oriented. He loves all his children and seeks to build them up *as* family and *through* family. This is the primary purpose of the Spirit's gifts to us: All of the gifts come from "the same Spirit," and each gift is "given for the common good" of God's church (1 Cor. 12:4, 7).

You and I need each other to grow up in Christ. I will love him and others better by using my spiritual gifts to help you grow as a Christ-follower and by responding appropriately and gratefully to your exercise of your spiritual gifts so I can become more mature in the faith as well. You can help me, and I can help you. Together, through the work of the same Spirit, we can grow into Christian adulthood within the family of God.

THE POWER OF COOPERATIVE CHOICE

Still another critical factor is the power of *cooperative choice*. Growth in the Christian life is not accidental but intentional; it requires effort, not only God's, but ours too.

Paul understood this truth—he believed all Christians are runners in a race. After describing the lengths to which he would go "for the sake of the gospel," he exhorts us, "Do you not know that in a race all the runners run, but only one gets the prize? Run in such a way as to get the prize" (1 Cor. 9:23–24). In other words, run to win! Be a competitor. Don't be lazy. Don't hold back. Don't think that God does it all and you do nothing. Give all you have. Compete hard. Go after not fourth, third, or even second, but *first* place.

What does this entail? In Paul's words, it takes "strict training" (v. 25) and running with purpose. "I do not run like a man running aimlessly," he says. "I beat my body and make it my slave so that after I have preached to others, I myself will not be disqualified for the prize" (vv. 26–27). Paul realized that he had to work to discipline his life. He knew that continual growth in the practice of Christlikeness demands it.

What prize was Paul seeking? "A crown that will last forever" (v. 25). In another letter he describes this crown as "the crown of righteousness, which the Lord, the righteous Judge, will award to me on that day—and not only to me, but also to all who have longed for his appearing" (2 Tim. 4:8). This reward is not a crown all Christians will receive. It will go to those who have stepped out of the grandstands and come onto the field to train and compete according to God's design. It will go to those who have disciplined them-selves, kept the goal in mind, and run to win. In short, it will go to those believers who have endeavored to live to the full. Not satisfied with being observers or playing at spirituality, they listen intently to what the Divine Lover wants, then they draw on his many resources and carry out the work of growth and service they have been saved to do.[6]

Paul's efforts paid off. The Christian faith was firmly planted in the Middle East, Asia Minor, and Europe. Thousands upon thousands heard the gospel and responded with belief. Skeptics were either converted or silenced. Ene-mies of the cross became friends of Christ. The sick and disabled were healed. Some were even raised from the dead. The despairing found hope, the depressed found joy. The addicted and chained were freed. The greedy became givers. In short, Paul showed sinners the Savior, and countless numbers embraced him.[7]

Paul's efforts were not flawless, nor did they always achieve their mark, as he readily acknowledged.[8] Despite this, he never stopped running the race for which God had commissioned him. He kept training and racing faithfully, "straining toward what is ahead" and "press[ing] on toward the goal to win the prize for which God has called me heavenward in Christ Jesus" (Phil. 3:13–14). Jerry Bridges says of Paul that he "never had an off season; he never slacked off in his efforts. [His] was a lifelong discipline."[9]

As we can see, Paul's understanding of the Christian life does not promote a passive "let go and let God" approach. Rather, his view represents more of an active "get going with God" strategy. We're runners, not benchwarmers. And we're not Sunday-only athletes or weekend warriors—we are to train every day, week in and week out. Our training must be disciplined and rigorous.

But with whom are we to cooperate in our efforts—in other words, who is our trainer? The third person of the Trinity, the Holy Spirit, the very One who trained up Jesus in his humanity. He conceived Jesus' human nature in Mary.[10] He "filled [the young child Jesus] with wisdom" so he could grow "in wisdom" (Luke 2:40, 51). He came upon Jesus at his baptism, making him "full of the Holy Spirit" (3:21; 4:1). He led Jesus into the desert to be tempted by the devil, empowering Jesus to withstand Satan's assaults.[11] Then "Jesus returned to Galilee in the power of the Spirit" (4:14) to begin his work of teaching, healing, exorcism, disciple-building, and evangelism.

Jesus knew the Source of his power. At the beginning of his earthly ministry, he told some of his fellow Jews, "The Spirit of the Lord is on me" (v. 18). The Spirit of God enlightened and empowered the Son of God in his humanity so the Son could do the work of the Father faithfully. As Jesus said, "I have come down from heaven not to do my will but to do the will of him who sent me" (John 6:38). The One who sent him was "the Father" (5:36), and the One who enabled Jesus to accomplish the Father's will was the Spirit.[12]

The same Spirit who made Jesus effective also works in us. He wants to make us like Christ, but we must daily choose to cooperate with his work in our lives. This cooperative choice is what Scripture calls being "filled with the Spirit." The first disciples were "filled with the Holy Spirit" on the "day of Pentecost" (Acts 2:1, 4), and the event radically changed their lives.

Before that epochal event, the marks of spiritual immaturity were all too evident in their lives and service. They were just average, ordinary men of their day. All were slow learners (see Luke 24:45). They were self-seeking (see Mark 10:37, 41). They were paralyzed with fear of the Jews (see John 20:19). In Jesus' hour of deepest need at the Cross, they all "deserted him and fled" (Mark 14:50). They were ordinary, weak, failing men and women, very much like us.

But when at Pentecost "they were all filled with the Holy Spirit" and abandoned themselves to his control, a startling transformation took place. The timid became brave and the weak powerful. Doubters became believers and the selfish self-forgetful. Slow learners became avid scholars. Individualists became willing to submerge themselves in team ministry.

They all became vividly conscious of Christ's presence with them. Joy and thanksgiving were the keynotes of their corporate life (see Acts 2:46–47). In their previous ministry they had caused little stir, but now they gained the reputation of being "the men who have turned the world upside down."[13]

The biblical command to "be filled with the Spirit" (Eph. 5:18) is in the present tense, indicating that we are to *keep on* being filled with the Spirit. It is not a once-for-all-time event but an ongoing decision of giving ourselves over to his influence. Just as the Spirit worked in Jesus throughout his life, and just as he worked in the disciples' lives from the day of Pentecost onward, so he will work in us. But we must welcome him on a continual basis. Remember, love is not rude. Love will not force its way into our lives. We must open the door to love, letting love do its life-changing work.

> [When we] live by the Spirit, [we] will not gratify the desires of the sinful nature, [the acts of which] are obvious: sexual immorality, impurity and debauchery; idolatry and witchcraft; hatred, discord, jealousy, fits of rage, selfish ambition, dissensions, factions and envy; drunkenness, orgies, and the like. [Instead, we'll gain] the fruit of the Spirit, [which consists of] love, joy, peace, patience, kindness, goodness, faithfulness, gentleness and self-control. (Gal. 5:16, 19–23)

In short, what we get when we daily cooperate with the Spirit's work is the life of abundance Jesus promised to all those who believe and follow him.[14] This life does not come to us all at once, but it does come in proportion to how we voluntarily move forward in the Christian life under the Spirit's guidance and power.

MIND RENEWAL AND THE HABITS OF LOVE

So how do we keep being filled with the Holy Spirit? How do we daily give ourselves over to his renewing work in our lives? The answer brings us to the last critical factor I want to mention: *mind renewal and the habits of love.*

Habits are fixed choices—the same choices we make every day until they become our custom, or simply the way we do things. We no longer ponder over whether to make these decisions. They've become automatic, routine. We go through the same motions each morning upon waking. We like certain foods fixed certain ways, and we prefer to eat our meals at about the same times each day. We have routines for driving our cars, greeting friends and strangers, getting ready for bed, and a host of other daily activities. These habits even include ways we think, whether about people in general, world or local events, our local church, the worldwide church, or Christian teachings. Habits are deeply ingrained and, therefore, not easily changed.

However, since habits are learned, they likewise can be unlearned. And new habits can be gained if we have the mind and will to learn them. I mention intellect and volition for a reason: *Both* must be engaged in mutual cooperation for old habits to be shed and new ones to form.

In Romans 12, Paul presents three essentials for spiritual growth: our will, our body, and our mind, all working together toward a common goal:

> I urge you, brothers, in view of God's mercy, to offer your bodies as living sacrifices, holy and pleasing to God—this is your spiritual act of worship. Do not conform any longer to the pattern of this world, but be transformed by the renewing of your mind. Then you will be able to test and approve what God's will is—his good, pleasing and perfect will. (vv. 1–2)

Our *will* is the seat of active causality. It's the capacity through which we exercise power, where we do one thing rather than another. Paul's expressed will to the Roman Christians was urging them to give their whole selves to God. And how were they to do this? They were to choose to offer their bodies to the Lord, refuse to be conformed to what opposes him, and seek to be transformed through mind renewal. The actions of offering, refusing, transforming, and renewing require volitional choices, the active power we exercise by our will. These decisive actions are performed daily until they become fixed into habits that express the way we normally live.

Along with the will, Paul focuses on our *body*.[15] He says our body must be offered up to God because it's through our body that we live: We speak, listen, help, teach, learn, and love through our bodies. You are reading words I have typed with my fingers; you are seeing them through your eyes or hearing them with your ears. I am reaching you through your body, and you reach out to others and receive them into your life through your body as well. Spiritual change requires the body.

Our will and body also require our *mind* before they can work. Yes, we can experience involuntary (or reflexive) bodily reactions, such as when a doctor uses a rubber mallet to tap a certain place on our knee. But for our actions to be purposeful, for them to be truly intentional, they must originate in our mind and then move beyond our mind to become real in the external world. The thought *I think I'll go to the grocery store to get some food items we need* engages my will and body so that the process leads to reaching for my keys, getting into my car, and performing all the other activities that get me to the store. My mind can think about the store and what foods I'd like to buy, and it can think through all the steps necessary to meet that objective, but my mind cannot accomplish this task in the physical world without the cooperation of my will and body. If my body is crippled so that I can't perform the function myself, someone else's body must get the job done for me if I'm going to eat.

The mind produces and reasons through myriad ideas and choices. The will then carries out the mind's decisions through the body. The more efficiently and cooperatively our mind, will, and body are working, the more we can do for ourselves and for others.

The problem is that our bodies, minds, and wills can grow weak through disease and abuse. This is what sin has done to us: We are conceived, born, and raised in corruption, and without being saved and transformed, we will also live and die in corruption. We do not come into this world as the Lord intended. We are not perfect creatures in perfect harmony with God, his world, ourselves, and our neighbors; we are instead out of sync with everything and everyone. Sin has changed us. Every aspect of who and what we are has been harmed in some way by sin. Sin is like a computer virus; once it infects us, nothing works as it should.

We exacerbate sin's impact when we submit to its ways. This is what Paul points out when he says, "Do not conform any longer to the pattern of this world." The "world" is not God's perfect creation but a corruption that first invaded through the free, wrongful acts of some angels and then our original parents—Adam and Eve.[16] This parasitic perversion spread to all human beings and to the natural created order; our moral depravity largely expresses itself through a pattern of behavior characterized by evil, what Paul calls "the fruitless deeds of darkness" (Eph. 5:11) and "the acts of the sinful nature" (Gal. 5:19). Consequently, we now live in "the present evil age" (Gal. 1:4), a world marked by foolishness,[17] one that has turned away from the all-wise God and submitted itself to Satan—the fool of fools, the king of liars, the "god of this age" (2 Cor. 4:4). Paul calls on us to reject the wrongful pattern we once lived out. We're not to conform ourselves to it any longer.

Leaving evil habits behind, we're to relearn new habits—habits that begin with new thinking, with *mind renewal*. This involves what we believe about God, his world, and ourselves, and what our new love relationship with him entails, including his role as well as ours. As our beliefs change, so will our attitudes and behavior. This is because, as J. P. Moreland explains,

> Beliefs are the rails upon which our lives run. We almost always act according to what we really believe. It doesn't matter much what we say we believe or what we want others to think we believe. When the rubber meets the road, we act out our actual beliefs most of the time. That is why behavior is such a good indicator of a person's beliefs.[18]

Our new thinking is to be *reality thinking:* believing that what's true is true and that what's good is good. Christianity calls on us to discard false beliefs, discovering and embracing what *is*. We, of all people, should be the ones who most prize the pursuit and possession of truth. It's truth that sets us free. It's truth that brings us to Love. The more we know what's true, the more aligned we can become with reality, including and especially with ultimate reality, which is God himself. In fact, *that's* what the Christian life is—rejecting false conceptions and becoming conformed to the ultimately Real. In the process we will gradually identify and overcome our evil beliefs and the behavior that issues from them, choosing the good instead.

As we do this work—living the Christian life with the Holy Spirit's help—we *will* change. We *will* undergo the transformation Paul mentions. We *will* become more conformed to whom and what God is and what he desires for us. In this state of growing renewal, we "will be able to test and approve what God's will is—his good, pleasing and perfect will" (Rom. 12:2).

Knowing that the mind, body, and will are all integral to the spiritual growth process, what new habits must we learn and cultivate so that they will work effectively together—with the support of the Spirit—to mature us in our love relationship with God? Revealed in Scripture and historically passed down by the church as the spiritual disciplines, they're what I call "the habits of love."

The spiritual disciplines are *spiritual* because they point beyond this world of the senses to the world of the Spirit. They are *disciplines* because they require effort and attention to cultivate and maintain. They are *habits* because they must become so entrenched in us that they are commonplace—activities as vital and normal as breathing. They are *loving* because they serve to deepen and strengthen our relationship with God and all he loves. These love habits, then, engage all we are and encompass all we have, focusing everything on the Divine Lover, the true Center of all life.

The idea of the spiritual disciplines as love habits is a paradigm shift in my own thinking. Like many other Christian writers, I long viewed the disciplines through the metaphors of training for and running a race, preparing for and fighting a war, being faithful in obeying God's commands, cooperating with him in the work of spiritual transformation, and deepening intimacy with him, seeing myself as a sinner saved by grace and him as my gracious Savior. While all these images are biblical and worthwhile, I have come to see that they can be best understood through the lens of love—what Paul recognized as the highest virtue and what Jesus said should most clearly delineate his followers.[19] Love is the ultimate focus, the image through which all other images take on vitality. Love is the essence of the Christian life—indeed, of all life—and the habits of love, when it comes to our relationship with God, are the spiritual disciplines.

Here's a taste of what I mean. When you love someone, you want to open up to him or her, be vulnerable, share your hopes and dreams, successes and failures, needs and wants, knowing you'll be received and heard. You also want that person to open up to you, laying bare the soul. In our connection with God, this connection is called *prayer*.

We also enjoy spending time alone with our human loves. We don't even have to speak; just being in each other's presence is enough. In the spiritual realm, this lingering is called *solitude* and *silence*.

We also want to know our loved ones as well as we can. We listen carefully to what they say, we closely watch what they do . . . in short, we focus on them to learn more about them. In our relationship to God, this is the spiritual discipline of *study*.

Have you ever had someone in your life whom you love and respect so much that you regularly seek her out for advice and counsel? This resembles what we do when we look to God for *guidance.*

We likewise enjoy (or at least learn to enjoy) our lover's friends and family. We spend time with them and serve them however we can, and what motivates us most is our love for our lover. On the spiritual side, these activities come under the names of *service, sacrifice,* and *fellowship.*

Every spiritual discipline, when viewed through the eyes of love, turns out to be the way to develop, maintain, and deepen our intimacy with the Lord. This breakthrough realization showed me how love is truly the essence of the life believers are called to live through Jesus Christ.

As you read on, keep in mind that *these love habits are not the essence of Christianity; the love of Christ is.* Neither are they the goal of the Christian life; transformation from sinner to saint in Christ is. *The habits of love are, however, the means to knowing Christ more fully, to loving him more deeply, to serving him more faithfully, and to becoming like him more effectively.* They are the way of Christ—his way, through the empowering and enlightening work of his Spirit, to incarnate himself in us. Therein we will undergo an abiding, comprehensive transformation into Christlikeness. We will find and experience the deeper Christian life, which is nothing less than a rich love relationship with God, his creation, and his family, the church.

The habits of love are many and diverse, treating different aspects of our lives in an attempt to help us bring every facet of who we are and what we do into conformity with our Lover's will. In this book I have chosen to cover the following disciplines:[20]

- simplicity

- submission

- prayer

- guidance

- study

- meditation

- journaling

- solitude

- silence

- confession

- forgiveness

- service
- sacrifice
- evangelism
- apologetics

In the following chapters, you'll find each of these habits explained, illustrated, and joined to our shared love with God. You'll learn why they're the habits of Christ's way, the regular means God uses to shower us with his affection and ones we use to express our love for him. You'll also find practical suggestions for turning these loving activities into spiritual habits.

I've written this book for you to *use,* not simply read. Knowledge learned is knowledge applied: For these time-proven practices to help you grow in Christ, you must discipline yourself to make them a vital part of your everyday life. They enrich our love relationship with God; this means we must move beyond reading words and understanding concepts to actually engaging the three persons of the Godhead. I want you to *experience* the Lover, the Loved One, and the Bond of Love. I want you to draw from their bountiful resources, seeing for yourself how sufficient and supportive they are. I want you to realize how incredibly valuable you are and how much you are cherished by the One who is love. This you must do with the Lord's help. Finding the way of Christ is good; learning it by personal application, with his help, is far better. I hope you will travel the most excellent way.

following LOVE'S WAY

4. Simplicity:
the God-centered life

There's a common misconception that believers frequently accept
and attempt to live out—namely, that the Christian life is about achieving
balance. The love habit called *simplicity* dispels this myth.

In seminary I was required to take a class on Christian living. One of the
texts was a generally good book by Charles Ryrie entitled *Balancing the Christian Life*. In it he says,

> There is nothing more devastating to the practice of spiritual living
> than an imbalance. . . . Too much emphasis on the mystical may
> obscure the practicality of spiritual living, while an overemphasis on
> practicality may result in a lack of vision. A constant reiteration of the
> need for repeated rededications could lead to a stagnant Christian life
> in which there is not consistent and substantial growth. An overempha-
> sis on confession could cause unhealthy introspection, while an under-
> emphasis might tend to make one insensitive to sin. Balance is the key
> to a wholesome spiritual life.[1]

Much of Ryrie's book applies this perspective to spiritual gifts, spiritual war-
fare, finances, temptation, confession, forgiveness, and a number of other

topics. The recurring theme: seeking balance in all areas of one's life in Christ.

As I continued my education, this *balance* idea kept coming up, not only from faculty but also from guest speakers and students. Amid incredible academic demands on our time and energy, we were told to carve out daily periods of devotional time with God, which were to be balanced with time given to family and friends, church attendance and ministry engagement, job requirements, recreation needs, and everything else we wanted or needed. Each facet of our crammed lives had to be in balance with every other facet.

It took me about a year to realize that this balancing act was not only impossible but unhealthy, verging on the insane. It didn't lead to balanced living, where everything was wholesome and in its proper place, but to fragmentation, where little was integrated with anything else. It created frustrating and strained relationships, where no one received what they needed, much less desired, from others. It churned out exhausted students who couldn't satisfy their own needs (including sleep). And, I believe, it contributed to increased divorce and adultery rates among the student body. Balancing the Christian life was an approach I chose to abandon.

Instead, I chose Jesus' way: I decided to live all out for God. Ironically enough, this approach came to me during my seminary studies. Working through the Gospels (especially John), I discovered that *Jesus lived an unbalanced life.* Rather than laboring to make everything "equal out," he oriented himself to his heavenly Father, and purposed through the Holy Spirit to say and do all that the Father revealed to him. Consider his own words:

> "I tell you the truth, the Son can do nothing by himself; he can do only what he sees his Father doing, because whatever the Father does the Son also does. For the Father loves the Son and shows him all he does. . . .
> "By myself I can do nothing; I judge only as I hear, and my judgment is just, for I seek not to please myself but him who sent me. . . .
> "I have come down from heaven not to do my will but to do the will of him who sent me" (John 5:19–20, 30; 6:38).

Jesus knew who he was: the Father's Son, eternal deity and full humanity. Jesus placed his Father first, looking to him for everything and ordering his life to this truth about reality. Rather than juggling and measuring, he lived with *one center,* God the Father, *one power base,* God the Spirit, and *one purpose:* to always do the Father's will. His commitment was so complete (*un*balanced) that seeing and hearing and believing on him was tantamount to seeing and hearing and believing on his heavenly Father. "'If you knew Me,'" Jesus said, "'you would know My Father also'" (John 8:19 NASB). Christ's life was fully conformed to the Father's revealed will.

THE HEART OF SIMPLICITY

Taking Jesus as my model, I began fleshing out what it means to genuinely follow in his footsteps, and the process took me to *the heart of simplicity*. Simplicity is about focus. Simplicity is about aligning our lives with the Source of life. Simply put, *simplicity is loving God with all we are and have; it is centering everything on our Divine Lover.* Jesus put it (and lived it) this way:

> "Love the Lord your God with all your heart and with all your soul and with all your mind. This is the first and greatest commandment" (Matt. 22:37–38).

From this, all the other commandments flow, and from simplicity flow all the other disciplines.

A close examination of this mandate shows that simplicity has four essential elements: divine love, personal relationship, one God, and total commitment.

Divine Love

The center of life is love, *agapē*. Our Lover created all things; therefore, love is the fabric of created reality. Our Lover also sustains all things; consequently, love is the power that perpetually envelopes created reality. Life originated and continues in love; thus, it makes perfect sense for us to approach our Lover out of love for him. The word for *love* in the greatest commandment is the imperative form of *agapē*—Jesus commands us to *agapē* God.

To our twenty-first-century ears, being *commanded* to love *anyone* sounds unreasonable. After all, isn't love a feeling, and don't feelings change, sometimes even moment to moment? Emotions can even well up within us and overwhelm us, even when we don't want them to, so how can we control them? How can we obey the command to love, if love is a feeling? The answer is, if love *were* primarily a feeling, we couldn't. Feelings cannot be mandated; they simply are. Emotions come and go, ebb and flow. They are relative to situations and persons, even to our own psychological state.

Commands, on the other hand, are absolute and authoritative, given with the expectation that they are to be obeyed no matter what. Recall what the centurion said when he asked the Lord to heal his servant from a distance: "Just say the word, and my servant will be healed. For I myself am a man under authority, with soldiers under me. I tell this one, 'Go,' and he goes; and that one, 'Come,' and he comes. I say to my servant, 'Do this,' and he does it." He expected his soldiers to obey his commands, and they did, just as Jesus expects us to obey the greatest commandment: *Love God.*

For love, then, to be commanded, it must not be a changing feeling. *Agapē* must be an activity, a force, a power, an act of the will that can always be carried out regardless of our emotional ups and downs. This is precisely what Paul reveals in 1 Corinthians 13. He tells us what love *does*—mentioning patience, kindness, rejoicing in the good, protecting, trusting, hoping, and persevering—and what love *doesn't* do—envy, boast, become prideful, act rudely, seek itself, become easily angered, keep a record of wrongs, delight in evil, or come to an end.

Agapē always behaves in positive ways and never in negative ones. Each verb Paul uses about love is in the present tense, indicating continuous action. In other words, *agapē* is always patient and never envious, always kind and never boastful, always rejoicing in the good and never delighting in evil. *Agapē* has no peaks and valleys, no variability.

This is how God loves us. His actions toward us are always full of *agapē*. Because he is *agapē* itself, his being is *agapē* unlimited—he does not, or cannot, will anything less than perfect love. He cannot *become* loving any more than water can become wet. Water *is* wet; God *is* loving.

While we, on the other hand, are not *agapē* itself, Jesus commands us to love God the way he loves us. Can we? Not on our own. *Agapē* in its fullness is perfect love consistently expressed; we are not perfect love, so we cannot express love perfectly. Even the first humans failed to love God with unswerving devotion: They doubted his word, questioned his intentions, swelled with pride and envy, and out of all this spurned his perfect love. Since they disobeyed him, the world has never produced a flawless person who could express anything perfectly. We pass on the propensity to sin from parent to child; the bent toward evil is embedded in us. We do not have to give in to it, but we do—all of us do. *Agapē*, then, which is devoid of sin in its fullness, is out of our fallen grasp; drawing on our own unaided abilities, we cannot *agapē* God, ourselves, or anyone else.

So has Jesus given us a standard that we have no hope of maintaining? Not at all. We *can* obey this command *with supernatural help,* and the Lover offers it. Just as water can make other things wet, so God, who is "love-in-eternal-action,"[2] can make us loving as well. How? In his letter to the Galatians, Paul tells us: *agapē* comes from the Bond of Love (5:22). The Spirit works in us to bring about *agapē,* and through that work the activities and benefits of love will follow: "joy, peace, patience, kindness, goodness, faithfulness, gentleness and self-control" (vv. 22–23). No wonder Paul can say that "against such things there is no law" (v. 23), for the essence of divine law *is* love. Law and love are ultimately unopposed to each other: Good law is loving, and true love is lawful. *Agapē* never fights itself but only what opposes it (evil).

Therefore, Paul exhorts us to "keep in step with the Spirit" (v. 25), which is to say, "Cooperate with the Spirit's transforming work and you will grow in your ability to express *agapē*." The Spirit is making us Christlike; because Christ came as *agapē* enfleshed, keeping in step with the Spirit means we'll enflesh *agapē* too.

Of course, this ability in us will not come about immediately or find its perfect fulfillment this side of heaven. The more the Spirit fills us, the more *agapē* will as well; the more Christlike we become, the more loving we will be. *Agapē* will grow in us and more fully express itself through us as we spiritually mature. The greatest commandment will remain for us a goal we will never completely achieve until we become fully like Jesus Christ—when we finally "see him as he is" (1 John 3:2). Nevertheless, a goal unachievable to its *fullest* degree in this life is still well worth striving for; that we won't have it *all* here doesn't mean we should abandon having *as much as possible* through the pursuit. The bottom line is this:

Do you want peace and joy? Love God.

Do you want to be patient and kind? Love God.

Do you want the benefits of goodness and self-control? Love God.

Do you want to become a faithful person—someone people can count on and trust? Love God.

Do you want to finally achieve self-control? Love God.

Do you want to receive and give love more consistently? Love God.

All of these flow from the Bond of Love. Cooperate with the Spirit, and he will give you these heavenly delights. The more you grow, the more these benefits will manifest themselves in you. The One who is *agapē* will give you *agapē* so that you can give *agapē* back to him and to others.

Person-to-Person Relationship

Christ's command to "love the Lord your God" indicates that the object of our love is a *personal Being*. The directive is not "love your country" or "love your job" or "love your hobby" or "love your sanctuary" or "love your spiritual gifts." Rather than inanimate objects or peripheral activities, we're called to devote ourselves to the triune, personal God. Like us, God is an *I;* he is not a thing, and neither are we. He has all the attributes of personhood infinitely; we have them finitely. Thus, we are to relate to him as our God, realizing and embracing that we are in a *person-to-person relationship* with our Creator, Sustainer, Savior, and Lord. By faith we have placed ourselves in his hands, and he has embraced us as his own. We are personally related to him, and he is personally related to us.

This is a two-way giving of love: We're to love God in response to his love for us, as the beloved disciple of Jesus says,

> Dear friends . . . love comes from God. Everyone who loves has been born of God and knows God. Whoever does not love does not know God, because God is love. This is how God showed his love among us: He sent his one and only Son into the world that we might live through him. This is love: not that we loved God, but that he loved us and sent his Son as an atoning sacrifice for our sins. (1 John 4:7–10)

We love him because he loved us first.

This intimacy shares many characteristics that are common in love relationships between humans. Several of these give us insight into what person-to-person *agapē* with God is really all about. Consider marital love.

Unity and New Life

At the establishment of marriage in Genesis 2, we read, "For this reason a man will leave his father and mother and be united to his wife, and they will become one flesh" (v. 24). Marital love is designed to bring unity between a man and a woman, and this union should embrace every part of a couple's life together: their spiritual development, their sexual expression and fulfillment, their child-bearing and child-raising, their psychological well-being, their careers, their finances, their social commitments . . . their everything.[3] Together they plant and grow a new life, one they could not create and enjoy apart from each other, a shared life forged out of two individuals dedicated to growing a union that expresses each of them yet produces more than their sum. Their shared life creates a new life.

Consider the product of a married couple's sexual union. The distinct twenty-three chromosomes of the mother and the distinct twenty-three chromosomes of the father unite within the mother and become a new human person. "[T]he conceptus is a new . . . individual with its own genetic code (with forty-six chromosomes), a code that is neither her mother's nor her father's" but uniquely her own. The combined genetic makeup of her parents brings about a uniquely new life that will have her own "gender, eye color, bone structure, hair color, skin color, [susceptibility] to certain diseases," and all the other attributes that mark her as a being who shares our common human nature yet will forever remain "unlike any individual who has been conceived before and . . . unlike any individual who will ever be conceived again (unless she is an identical twin)."[4] The baby is a growing person, her own person. She is not her mother or her father, and she is more than the sum of her parents: She is a new life.

The same is true of a married couple. A man and a woman, when he becomes her husband and she becomes his wife, combine their lives and bring themselves into their new relationship. Together they share their dreams, hopes, and fears, creating and shaping new ones. They postpone or sacrifice individual pursuits in order to achieve something bigger and better. Their self-centeredness gives way to other-centeredness: Meeting his needs becomes her priority, and meeting her needs becomes his. They seek to become of one mind and heart, reaching out to each other, reshaping each other, even becoming more like each other. As times goes on, they pick up some of each other's mannerisms, attitudes, and perspectives. Their growing conformity to each other is transforming to the relationship, and together they are building something that only united lives can create. They are giving birth to and growing a new life—a life that shows the contributing marks of each partner, but a life that is far more than either person could create independently.

Likewise, when we become believers, we are united with Jesus Christ and thereby begin a new life together with him. Our old life of sin "was crucified with him so that the body of sin might be done away with . . . because anyone who has died has been freed from sin" (Rom. 6:6–7). No longer in bondage to our sin-ridden past, we have been resurrected to a new life through the risen Christ: We are now "dead to sin but alive to God in Christ Jesus" (v. 11), living a "new life" (v. 4) in union with our Lord. Everything has changed; we have abandoned the life we once knew and entered a new life, given by God as an offering through Jesus. Our faith in the Son gives us entrance into this new life in which we are reconciled (rightly related) to God.

However, once again, this new life is not immediately made complete; it is filled out as we grow up in our relationship with God, cooperating with the Spirit's work of restoration and transformation. In this way, God gives us the privilege of being his co-workers. The structure of our new life is of his making, but the process of maturing—filling it out—will be a joint effort. In other words, together, God and we will grow a life that neither God nor we could grow alone. Just as a flourishing human marriage requires the cooperation of each partner, so the growth of a new life begun in Christ requires our cooperation with the Spirit. Dying to the old world, we enter and grow up in a new one.

This new life through our union with Christ affects our *everything*; nothing is untouched. God is at work in us to transform all we are into all the good we can be. He is reshaping our character and actions. He is impacting all our relationships and interpersonal skills. He is seeking to change our mind and will. What we value is also shifting: What we once "couldn't live without" we have come to see as far less valuable, maybe not important at all, perhaps even sinful. We are changing within, becoming more deeply one with Christ as his life is altering ours. We are becoming like our Lord; his life is becoming our life. He is raising us up, uniting us to him, his Father, and his Spirit. He is seeing the answer to his prayer "that all of them may be one, Father, just as you are in me and I am in you. May they also be in us" (John 17:20–21).

In this uniting process, we do not lose ourselves but gain ourselves—our *best* selves, our *true* selves. Divine Love is committed to our full purification into Christlikeness, the very fullness we were created to be. This demands the purging of all that stands in the way of this goal's achievement: All blemishes, all distortions, all that corrupts must go.

Yet this is only half the story. Purging is the work of *restoration*, getting us to the goodness that is already our potential but becomes actual once sin is out of our lives. This is like discovering a badly nicked and poorly painted table, and then removing the paint and sanding the surfaces to reveal the invaluable, precious wood and restoring it to its pristine beauty.

The other half is *transformation*, the stage of the process that takes us beyond restoration to metamorphosis. This is where unity reaches its optimum; it is where we "participate in the divine nature" (2 Peter 1:4). We become as much like God as we can while retaining our humanness. We become as fully good, fully knowledgeable, fully harmonious, fully loving, fully joyful . . . as fully perfect as a finite human can be. We do not become God, which is impossible; we become like him in all the fullness a human being can become. We become united to our Creator while keeping our distinct identity as his saved creatures.

We become like the ceiling of the Sistine Chapel. Before Michelangelo painted it, he had to prepare it to make possible the work of art he had envisioned it could become. Once the ceiling had been restored and adequately prepared, he then set about transforming it into "a sublime work of Christian art" depicting "the history of humanity" portrayed in the Bible.[5] Similarly, God is in the process of making *us* his *greatest* created work of art, creatures displaying the Creator's sublime magnificence and therein finding maximum fulfillment. The first stage in this process is restoration; the second stage is transformation. Both further and deepen our unity with our Divine Lover.

Intimacy and Vulnerability

As person-to-person relationships develop, they become increasingly transparent. I share more about me, and you reveal more about yourself. The more I find I can trust you, the more encouraged I am to further open up to you, and vice versa. The more we reveal, the more vulnerable we become as long as our mutual trust goes unviolated. Greater revelations deepen our intimacy and encourage greater degrees of vulnerability. If the process continues, we'll learn more about each other than perhaps anyone other than God knows.

The best, longest-lasting relationships are those where deep intimacy and transparent vulnerability are the abiding hallmarks. This is as true in our relationship with God as it is with people, whether with a spouse, another family member, friend, minister, or colleague. We *need* such relationships, especially with the One who knows us fully and loves us perfectly.

Our loving God desires to have this kind of intimacy with us. Jesus said that the Father has a special love for those who love his Son, and that Father and Son will make their "home" with them.[6] Jesus says those who do the Father's will are members of his spiritual family; as far as he is concerned, they are his true relatives.[7] And the One whom Jesus calls Father we can as well, even using the term *'Abbā*—the same word Jesus used to express his familial intimacy with the heavenly Father.

Along with being loved by God, regarded as part of his family, and being able to call him *'Abbā,* we can also be his friends. Jesus says,

"You are my friends if you do what I command. I no longer call you servants, because a servant does not know his master's business. Instead, I have called you friends, for everything that I learned from my Father I have made known to you" (John 15:14–15).

In Christ, we have the kind of love relationship with God resembling the best that family and friendship have to offer. God makes his home with us: He lives with us, unites us to himself, opens himself up to us, revealing more and more of himself to us as he reveals more and more of ourselves to us.

God has nothing to learn about us; he is already completely acquainted. Nevertheless, he gives us the chance to know him also, if we'll just entrust ourselves to him. The choice for intimacy is ours.

Honesty and Truth

Along with intimacy and vulnerability come honesty and truth. Truth is telling it like it is, and honesty is telling the truth even when doing so might hurt or make us look bad.

Truth-telling at all costs is best achieved in an authentically loving relationship. A husband can confess inadequacies to a wife who loves him no matter what. A child can tell the truth about disobedience to a father who has consistently shown that he has his child's best interests at heart.

Dishonesty is usually motivated by the fear of rejection or the fear of ridicule. *Love casts out both fears:* "There is no fear in love. But perfect love drives out fear, because fear has to do with punishment" (1 John 4:18). A husband will not be afraid of his wife's making fun of his shortcomings if he knows she loves him; he can look to her for understanding, comfort, and support, as ridicule will be far from her. A child will not be terrified of revealing a misbehavior to her parents as long as she knows they will listen to her struggle, help her learn from it, and overcome it so that next time she'll have the courage to do what's right.

Truth and honesty drive our love relationship with God: Just as he is love, Jesus says that he is "the truth" (John 14:6), and Paul adds that the "truth is in Jesus" (Eph. 4:21). The psalmist exclaims that God's "truth reaches to the skies" (108:4 NASB) and that the "works of His hands are truth" (111:7 NASB). God's "word is truth," and Jesus prayed that the Father would sanctify us "in the truth" (John 17:17 NASB). Moreover, God always tells the truth; he's never dishonest. People lie, but God is always found to be true.[8]

God will always shoot straight with us. He will not deceive us or lie to us; he will tell us the truth, for true love *always* speaks truthfully. For the very best to be realized, the worst that blocks the way must be revealed. We cannot rise to the heights unless we acknowledge our status in the depths and resolve to make the climb with the Spirit's help. Out of his love for us, God exposes even our worst while showing us how great we can become through his supernatural work.

Just as our Lover lives honestly with us, he expects us to live honestly with him. Since he already knows everything about us, there's nothing we can hide from him. So why try? When we sin, we ought to confess it. When we delight over some good, we must thank him and praise him for it. When we don't understand what he's doing, we should share our confusion with him. When he acts in a way we feel is inadequate or insensitive, we should tell him how we feel, even if we're angry or disappointed. He can handle whatever we hand him, and he will always receive it with a heart filled with *agapē* for us.

Acceptance and Safety

When we're in a love relationship, we're in an environment marked by acceptance and safety. We have a shelter from life's storms and a place where we can grow. We're loved as we are, but we're also encouraged to develop our full potential. In such a relationship we have the support to dream and to pursue our dream, as well as the freedom to fail without facing condemnation. We have, in other words, the right setting to relax. I'm not talking about the kind of relaxing that leads to laziness; rather, it's the relaxation that says, "I enjoy a love that's not earned but received, a love that takes me just as I am and then gives me what I need to mature into the person only love can help me become, a love that gives me room to fail while showing me how to succeed." Here we can find rest in the midst of the work as well as fresh springs of creativity to tackle the challenges facing us.

In Christ we have God's complete acceptance. Through our faith in Jesus, God reconciles us to himself, forgives us our sins against him, cleans out the pollutants within us, and baptizes us in his Spirit, giving us the supernatural power we need to grow up and mature in him.[9] Here we find the "good works" we are saved to accomplish (Eph. 2:10). We also find a place of rest— a rest that begins now in the person of Christ and will be ultimately fulfilled in the new heaven and new earth yet to come.[10] Through the Spirit, we have the power to do even greater works than Jesus did during his first-century ministry.[11] God gives us incalculable resources, then dares us to dream dreams far bigger than ourselves, dreams that encourage us to pursue what is impossible for us to achieve alone but entirely possible when we pursue them arm in arm with our Divine Lover. "What is impossible with men is possible with God" (Luke 18:27).

In this loving environment of acceptance and safety, we gain the courage to face the world: "If God is for us, who can be against us?" Can anyone or anything separate us from God's love? "No," Paul replies, "neither death nor life, neither angels nor demons, neither the present nor the future, nor any powers, neither height nor depth, nor anything else in all creation, will be able to separate us from the love of God that is in Christ Jesus our Lord" (Rom. 8:31, 37–39). If the love relationship is this strong—if we finally trust that *nobody* and *nothing* can cut us off from the Source of love and life—then we can set aside our fears and even take monumental risks. Fears of failure and ridicule, misunderstanding and inadequacy, obscurity and fame . . . whatever worries we harbor are fleeting shadows in the bright light of *agapē*.

Our love connection with God—the best gift we can ever receive—is safe from all intruders, from all potential or actual enemies. It is ours forever if we will accept it and embrace it as our own. What could possibly matter more than this? If we are in our right minds, thinking clearly, we must answer, "Absolutely nothing matters more than having God's love in my life." When we have God's love, we have everything good, for his love encompasses all he is and all he does directly or indirectly.

> Thus Saint Augustine says in the *Confessions* that he who has God has everything, and he who has God and nothing else lacks nothing, and he who has God and everything else does not have anything more than he who has God alone.[12]

Or, to put it in the words of C. S. Lewis, "Aim at Heaven and you will get earth 'thrown in'; aim at earth and you will get neither."[13] We aim at heaven by loving God with our everything, and in return we receive his everything, including all of creation.[14] There's no better exchange than this.

So when Jesus reiterates the greatest commandment, "Love the Lord your God," he is reminding us that the greatest intimacy we can ever enjoy is what we can have with God himself, the ultimate and eternal Center of perfect relationship. God offers us the incredible privilege of being in relationship with him—the love relationship for which we were made, the one in which we will find our highest fulfillment now and forever. Augustine exclaimed in prayer, "Thou hast made us for Thyself and our hearts are restless till they rest in Thee."[15]

The One God

So far we've seen that divine love and personal relationship are essential to simplicity. The third essential—one God—takes us to the object of our supreme devotion.

"Love the Lord your God," Jesus said. "*The* Lord" points to the fact that there is but one God (Jesus did not say "*a* Lord"). Moreover, he quoted from the fifth book of the Hebrew Scriptures (Deuteronomy), which is where the greatest commandment is first found, appearing immediately after the *shema,* Judaism's basic confession of faith: "Hear, O Israel! The LORD is our God, the LORD is one!" (6:4 NASB). Earlier in the same book, Moses challenged, "Acknowledge and take to heart this day that the LORD is God in heaven above and on the earth below. There is no other" (4:39). So when Jesus cited the passage following the *shema* as the greatest commandment (6:5), he was re-affirming that there is one God; no others exist.

In loving this one Lord as we're commanded, we declare him to be *our* God: "Love the Lord *your* God," said Jesus. *Your* God? Does this suggest that I could have a God different from yours? How could this be? If there really is only *one* God, how could you or I love any other? Is it possible for us to love something that isn't actually there to love?

Unfortunately, the answer is yes. Human beings are immensely imaginative. Throughout our history, we've granted divine status to just about everything around us: the stars and planets, rocks and trees, large and small animals, wind and fire, lightning and thunder, angels and demons. We've even worshiped ourselves and the work of our own hands. In the process, we've given ourselves to fraudulent imposters, fictional deities, figments of our imagination. We've prostituted ourselves, given our love to that which, at worst, cannot love us back at all and, at best, cannot love us anywhere near the degree that the only living God can and does.

We need a real Lover, a Lover who can give us the fullness of *agapē.* The only One who meets these qualifications is the God who actually exists, the Lover who is *agapē,* the One who must become *our* God, yours and mine. The only way this can happen is by our will; we must choose to receive God's love and to love him back. Dreaming about it won't produce it; talking about it won't create it; reasoning through it won't achieve it; attending church won't bring it about. *We must each choose to devote ourselves to him.* Because he is the one and only God, he is already our God by ontological fact. But he becomes our God in mutual loving relationship through the act of our individual wills. Again: Apart from our respective choices, he remains our Creator,

Sustainer, and Judge but is not our Friend, Father, and Beloved.

The choice Joshua set before the Hebrews long ago applies to us as well:

> If serving the Lord seems undesirable to you, then choose for your-
> selves this day whom you will serve, whether the gods your forefathers
> served beyond the River, or the gods of the Amorites, in whose land you
> are living. But as for me and my household, we will serve the Lord. (Josh.
> 24:15)

Total Commitment

Choosing to love the one and only God is not a one-time decision any more than choosing to love one woman for the remainder of life takes place once. Loving someone occurs day by day, hour by hour, moment by moment. It takes place on good days and bad days, whether we feel like loving or not. We love by choice and by ongoing choices regardless of the circumstances. Therefore, to fulfill the command to "love the Lord your God," we must love him and keep on loving him always. *Agapē* "always perseveres" (1 Cor. 13:7).

But there's more, for Jesus goes on to tell us that we must love God with all our heart, all our soul, and all our mind. The ultimate Being deserves our ultimate commitment—precisely what this commandment requires. God gives us his all, and he expects us to give him our all in return. His all-out devotion to us demands our all-out commitment to him. He must be our first and highest love. Nothing must come before him, and nothing must receive more than him. We must be totally sold out to him and to him alone.

The irony is that only by loving God fully can we love anyone else truly: He is the key to all other loves. If our love for him is as it should be, our love for others will become as it should be. We will not love our spouse as if he or she is divine; we will love our spouse as someone beloved of God first and loved by us second. Only God can love our spouse perfectly, and our spouse deserves from us the kind of love that only God can grow in us and flow through us. So when we're loving God as we should, our spouse is being loved as she should; rightly loving God leads to rightly loving others. This is why the second-greatest commandment is to "love your neighbor as yourself" (Matt. 22:39). I will love myself and my neighbor best when I am loving God most.

SIMPLICITY IS . . .

Given the four essentials of simplicity conveyed in the greatest of all com-mandments, we can now see that *simplicity is the habit of centering our ulti-*

mate loving devotion on the living personal God. We must not let anything on earth or in heaven become a rival to his place in our lives. He is the Center; all else is dependent on him. We do not *make* God the hub of our lives, as if he needs us to put him in his proper place. Simplicity requires that we see that God *is,* in fact, the hub of everything he created. Simplicity calls on us to recognize what is already true and then align ourselves with that truth. And not only align ourselves, but devote ourselves—commit all we are and have— to serving and loving the God of that truth.

CENTERED LIVING

While in seminary, I started doing exactly this. For example, I realized that since God is the Center of all life, every moment of my day needs to be lived in light of that fact. A half-hour devotional time did not end my commitment to God until the next morning; my entire day had to somehow honor the fact that my existence is to revolve around him. So I worked to turn my whole day into an offering. My life would be my devotion to God: my studies, my relationships, my work and play, my speech, my political positions, my thought life, my diet, my finances, my church attendance, my personal and corporate worship. Nothing would be left out. I sought to order everything to God's truth and will.

This process did not lead to stale legalism, where dos and don'ts define what a person is and does. Rather, it led to newfound freedom. Trying to gain an unachievable balance went by the wayside; my fragmented life gave way to a united life of "undivided devotion to the Lord" (1 Cor. 7:35). Instead of chopping up my day between time with God, time in classes, time with family and friends, time at work, time to eat and sleep and do assignments, I saw God permeate every moment of my existence. I began seeing him in all of life and seeking to live through it all as he would desire.

In my classes, I studied about God and his ways in the world. In my homework, I deepened my understanding of the Lord and what he wanted of me and for me. In my relationships with others, I started seeing them as God did—some as unbelievers who desperately needed him, some as believers who needed more of him, and all as his image-bearers deeply loved by him. In my work, I treated my colleagues as objects of divine love, and my productivity as service to God. Even while playing with my children, I took teachable moments to help them see that he loves them and that he loves play too. Throughout each day, I prayed, asking him to help me see his presence and draw more readily on his wisdom and power, to show me how to meet the needs of my loved ones and his. He always answered this prayer.

By the time I graduated from seminary in 1984, I ended up with a wonderful education and an even better experience of divinely centered living. My shift in perspective turned my four-year program into a six-year effort. I slowed the pace. I focused on those things that clearly mattered most. I sacrificed great grades for good (and some grades not so good) in order to give my wife and children more of what they deserved from me, and so that I could learn enough to keep learning for a lifetime.

On the personal side, fellow seminarians would often ask me how I found so much time to spend with my family. They were amazed that I could keep up with studies and a host of other activities and still help clean the house, tend the yard, take my wife on frequent dates, spend hours with my kids, and serve as a mini-pastor at my church. "How do you manage it all?" they'd inquire.

My answer was less articulate then, but this is how I would say it now:

> Life is not about managing, about juggling this task and that relationship and finding a way to meet the demands of both. Of course, the managing task is an important one, but it's not a defining one. What life is really about is living and loving, and I began to more fully experience both when I stopped trying to squeeze God into the nooks and crannies and took seriously the fact that he is the Center and Source of life.
>
> This required a realignment on my part. And that change began with a change of mind that led to a change of will. The intellectual shift involved coming to grips with the truth that God is not just number one in my life; he is *all* the numbers, and nothing must take his place. The volitional shift began when I made pursuing this truth an all-consuming activity. In the process, God keeps giving me more of himself and all that's genuinely important. With him as my everything, he gives me more of his perspective on everything. I increasingly soak up his attitude, his love, his desires, his knowledge, and his power to live my life with his priorities.
>
> As a result, I keep learning what the Lord values most, then making those values my most precious ones. Among those high-ticket items are people, especially those under my loving care. People will endure forever, and it's for them that Christ came and gave up his life. So I must give myself to them too, especially those closest to me. That means my family deserves more from me than I give to others. As I personally

embraced that divine priority, my family and I benefited immeasurably through the realignment choice.

This centering habit has produced the best win/win scenario I've ever seen. My life still manifests struggle and hurt, but I can handle it far better. I still sometimes fail my Lord and others, but much less often than before. All in all, I have found that what God said to Paul is true for me as well: "My grace is sufficient for you, for my power is made perfect in weakness" (2 Cor. 12:9).

I say all this to give you a glimpse of what God-centered living can do. My experience is common. When you see that God is truly the heart of your life, and when you take the steps to alter your perspective, attitude, and behavior accordingly, you will find yourself profoundly changing for the better. You will find your fragmentation pulling together around one Center. You will see first things finally taking first place in your life. You will regard people differently, and they will see differences abounding in you. Your days will lose their frenetic pace, containing less and less clutter.

Is this the life you want? If so, you must *choose* it. Thomas Kelly notes, wishing will not deliver it:

> Life is meant to be lived from a Center, a divine Center. Each one of us can live such a life of amazing power and peace and serenity, of integration and confidence and simplified multiplicity, on one condition— that is, *if we really want to.*[16]

Assuming this is what you seek, the process begins with *simplicity.*

How, then, can simplicity become a love habit? What practical steps must you take for your life to revolve around the true Center?

The first step is *recognizing that God is the heart of all goodness.* Life and love flow from him. He cannot be *made* the Center of anything; he already *is* the Center of everything. You must embrace this truth in your mind.

Having acknowledged that God is the Center of all reality, the second step is *thinking through how this fact should reshape your life.* How should it change your relationships, the way you earn, spend, save, and invest your money, your involvement in church, your work life, your recreation? Everything must be reevaluated in light of who God is and what he requires.

As you accept the fact of God's centrality and see how your life should change as a result, the third step is *exercising your will by asking God to give you the necessary wisdom, power, and courage to make the needed changes.* Then you must determine to step out, begin making those alterations, and keep on living them through the Spirit's exceedingly abundant strength.

While these steps are easy to state, it takes more investment to turn them into reality. In the following chapters, you'll see in more detail how you can simplify your life, for the love habit of simplicity is fleshed out through the other disciplines. Just as the greatest commandment is the pinnacle of all the others, the one from which all the rest flow, so simplicity is the greatest love habit. From it all the others take their lead, and to it all the others point and seek to fulfill. Simplicity, centering our ultimate loving devotion upon God, is the starting line and the finish line—in fact, it's the entire race. All the other habits help us to navigate the course and finish as victors.

The next discipline we'll address—the love habit of submission—is the logical and relational consequence of simplicity's truth.

5. Submission:
freedom in surrender

Rudy, *one of my favorite movies,* is about a high school graduate who desperately wanted to play football at Notre Dame. Rudy grew up in a family who watched the Fighting Irish religiously, revering the school and the team, but only Rudy, a little guy with a huge heart, had the hunger to actually set his sights on playing in South Bend. To achieve his dream, he needed to get in as a student, which proved to be the most difficult task of his young life. He had to begin as a freshman at Holy Cross, and no matter how hard he studied, he kept falling short of earning the grades necessary to be granted admission into the more prestigious university (and, thus, to try out for the nation's most renowned college football team). Rudy kept praying and laboring for his dream's fulfillment, but discouragement and frustration eventually emerged.

On one of his darkest days, he went into his church to pray. One of the priests who'd befriended him took note and sat down in the pew behind him. Rudy then turned and poured out his pain, wondering aloud if he needed to pray more or work even harder. With each suggestion he made, the priest calmly answered, affirming him and his efforts. Out of sheer angst, Rudy finally asked if there was anything else left to do. He believed the faithful minister knew God best and, therefore, held the answer to his desperate dilemma, the key to unlocking the divine secret for getting into Notre Dame. The priest, however, knew otherwise; he told the young man, "Son, in thirty-five years of religious studies, I've come up with only two hard, incontrovertible facts: There is a God, and I am not him." With this counsel, he redirected Rudy to the One he needed to keep seeking, the One who "causes all things to work together for good to those who love God" (Rom. 8:28 NASB).

After I saw *Rudy*, the minister's words kept echoing in my soul: *There is a God, and I am not him.* The more I pondered them, the more I understood that they express a fundamental biblical truth, a touchstone of the Judeo-Christian faith: God is God and we are not. He is the ultimate Being; we are beneath him. He is the hub of all things; we are some of the entities around him. He is the Creator; we are some of his creatures. He is the Sustainer of all; we are some of the beings he sustains. You and I are not what life is about; all things, great and small, revolve around the one and only Center—God himself. He is life's rhyme and reason, and he has given us an important part in the working out of his will.

If we applied this truth to our love relationship with the Lord, we'd say that he is the Lover of all lovers and that we are some of the lovers he loves. He *is* love, and he bestowed upon us the ability to love. He loved us first, and we can love as we should because he always loves us well. Most important, regarding our love relationship with God, he is the First in all things. We are not on a par with him; our relationship with him is not one of equals but of unequals. He is above us in every way, and we must love him as the superior Lover that he is.

From the vantage point of the love habits, we see from this truth that *simplicity leads to submission.* Simplicity says, "Center your ultimate loving devotion on the one and only personal God." Submission adds, "Ultimate devotion requires ultimate service, so in *loving* God with all you are and have, be sure also to *serve* him through all you are and have."

Simplicity points us to the Being whom we should love fully. Submission tells us that our love for this Being must be worked out in complete surrender to his all-good, all-loving will. We were made to love, and especially to love God. For our love to be loving, it must be obedient to the One who is love itself.

I'm well aware that "submission" has a despicable ring to contemporary ears. For many people, it smacks of slavery and humiliation, conjuring up images of victimization, abuse, and domination. But when Scripture speaks of submission in the context of the Christian life, it carries a different idea altogether. The best way to see this is by looking to him who is the way, the truth, and the life,[1] for it is Jesus Christ who best exemplifies the epitome of submission and its power as a discipline.

SUBMISSION, JESUS' WAY

The life of Christ shows us that submission is a sacrificial act of *agapē*. Submission is not subjugation—forcing someone to bow to another's strength, as a conqueror coerces a defeated enemy to kneel before him. Nor is submission an act of subordination, where too often a person is mistreated by another as insignificant or unworthy. Jesus demonstrates that *submission is voluntarily yielding one's will to another's out of love for that person.* We can see this first by looking at the very act of the Son's incarnation, then by turning to how he lived his life while on earth.

Incarnate Love

When the Son of God joined his divine nature to a human one, he took on "the very nature of a servant" and thereby "humbled himself" (Phil. 2:7–8). In other words, the Son freely and lovingly chose to become one of us so he could save us from our self-destructive path. As God, the Son is eternally coequal with the Father and the Spirit; he is not inferior in any way within the Trinity. Yet because all three persons of the Godhead love us, the Son eternally decided, in harmony with the Father and the Spirit, to dwell among us as a man and surrender the exercise of his divine attributes and prerogatives. In the process he did not lose anything of his deity; he remained fully God. But at the same time, he also chose to live as a full-blown human being, enduring the limitations that mark us as human.

> [For our sake the Son] put himself at our level, so that he actually thought and acted, viewed the world, and experienced time and space events strictly within the confines of a normally developing human person. Under these conditions of humanness . . . God the Son . . . learned as we learn, felt as we feel, laughed as we laugh, was surprised as we are surprised, suffered to the full our sorrows and disappointments, hurt as we hurt, died as we die.[2]

As God, the Son submits to no one—he is above every creature. "He is before all things, and in him all things hold together" (Col. 1:17). Everything that exists, he (along with the Father and the Spirit) brought into being. No created being is greater than God the Son, for each owes its existence to him. He is the Lord of all creation.

Furthermore, the divine persons are not above or beneath each other; there is no inherent hierarchy in the Trinity. All three are equally divine, equally absolute, equally supreme, equally first. They are eternally united in nature and completely harmonious in will. Each divine person deserves the highest honor and wholehearted devotion from all who are under them: They are the one and only God.

However, when the Son joined humanity, he voluntarily placed himself under the authority of the Father and the Spirit during his earthly sojourn. The Son put himself in our place. The Creator became part of his creation, trading heavenly majesty for earthly humility. The King put aside his glorious robes and angelic attendants, becoming one of his own subjects. He allowed a carpenter's wife to carry him in her womb, give him birth in a cave, place him in a feeding trough, and nurse him from her breasts. The Ruler of the universe put himself under the authority of human parents, under the authority of the religious teachers of his own written Law, under the civil authorities of his unwritten (yet universal) moral law, and under the natural world governed by the very laws of physics he himself created and set in motion. The eternal King placed himself under the powers he established by his own decree. The everlasting Sustainer of all life chose to become enfleshed and breathe his own air. Greatest of all, the Son, who by his divine nature deserves all that the Father and Spirit likewise do, subjected himself to their authority: God the Son, in his humanity, bowed to God the Father and God the Holy Spirit. The Trinity modeled submission in the Son's incarnation, not by divine command but chosen in concert with the Godhead's united will.[3]

Full Obedience

After the Son of God became a man, he was fully obedient to the Father's will through the guidance and power of the Spirit. In his human nature, the Son yielded himself to the Father's will, seeking to say and do whatever the Father wanted. He even went so far as to obey the Father to the point of "death—even death on a cross!" (Phil. 2:8).

What motivated Jesus to make such an incomprehensible sacrifice? Only one thing has such dynamic power: *agapē*. "Just as the Father has loved Me,"

Jesus said, "I have also loved you" (John 15:9 NASB). God's love reached down to us through Jesus Christ. Because of his love for his Father and for us, the Son of God entered history as Jesus of Nazareth. *Agapē* led to the ultimate act of submission.

Why? Because *agapē* is "not self-seeking" (1 Cor. 13:5). Love, by its very nature, gives itself away; it endeavors to meet the needs of others, to do what is good for them. Love is fulfilled through surrender to service: *True love is naturally submissive.* When we love someone unselfishly, we desire their best and seek to secure it while still loving them through even their worst. We surrender our agendas, our timetables, our rights, our dreams, our desires— all to give the ones we cherish what they need and appropriately desire. Christ showed us that "to love is to submit, and to submit is to love."[4] This he did throughout his life, even to the point of his death.

It is in the context of Christ's death that we learn the most about the love habit of submission, for in that setting Jesus spoke to his disciples about this life-shaping discipline.

Submission by Crucifixion

About a year before Jesus was crucified, he told his disciples and a crowd that had gathered around him, "If anyone would come after me, he must deny himself and take up his cross and follow me" (Mark 8:34). This must have been startling to his audience. The imagery of the cross signified a death so disgraceful and brutal that Jews almost always condemned it and many Romans often despised it. The Jewish response was primarily based on Deuteronomy 21:23: "Anyone who is hung on a tree is under God's curse." Cicero, the famous orator and statesman of ancient Rome, articulated repugnance: "The very word 'cross' should be far removed not only from the person of a Roman citizen but from his thoughts, eyes, and ears."[5]

In Jesus' time, only the Romans could legally carry out the death sentence in Jewish provinces. Crucifixion was one method of execution, despite the protests of some highly respected Roman citizens, but its use was restricted. Death by crucifixion was generally applied to crimes perpetrated against the state, and the condemned were never Roman citizens but almost always rebellious slaves, seditious foreigners, lawless pirates, political traitors, or religious subversives. Eyewitness accounts, archaeological discoveries, and the laws of the era show that crucifixion was lengthy, agonizing, and humiliating.

The condemned was first stripped naked, and "the executioners were allowed to distribute [his] clothing among themselves."[6] He was also scourged with a whip that had shards of iron or bone attached to the ends of the thongs. Each blow shredded skin and drew blood; sometimes the offender died during the beating. Because scourging could be so traumatic and even fatal, it frequently took place at the execution site.

In torment, naked, and with blood streaming from gaping wounds, the condemned was either strapped or nailed to a rough wooden structure that could take any one of four shapes: a single post or stake; two posts crossed to form an X; a post with a high crossbeam forming a T; or the traditional cross shape: †. If spikes were used for the limbs, they were several inches long and large enough to hold the condemned in place. In one archaeological find, the remains of a man crucified and buried in first-century Jerusalem showed that executioners had pounded spikes into his forearms, just above his wrists, and had driven a spike through "both heel bones after first penetrating an acacia wood wedge or plaque that held the ankles firmly to the cross."[7]

With his extremities attached to the wood, the only support the dying man usually had for the rest of his body was a peg pounded into the midsection of the cross—a small, uncomfortable seat. The cross itself stood quite tall when the Romans wanted people to see it from some distance away; "usually, though, the pole measured no more than about seven feet. This meant that wild animals could tear the crucified man apart."[8]

Those who suffered crucifixion could live for several days. Death usually came by suffocation or exhaustion but also sometimes through other factors such as exposure, shock, disease, and hunger. When the process was too slow for the executioners, they would break the legs of the condemned, making it impossible for him to support the operation of his diaphragm and therefore the mechanics of his breathing. When he finally expired, his corpse was often left hanging, subject to the weather and to carnivorous creatures.

While waiting to die, the crucified were "tortured by cramped muscles, unable to swat crawling and buzzing insects, hungry, thirsty, and naked before a taunting crowd."[9] Their only relief came from women who might give them "an anaesthetizing drink (wine and spices)" before death.[10]

Why did Jesus use such a horrifying and inhumane method of execution to describe Christian discipleship? The key to his teaching lies in the phrase "take up his cross." Note that he does not say "take up *my* cross," referring to the means of *his* death. Instead he points to my cross, your cross, and the cross of anyone else who decides to follow him. In other words, cross-bearing does not necessarily entail terrible torture or cruel death such as Jesus suffered. What, then, does it mean for me to take up my cross? And what does cross-bearing have to do with the love habit of submission? The answers lie in the rationale behind crucifixion and in a customary practice associated with it.

Crucifixion was not a sentence handed out primarily for *retribution;* that purpose was secondary. The main reason for crucifying a person was *deterrence.*[11] The Roman Empire tolerated much diversity of belief and practice within its borders, but it refused to put up with what it deemed "subversive activities": The state's rule had to be upheld at all costs, for Rome's hegemony was paramount. Thus rebels were forced to submit *publicly* to its final authority in order that others would think twice about contravening Roman rule. The best way to do this, the authorities reasoned, was by visibly displaying submission to the state through death by crucifixion.

Indeed, this even began en route to the execution site. Offenders were forced to wear a tablet around their neck stating the reason for their conviction; they were also made to carry their own crossbeam through public areas along the way. Once the condemned were hung on the cross, the conviction notice was nailed above their head so that everyone who saw them could plainly see the fatal consequence of rebelling against Rome.[12]

Therefore, to Romans and Jews in Jesus' day, cross-bearing and crucifixion meant finally submitting to the authority one had rebelled against.

We can see this purpose at work in the biblical account of Christ's final hours. To get the Roman governor Pilate to carry out the death sentence on Jesus, some Jews challenged Pilate's loyalty to the empire: "If you release this Man," they charged, "you are no friend of Caesar; everyone who makes himself out to be a king opposes Caesar" (John 19:12 NASB). In other words, they attempted to motivate Pilate to do their bidding by attaching a label of subversion to any act leading to Jesus' freedom. Later, when Pilate asked the crowd, "Shall I crucify your King?" the chief priests answered, "We have no king but Caesar" (v. 15 NASB). Once again, the issue of loyalty to the state was used as the central rationale for urging Pilate to put Christ to death.

Pilate had heard Jesus say that he was indeed "a king" (18:37), yet he had also heard him say that his "kingdom is not of this world," that it is "from another place" (v. 36). We're not told what Pilate understood by all this, but one thing is certain: He did not believe Jesus had committed any wrong, much less attempted to rebel against Rome's authority. Pilate told the accusers, "I find no basis for a charge against him" (v. 38). Still, under public pressure, Pilate gave in and turned Jesus over for execution. He also ordered that the conviction notice to be nailed above Jesus' head while he hung on the cross should read: "JESUS OF NAZARETH, THE KING OF THE JEWS" (19:19). By this charge, Pilate used Christ's execution to disavow any hint of disloyalty to Rome. The death sentence also served to remind Rome's Jewish subjects that they and their King were under Roman rule as well.

The biblical account of Jesus' death, then, fits with the other historical evidence regarding the intended meaning of crucifixion: To die in this manner under Rome's authority meant that the condemned rebel had finally submitted to Roman rule. Caesar's authority was deemed absolute.

Clarification About Cross-Bearing and Submission

Regardless of what Rome wanted to communicate through crucifixion, Jesus used the imagery to convey something higher and richer. When he spoke of cross-bearing in reference to Christian discipleship, the authority he had in mind was not Rome but heaven, not the emperor but the Father, not Caesar but Christ himself. The context of Mark 8:34 further supports this.

Just before Jesus talked about cross-bearing, he "spoke plainly" to his disciples about his impending rejection, death, and resurrection (Mark 8:31–32). Upset over this, Peter pulled Jesus aside and rebuked him; apparently he tried to persuade Jesus to travel a different path, which meant disobeying the Father's will. Jesus would have none of it, resolutely countering Peter's rebuke with one of his own, stating in the starkest terms, "Get behind me, Satan! . . . You do not have in mind the things of God, but the things of men" (v. 33). The disciples had to understand that obedience to the Father's will was supreme, regardless of the cost. The Son had freely and completely submitted himself. If his disciples were to follow in his footsteps, they had to submit to him as he had to his Father—without reservations, even to the point of death, if necessary.

At this juncture in Christ's ministry, they did not yet understand all that submission required. But on the eve of their Master's execution, they saw how far submission could reach into the human soul. Before his impending betrayal, Jesus wrestled with his Father's will more than at any other time in his earthly life. In the Garden of Gethsemane, he "fell with his face to the ground and prayed, 'My Father, if it is possible, may this cup be taken from me. Yet not as I will, but as you will'" (Matt. 26:39). He had repeatedly predicted his crucifixion and labored to prepare his followers. Still, when such an excruciating death loomed imminent, he became overwhelmed, even terrified. He agonized over what was to come, pleading with his Father to change the plan. Through it all, however, Jesus voiced his commitment to surrender his will, even if this meant suffering an unimaginable death.

Their Master's submission to the divine will, especially through such turmoil, clearly impressed itself upon the disciples. Three of the four gospels record the prayer session in Gethsemane, and each emphasizes Jesus' intense struggle, as Bible scholar Curtis Mitchell points out:

> Luke records Christ simply as kneeling; Matthew pictures Him as prostrate upon the ground, and Mark says He repeatedly fell to the ground! Putting all three [accounts] together, Christ probably first fell to His knees and as the agony intensified, He literally prostrated Himself. Then, in the height of the prayer struggle, He was in such torment of soul that He was literally writhing in anguish upon the ground. In all probability neither the kneeling nor the prostration were the normal positions Christ assumed while praying. Their very mention and emphasis in this account argues that such behavior appeared unusual to the disciples. They probably had never seen Him conduct Himself in such fashion before. Actually the account indicates that the emotional agony of soul caused Christ to end up prostrate upon the ground. By that I mean He did not assume the kneeling or prostrate positions in order to pray (or even in order to pray more effectively), but rather our Lord, oblivious to His physical position in the intensity of His prayer battle, ended up prostrate upon the ground! . . .
>
> The language of this prayer pictures a small child crying out in desperation to His daddy in the most intimate language possible![13]

Jesus certainly agonized over obeying the Father's will, but in the end he "humbled Himself by becoming obedient to the point of death" (Phil. 2:8 NASB). For Jesus, submission to the Father meant total surrender, not to a despot but to an all-loving, all-knowing, all-powerful Parent who would never permit his child to undergo unnecessary suffering.

In light of all this, the meaning of Mark 8:34 and the discipline of submission take on new significance. The passage shows that submission has two requirements, two steps we must take to activate this love habit.

The first step is *self-denial.* "If anyone would come after me," states Jesus, "he must [first] deny himself" (Mark 8:34). To see self-denial as Christ means it, we must see it through the lens of submission. If we are in rebellion against God like Peter was, it is because we are putting ourselves and our will first. Rather than aligning ourselves with God, seeing him as the Center of life, we are setting up ourselves as the standard. We and our will take center stage; in reality, though, there is but one first—the Divine King. If we are to follow him, we cannot be fighting against him, so denying ourselves means ceasing our rebellion against the Lord. Submission begins with acknowledging the truth central to simplicity, the same truth the priest spoke to Rudy: There is a God, and we are not him. When we recognize that God is first and stop rebelling against this truth, we have taken the first step of submission. Submission to the truth of simplicity marks the follower of Christ.

Also notice—and this is very important—that self-denial does *not* mean losing our identity or hating ourselves. I've read numerous Bible scholars and heard many preachers present one or both of these interpretations of Jesus' words, but I have not found either view convincing or consistent with God's action in human history.[14] Instead, I find that the biblical text teaches this: (1) It is by following Christ that we find our true identity—namely, to become more fully who we were created to be in him; and (2) it's by following him that we discover the path of genuine, unfailing love—a love that shows us how to love ourselves, our neighbors, and our God.

We do not lose ourselves in Christ; we actually gain ourselves. We learn who we really are, how great we can become. And we do not hate ourselves in Christ; we find out how incredibly loved we truly are. Self-denial does not equal loss of self but only the loss of what corrupts the self and turns it against the very One who loves it most. We should not hate what he loves but love it as he does. Nor should we desire to lose what he sent his Son to save: The well-known and dearly loved John 3:16, spoken by Jesus, should be enough to convince us that whatever self-denial means, it cannot mean that we should hate ourselves or seek to abandon who we are. God's work of redemption proves how magnificent is his sacrificial love for us—for each and every individual among us.

So as we have seen, submission's first step is self-denial. We are to stop rebelling against God, acknowledging that he is God and we are not.

Jesus did not need to exercise this first step of submission, because he always obeyed—he never rebelled against the Father. In Christ was no sin. Perhaps this is one reason he never equates self-denial with carrying *his* cross. Our need to bear our own cross requires that *we* cease rebelling against the Lord.

On the other hand, if submission meant only that we stop fighting against God, it would not suffice. Unless submission goes beyond this point, all we have between God and us is a cease-fire. Our fists would stop shaking at him, no more insults and hate-filled speech would pour from our lips; our lies, deceptions, and acts of one-upmanship would halt, and all that's hurtful to us and to him would desist. Nevertheless, as good as all this would be, it would bring nothing positive into the relationship: It would be as if we were yelling and cursing at God, then suddenly stopped and did nothing more. To his loving advances, we'd simply remain unmoved, which is an intolerable position for love. Love yearns to be received and accepted; love hungers to give its everything to those who will embrace it. The cessation of hostilities to love's advances is only a beginning. Love, to fulfill its purpose, must be pursued, trusted, followed, and obeyed.

Knowing this, Jesus gave us submission's second step: Take up your cross and follow me. We must *bear our cross and follow love's lead.*

"Stop rebelling"—self-denial—is a negative action. "Start submitting"—cross-bearing—is a positive action. As rebels who have laid down our arms, we must now surrender ourselves and our ways to the rule of our King. We must surrender to his advances, give in to his sweet embrace. Only then will our self-denial lead to our self-fulfillment. Only then will we realize what Jesus said we could possess: "Whoever wants to save his life will lose it, but whoever loses his life for me and for the gospel will save it" (Mark 8:35). Surrendering our all to Christ, taking up our cross and following him in everything, we receive from him nothing less than the full riches of everlasting salvation. Submit to Christ and you will get more than you could ever dream or imagine, including a fully glorified, richly renewed you. Keep rebelling against Christ, and you will end up with nothing, not even your soul.[15]

Love requires our all to do its redeeming, restoring, and transforming work. The love habit of submission is essential to fulfilling love's work in our lives.

SUBMISSION'S POWER

Christ's lifetime habit of submission demonstrated the discipline's power. His full obedience to the Father led to receiving the Spirit's authority to heal the sick, exorcise demons, resurrect the dead, walk on water, escape premature death, teach with astonishing authority, bring Jews and Gentiles to salvation, lead his disciples into becoming leaders themselves . . . in short, to establish and further a ministry of such proportions that the world has never again been the same. French general Napoleon Bonaparte noted Christ's unsurpassed impact: "I search in vain in history to find the similar to Jesus Christ, or anything which can approach the gospel. . . . Nations pass away, thrones crumble, but the Church remains."[16] British historian William Lecky, an opponent of Christianity, wrote,

> It was reserved for Christianity to present to the world an ideal char-
> acter which through all the changes of eighteen centuries [now twenty
> centuries] has inspired the hearts of men with an impassioned love; has
> shown itself capable of acting on all ages, nations, temperaments and
> conditions; has been not only the highest pattern of virtue, but the
> strongest incentive to its practice. . . . The simple record of these three
> short years of active life has done more to regenerate and soften man-
> kind than all the disquisitions of philosophers and all the exhortations
> of moralists.[17]

Jesus' submission to the Father created staggering consequences for life now and in the hereafter. We did not need to wait for the centuries following him to see it; the results bore fruit immediately, even in the redefinition of crucifixion.

Rome used crucifixion as an awful symbol of the state's ultimate authority over the life of its citizens. Christ, on the other hand, turned that symbol into a beautiful expression of the Father's supreme authority over all authorities. To Pilate's question, "Don't you realize I have power either to free you or to crucify you?" Jesus replied, "You would have no power over me if it were not given to you from above" (John 19:10–11). Paul said, the state receives its authority from God: "There is no authority except that which God has estab-lished" (Rom. 13:1). Jesus went to the cross because he chose to yield to the Father's authority, and Rome was able to crucify Jesus because the Father per-mitted it to achieve a higher good: the salvation of all who would receive Christ by faith. The Crucifixion exhibits the Father's supreme authority and the Son's supreme obedience to the Father.

Rome forced cross-bearing. If you failed to submit voluntarily to Rome's authority, you would be compelled to give in to it with your last breathing act on earth. Christ, however, made cross-bearing volitional. Love does not coerce submission: If we want the fullness of divine love, we must decide to follow him who incarnated love to the world. As the Son chose to live under the Father's loving rule, so we must choose to live under the Son's loving rule. When we submit to Christ, we automatically submit to the Father, because the incarnate Son always followed the Father's will—the persons of the Trinity always act in harmony.

Roman cross-bearing epitomized terrible suffering and drawn-out death, offering no hope for life here or beyond the grave. On the other hand, while suffering and martyrdom could become part of a believer's cross-bearing, Jesus places the emphasis on life: "Whoever loses his life for me and for the gospel will save it" (Mark 8:35). Taking up one's cross means finding life and preserving it. Only by trusting in Christ could one have real hope that bearing and dying on a Roman cross could usher him into a blissful, life-fulfilling Paradise.[18]

Rome used cross-bearing to force the rebellious into submission and to ensure their deaths in the process. Christ's act of submission, however, made our liberation possible. Because of his obedience to the Father, we can be set free from all that enslaves and have abundant life, now and forever.[19] When we take up our cross and follow Jesus, we discover the truth of what Paul said to the churches in Galatia: "It is for freedom that Christ has set us free. Stand firm, then, and do not let yourselves be burdened again by a yoke of slavery" (5:1). There is true freedom in surrendering to God.

Jesus Christ demonstrates that submission to God's will has incredible liberating and transforming power in life and over death. Its exercise can change our lives and countless others forever.

SUBMISSION'S SUBJECTS

Now that we know submission is biblical, powerful, and loving, to whom should we submit? I say *to whom* because "there is no way to surrender the will except by surrendering it to another will."[20] Submission occurs between persons, not between things or between persons and things.

We may wonder about this since addiction is so rampant today: Hasn't the alcoholic surrendered his will to booze? Hasn't the drug abuser given herself over to prescribed or illegal drugs? Hasn't the workaholic yielded to the demands of his company or clients? *The answer in each case is no.* Every addict has submitted not to things but to other persons—past and/or present—to whom they have yielded control or from whom they seek to wrest control. The drug addict might be fighting against the will of her overprotective mother or domineering father. The sex addict may be submitting to perversions enacted on her when she was just a child. The workaholic could be attempting to prove his worth on the job to his perfectionist boss, or to mocking classmates who ridiculed him relentlessly yet are long gone from his life. Whatever the addict's situation, you can bet she's either surrendering to or warring against the will of other persons. Submission occurs between wills and is therefore intrinsically personal.

To whom, then, should we surrender ourselves? Our ultimate and absolute submission belongs to only one—the Lord. "Love the Lord your God with *all* your heart and with *all* your soul and with *all* your mind" (Matt. 22:37, emphasis added). We are to hold nothing back in our submission to him. He deserves our all and he requires our all, making no exceptions even for the Caesars of the world.

In the chapters that follow, we'll see a wide variety of ways to practice the love habit of submission. All the spiritual disciplines are means to bringing every aspect of our lives under the supreme and loving authority of God. But reading about them and learning more of them will not lead to the sweet surrender that brings honor and glory.[21] Each of us must be willing to acknowledge that God is God and we are not (simplicity), then submit our whole selves to the will of God, day in and day out (submission).

One truth this entails is that *we play an essential role in choosing our Master.* Paul is crystal clear:

> Don't you know that when you offer yourselves to someone to obey him as slaves, you are slaves to the one whom you obey—whether you are slaves to sin, which leads to death, or to obedience, which leads to righteousness? (Rom. 6:16)

We freely give ourselves either over to sinners (such as ourselves) or over to the Sinless One. When we surrender to sinners, we reap sin, and the wages of sin is death. When we surrender to God and obey him, we become increasingly righteous through the Spirit's renewing work and receive life. That Paul saw the reality of godly surrender in the Roman church is evidenced by the words that followed his question:

> But thanks be to God that, though you used to be slaves to sin, you wholeheartedly obeyed the form of teaching to which you were entrusted. You have been set free from sin and have become slaves to righteousness. (vv. 17–18)

The Roman Christians rejected their sinful ways, entrusted themselves to God through Christ, and "wholeheartedly obeyed" the truth they'd received from fellow believers. As a result, they were now reaping "holiness," which results in "eternal life" (v. 22).

Do you want to be free from sin's wages and power? Do you want the full benefits of divine love? Then acknowledge the Father, trust in his Son, and seek to surrender every part of your life to his Spirit. Give your finite all to God, and he will give you his infinite all. There's no better exchange.

The same God who calls on us to abandon ourselves wholly to him also tells us there are others to whom we must submit. Until we become adults, we are to obey our parents; our parents, especially while raising us, are to serve us by raising us "in the training and instruction of the Lord" (Eph. 6:1, 4). In the world of work, employees and employers are to look out for the interests of one another, serving "wholeheartedly, as if you were serving the Lord, not men, because you know that the Lord will reward everyone for whatever good he does" (vv. 7–8). Spouses are to love and serve each other sacrificially and respectfully.[22] Christians are to "submit to one another out of reverence for Christ" (5:21), including to church leaders.[23] And we are to submit ourselves "for the Lord's sake to every authority instituted among men," showing "proper respect to everyone" (1 Peter 2:13, 17). In other words, we're to love and serve our neighbor as we love and serve ourselves, doing all out of our "undivided devotion to the Lord" (1 Cor. 7:35).

Our submission to fellow human beings flows out of our all-embracing submission to the sovereign Lord. Because he loves others, we must love them too. Because he humbled himself to serve others, we must humble ourselves to serve them also. Because his Son placed himself under the authority of others, so must we. The Lord is the One we imitate and obey in all ways to which he calls us. Our coverage of the other love habits in subsequent chapters will help us see more specifically how far his call extends and how we can fulfill it.

SUBMISSION'S LIMIT

Before we move ahead to the discipline of prayer, I want to mention one last matter regarding the love habit of submission: its limit.

Submission is absolute only in reference to God. We are always to submit to him, but exceptions arise regarding submission to other people or to evil spiritual entities.

Concerning spirits, Scripture is adamant that we are never to obey those at war with God. Paul exhorts us to "struggle . . . against the rulers, against the authorities, against the powers of this dark world and against the spiritual forces of evil in the heavenly realms." In the face of these demonic enemies, we are to "put on the full armor of God" and "stand firm." We must resist the "devil's schemes" and with "the shield of faith . . . extinguish all the flaming arrows of the evil one" (Eph. 6:11–16). We can make no peace with Satan and his fallen angels: They are arrayed against God and his people, relentlessly seeking to subvert and corrupt all that is good, and because of their unrepentant rebellion, they are doomed to destruction.[24] As followers of Christ, we cannot submit to the demonic beings dedicated to our King's overthrow. We're on his side; therefore, we must commit ourselves to fighting for him and his kingdom.

Concerning fellow humans, when they demand our submission in ways that challenge God's position or directives, we are under no obligation to obey. More than that, we are obligated to disobey in ways honoring our Lord. For example, when Shadrach, Meshach, and Abednego—Hebrews captured by the Babylonians—were ordered by imperial decree to worship the image of a human king, they rightly refused and ended up being tossed into a blazing furnace, from which God spared them even getting slightly singed.[25] Centuries later, when certain religious officials ordered the apostles to stop teaching about Jesus, they refused, stating as their reason, "We must obey God rather than men!" (Acts 5:29).

When it comes to submission, then, our ultimate and absolute obligation is to obey the Divine King. Everything else is ordered to and subject to this.

Consequently, when someone—whether it is a demon disguised as an angel, a parent pretending to be a caring provider, a spouse faking faithfulness and love, or a church leader abusing authority—attempts to lead us away from the One we serve (and even to oppose him), we are morally obligated to disobey. Our loyalty to the Lord may bring upon us painful consequences, even the sacrifice of our very lives, but such suffering is insignificant compared to the blessings that will flow to us and through us for upholding our undivided commitment.

The life and death of Jesus Christ are ample proof of this: Because he refused to obey some of the religious authorities of his day and instead fully submitted his will to the Father's, he was crucified, but the Father would not allow even death to hold his faithful Son. The Spirit who empowered the incarnate Son in life also raised him from death to life immortal, thereby vindicating him and his redemptive work.[26] This same Spirit empowers the followers of the Son, enriching their lives with love's unlimited blessings, preparing them in this life for the incorruptible inheritance awaiting them in heaven. This is why Paul could conclude that "our present sufferings are not worth comparing with the glory that will be revealed in us" (Rom. 8:18).

While submission may *bring* us temporary suffering, submission will never *leave* us with it. Submission to our Lover will always result in the fullness of joy that only he can give. Jesus promised,

> If you obey my commands, you will remain in my love, just as I have obeyed my Father's commands and remain in his love. I have told you this so that my joy may be in you and that your joy may be complete. (John 15:10–11)

Submit to him, without reservation, so that his joy may grow in you. Begin the process by yielding to the truth of simplicity: God is God and you are not; he is the Center of life, not anyone or anything else.

6. Prayer:
connecting with God

"Lord, teach us to pray" (Luke 11:1).

The disciples had often watched their Master go off alone to pray. They'd heard him pray in their midst when the crowds were not around. And they'd seen him pray in public, even when throngs of people were pressing in. They knew his prayers produced results—demons fled, the blind regained sight, diseases disappeared, the dead rose, water became wine, the winds and seas bowed in obedience, the wisdom of the worldly was stripped of its foolishness.

Lord, teach us to pray. Help us tap into your resources. Show us how we also can have an intimate, vital relationship with the heavenly God.

This is what the disciples wanted.

This is what every follower of Christ desires.

This is what Jesus wants for us.

Why, then, is prayer often the activity of last resort? "When all else fails, pray" may not be what most believers say to each other, but it is the way far too many live, trying first on their own to meet their needs or reach for their desires. Why? I think one major reason is that many Christians are closet skeptics when it comes to prayer. They don't really believe that heaven hears them, so they pray only when they can't seem to get what they want on their own. A dialogue I had with one such skeptic went something like this:

"When I pray, nothing happens," she said with a trace of anger and desperation.

"What do you mean, 'nothing happens'?" I asked.

"I mean I get no response. I might as well be talking to myself." Her eyes penetrated mine as she spoke; then, point made, she looked away, frowning.

"Let me see if I understand you," I said, somewhat slowly and cautiously. "You come before God in prayer and ask him for something or share something with him, but all you get in return is stony silence. He says nothing. He does nothing. And nothing happens in your life to indicate in any way that God heard your prayer."

Without turning her face back toward me, she defiantly answered, "That's right. That's what I'm saying. I pour my heart out to him, but he does nothing in return. It's a one-way street that dead-ends."

"Hmm. That puzzles me," I responded, looking off into the distance. "You mean that when you pray you never walk away feeling better about the situation? You never have a better idea what to do? You never hear a still, small voice pointing you in a certain direction? You never find yourself more sensitive to another person's needs? None of these things ever happen to you?"

She turned and gazed at me with a quizzical look. "Well, yeah, I've had things like that occur."

"Then you've received answers to your prayers."

"Those are answers?"

"They sure are. What were you expecting?"

She thought for a minute, then replied, "Well, I suppose I expected God to answer my prayers in a certain way. You know, I prayed for God to heal someone, and I thought he would make them well again. I asked him to move my boss to give me a raise, and thought my next paycheck would show that I got it. I expected God to give me what I asked him for, when I wanted it."

"So when he didn't deliver according to your expectations, you thought he wasn't answering you. Right?"

"Yeah, I guess so."

Great expectations. We all have them, and when we come to God—the all-powerful, all-knowing, all-loving, and all-merciful Being—our expectations soar. And why not? Scripture and church history are filled with stories of the Lord answering his people's prayers, often in dramatic ways. He heard the Hebrews' prayers and freed them from slavery in Egypt, brought them into the Promised Land, and helped them conquer it. He provided his people with food from heaven and water from rocks. Through his Son, he healed the disabled and sick, freed the oppressed, fed the hungry, forgave sinners, and raised the dead. All this is truth, but it is only part of the story.

In the Gospels, we do see Jesus working wonders among the people, but his ways are frequently incompatible with their expectations. For instance, when his close friend Lazarus is gravely ill, Jesus ignores the pleas of Mary and Martha to rush to their brother's side. Only after he learns of Lazarus's death does he begin to travel to their home. Once he arrives, the sisters place the onus of responsibility for Lazarus's death on him, saying that if he'd come when he heard about Lazarus's condition, he could have saved their brother.

While what they said is correct, it would not have achieved what the Father wanted his Son to do: raise Lazarus from the dead in front of many witnesses. By obeying the Father, Jesus was glorified and "many of the Jews who had come to visit Mary, and had seen what Jesus did, put their faith in him" (John 11:45). Jesus clearly answered the pleas of Mary and Martha, but not in the way they wanted. As a result, he accomplished far more in a much better way by responding according to the Father's desires.

Through Isaiah, God declares, "My thoughts are not your thoughts, neither are your ways my ways. . . . As the heavens are higher than the earth, so are my ways higher than your ways and my thoughts than your thoughts" (55:8–9). When it comes to prayer, we must never forget this. Though God will always answer, he is not a vending machine. We can't just drop a prayer into the God-slot, make our selection, and expect the answer we want when we want it. The Lord is wiser and more loving than that; he will frequently not answer in the way we expect. It may be yes or no, now or later, soon or never. He may respond far beyond our wildest imaginations, or he may not give as much as we want but enough to meet our need. When we pray, we must be ready to accept his answers according to his timetable. Prayer, in other words, requires our submission to love's ways.

Because God always has our best interests at heart, knowing us and our situation exhaustively, we can completely trust him to answer our prayers for our good. This is what we should expect from our Divine Lover, and it's an expectation on which he will always deliver.

WHAT PRAYER *IS*

No single definition can exhaust the many elements of prayer. Like a multifaceted jewel, the essence of prayer glimmers in different ways depending on how it reflects the Light. But if we could examine the jewel long enough to see what all of its facets have in common, we would find that the shared quality is *communion with God*. Like no other love habit, prayer ushers us into the very presence of eternal Love.

This is how it should be. God's relationship with us is personal and loving. Scripture describes him as our Groom, preparing us for a wedding day in which we will appear before him splendidly holy, beautifully pure. He is also our Friend, who enjoys lingering with us and joining in conversation. God is our Father, seeking parental reconciliation and intimacy with his prodigal children. He is our Teacher, instructing us in the way, the truth, and the life; and he is our Master, calling on us to serve him freely, faithfully, and wholeheartedly. God is our King and High Priest, our Vindicator and Commander. He is our greatest and fully faithful Lover.[1] We live and work and play and have our being within the created world of the infinitely personal and loving God; he has established prayer as the primary way for us to keep in personal contact with him and for him to stay in personal contact with us.

Communion between persons requires communication and lots of it. When those persons love each other, communication between them is even more important. Lovers hunger to know each other as fully as they can. They want to know what the other likes. They share and build on common beliefs, while exploring and trying to reconcile their differences. Lovers reveal their secret sins and shortcomings, seeking to shoulder them together. Lovers share their hopes and dreams, successes and failures. Lovers in marriage even surrender their bodies to each other, using them to express an intimacy that words cannot fully convey. Communication and communion go hand in hand, not only between human lovers but also between us and our heavenly Lover. In the spiritual realm, communal communication is called prayer.

WHAT PRAYER IS *NOT*

There are many misperceptions about prayer. You may have heard people say that you must pray a certain way, or pray about certain things, otherwise your prayers will not be effective. That is simply not true; the Bible reveals that the life of prayer is as diverse as life itself. Here are a few prayer facts that even a one-time reading of Scripture clearly conveys:

- *There are no right prayer formulas.* Prayer can be a simple petition, a long praise, a brief thank-you, a cry of pain, a heartfelt song, a combination of intercessory requests and worshipful proclamations.

- *There are no right prayer positions.* You can sit in a chair or on the ground or in a boat, bend one knee or both, stand straight or slump, lay face-up or prostrate, have your eyes open or closed, raise your hands upward or cross them in front of you or behind you or leave them dangling at your side.

- *There are no right prayer words.* The prayers in Scripture are as varied as human experience and emotion. Some call for judgment, others for mercy. Others are filled with anger, while many express deep remorse. Some praise God for hard-fought victories, as others ask for his help in unexpected defeat.

- *There are no right prayer places.* Prayers are offered to God on grassy hillsides, on raging battlefields, beside refreshing streams, next to dried-up riverbeds, in cities, fortresses, and country homes, on the jobsite, in prisons and deserts, on the high seas, and, in one prophet's case, from the belly of a great sea creature.

- *There are no right prayer times.* You can pray anytime, day or night. Prayer can last seconds, minutes, hours, or even days. Prayer can be offered on any occasion and during any circumstance.

- *There are no right prayer feelings or thoughts.* Prayer can communicate serenity and anxiety, joy and sorrow, understanding and confusion, love and hatred, wisdom and foolishness, faith and doubt.

In short, nothing is off-limits in prayer. God can take anything we dish out, delivered anywhere, anytime, from any position. He knows us better than we know ourselves, and he knows our feelings and thoughts even if we never articulate them. We cannot keep anything from him,[2] so why should we try? We don't have to sugarcoat our hurt, cover up our anger, deny our faithlessness, or conceal our dishonesty. We can tell him every-thing and know that we are loved no matter what. We will never find a better deal than this.

KINDS OF PRAYER

There are many kinds of prayer, for while all prayer communicates, not all communication is of the same variety. When human lovers make requests, they are *petitioning* each other. When one attempts to meet the other's need or desire, she is *interceding* on his behalf. When one exposes his mistakes, he is *confessing*. In each case communication occurs, but in diverse ways. The same is true with prayer: In our communion with God, we will engage in various kinds of communication, and each kind will typically bring different answers to our prayers. For example:

Intercession involves praying for the needs of others, so the answers are fulfilled needs.

Petition is concerned with asking God for something, often for oneself. An answer to a petition is receiving what was requested or something that God deems better.

Confession is asking God's forgiveness of sins, which he grants, even though we may still reap consequences of our wrongdoing.

Thanksgiving is the prayer of gratitude, focusing on thanking the Lord for who he is and for what he has done, is doing, or will do. The answer to the prayer of thanksgiving is often a deepening of the heart's attitude of gratitude. The more we give thanks, the more we become grateful people.

Adoration is worshipful prayer. Through adoration we express our deep reverence for God, our focus of praise. He is the One we glorify and herald as the Lord of Lords, alone worthy of our complete devotion. An answer to our adoration is a better understanding of our status as creatures: We come to realize that we have power, but God is all-powerful; that we have knowl-edge, but he is all-knowing; that we can do some things for ourselves, but we cannot do anything apart from him. Adoration can help us achieve a proper self-understanding, critical for our development into spiritually mature adults.

In a significant sense, all these forms of prayer have a petitionary quality to them—that is, they either ask God to do something or convey a response based on something he has done or will do. When we intercede on someone's behalf, we ask him to do something for her. When we confess sin, we ask him to forgive us for it. When we thank him, we show our gratitude for what he has done or will do, often in response to our petitions. And when we adore him, we worship him for who he is, usually because of something he's done or has promised to do for us or those we love. Jesus' prayer life and teaching on prayer exhibit this fact: Prayer is largely petitionary in nature.

In order to grasp this, we'll look at how Jesus taught us to pray; in the process, we'll discover how we can pray Jesus' way.

PRAYING JESUS' WAY: THE DISCIPLES' PRAYER

When the disciples asked Jesus to teach them to pray, he gave them what has come to be known as the Lord's Prayer, but it might be more accurately called "the disciples' prayer." Jesus taught what types of things we should routinely bring before the Lord, and while the full teaching of Scripture is that we can pray about anything, Jesus highlighted certain issues that should occupy most of our attention. Since these represent what God sees as most important (otherwise, why would his Son point them out to us?), they should become especially important to his people. In short, this prayer supplies a model for how Christ-followers should normally converse with God.

The disciples' prayer was recorded by both Matthew and Luke, and although the accounts are similar, the fuller version is found in Matthew (6:9–13). It begins with an address to God and then follows with six petitions:[3]

Our Father in heaven,	*Address*
hallowed be your name,	*First Petition*
your kingdom come,	*Second Petition*
your will be done on earth as it is in heaven.	*Third Petition*

Give us today our daily bread.	*Fourth Petition*
Forgive us our debts, as we also have forgiven our debtors.	*Fifth Petition*
And lead us not into temptation, but deliver us from the evil one.	*Sixth Petition*

Now let's look at each element of this prayer so we can see more clearly what Jesus is teaching us about praying to God.

The Address

"'Our Father in heaven'" opens the prayer, indicating to whom we should pray and how we should think of ourselves as we pray.

Prayer should be directed to *our* heavenly Father. By attaching the personal pronoun to the word *Father* (*'Abbā*), Jesus is teaching us that we have a close, childlike relationship with God, similar to what he has with the Father. Indeed, Jesus was the first to call God his *'Abbā* (Mark 14:36); the word is Aramaic, originally coming from baby language and meaning "Daddy." *'Abbā* came to be used by older (even adult) children as "the father" and "my father," and, throughout its history, the word retained a warm, intimate ring. So when Jesus finally used the term in reference to God, he was expressing their close, familial relationship; he was the Father's one and only eternal Son.[4] As Jesus called God *'Abbā,* so can we, the ones who have become God's adopted children through faith in his Son.[5] In him we have a loving, trusting, and respectful intimacy with the Father.

When we pray, then, Jesus tells us we should come to God as a child comes to his earthly father, trusting that our heavenly Father loves us, cares for us, and will give us what is best for us:

> "Which of you, if his son asks for bread, will give him a stone? Or if he asks for a fish, will give him a snake? If you, then, though you are evil, know how to give good gifts to your children, how much more will your Father in heaven give good gifts to those who ask him!" (Matt. 7:9–11).

Notice also in the opening address of the disciples' prayer that the Father is described as the God "in heaven." God is not Mother Earth or anything else in the created order: He is the heavenly God, the One above earth and all other created things. He is not to be confused with what he's made: He's the Creator who transcends everything and everyone, the Lord over all creation.

Furthermore, the Father is the person of the Godhead we should address in our prayers. We can, of course, pray to the Son and the Spirit because each is also divine. However, it was Jesus' own habit to address the Father, and in the model prayer he instructs us to imitate him.[6] Nowhere does he say that we cannot or should not pray to him or to the Spirit, but if we are to take his teaching seriously, we must recognize that he tells his followers to direct prayer, *as a matter of routine,* to the heavenly Father.

One more thing I'd like to note: Jesus did not say, "Pray to 'your' Father or 'my' Father," but to "*our* Father in heaven." In fact, throughout the model prayer, Jesus uses plural pronouns in the places where believers refer to themselves. When we pray, therefore, we must never forget that we pray as fellow members of the everlasting family of God. Each of us is part of the church, the body of Christ; in him, I am your brother, and you are my brother or sister. This means we all share the same Father, so regardless of our unique beliefs or practices, none is greater than what unites us—*a common family relation with one Father through faith in one Son by the power of one Spirit*. Love unites all who submit to it, and our approach to prayer should reflect it.

When, therefore, we go to prayer with our family status in mind, we'll be much less likely to hold on to envy or malice, especially when it concerns fellow brothers and sisters in Christ. We'll more readily pray *for* each other rather than *against* each other, to humble ourselves and readjust our desires for the sake of others in God's family.

First Petition: Revere

After the address to the heavenly Father, the privilege of making requests begins right away. Jesus does not want us to hesitate to ask for things. Just as a child goes to a parent with desires, so we are to go to our Supreme Parent with petitions we want him to answer.

Among all that a believer might ask, Jesus teaches us that one request we should regularly make is that our Father's name be revered: "Hallowed be your name" (Matt. 6:9). In Exodus, God revealed his name to Moses as *YHWH,* the great "I AM" (3:14). Only the consonants "YHWH" appear in the biblical text because in Hebrew vowels were never written, only pronounced. God's people later held the divine name so sacred that they refused to speak it; whenever "YHWH" occurred in the text, they would say *Adonai,* which means "Lord." Biblical scholars are unsure how "YHWH" should be pronounced, but their best guess and the overall consensus is

Yahweh. In the Exodus 3 context, *Yahweh* is linked with the Hebrew verb *hayah*, which means "to be," hence a major reason for the translation "I AM."[7] In other words, God is the One who is. He can say, "I BE" or "I AM" because that is what he is by nature, whereas we are—exist—only because he has created us to be. My existence is created by him; His existence is uncreated and eternal.

With this name, God reveals to us that he is personal, active, unchanging, and self-existent.[8] Consider the *personal* aspect first. God is the ultimate *I* ("I AM," not "IT IS") who relates to other persons, especially to his chosen people. In fact, he is tri-personal: Father, Son, and Holy Spirit.

He is also the God who acts and who acts *effectively,* completely unlike the idols of human creation. In the Exodus account, Yahweh is the One who defeats all manmade gods, showing the Egyptians and the Hebrews that he is the only true and all-powerful God.[9]

Furthermore, Yahweh is *always the same.* He is (not *was*) "the God of Abraham, Isaac and Jacob," the very same God who promised to deliver his people from bondage and lead them into the Promised Land—"a land flowing with milk and honey" (Ex. 3:16–17). He is the covenant-keeping God, the One who can always be trusted, who keeps his promises, who remains ever consistent.

And Yahweh is AM-ness, IS-ness. He brings all other things into being, but he alone *is* Being. Only he is self-existent, the infinite fullness of Being and therefore the uncaused Cause of all other beings. Everything else has come into existence because he brought it into existence. John says, "All things came into being through Him, and apart from Him nothing came into being that has come into being" (John 1:3 NASB), and Paul adds, "By Him all things were created, both in the heavens and on earth, visible and invisible . . . all things have been created through Him and for Him" (Col. 1:16 NASB).

When Jesus, then, teaches us to pray to the Father, "'Hallowed be your name,'" he is asking us to uphold as sacred the personal character, unchanging nature, and active faithfulness of the only God who *is.* He wants us to ask God to reveal and protect his name, which is nothing less than the fullness of who he is and what he does. Who is the best revealer and vindicator of God? "Hallowed be your name" tells us that *God himself* is.

I began to learn this lesson during my first year as a Christian. I was a poor college student at the time, helping to support my small family and earn part of my way through school as an assistant manager of a huge apartment complex. As one of my duties, I worked with Barry, another young man, to prepare vacated units for new residents. This required some painting and a lot of cleaning.

One day we were working together, and I was talking about Jesus and his second coming. I was excited about my new relationship with Christ, and I wanted Barry to know him as I did. Barry, though, was unimpressed and a bit annoyed. He threw out a few half-cocked objections, which I was barely able to answer at the time. For the most part, he simply tried to ignore me and the message. His response led me to say, "You really don't believe Jesus Christ is real, do you?"

"Nope," he flatly answered while cleaning out an oven.

"What would convince you that he is real?" I countered, standing nearby.

"I don't know. Maybe him showin' up right now and sayin' somethin' to me." Barry kept on working, not making eye contact.

My mind raced. *Would Jesus do that? Would he make an appearance for Barry?* Since I wasn't sure, I decided on a different test for truth. "Since you don't believe Jesus is real, I'm going to pray that you don't get any sleep until you recognize he's real and ask him by faith to save you."

Barry removed his head from the oven and looked straight at me. "Why would you do that?"

I saw a bit of anxiety on his face, as I sensed a tinge of fear within me. *What have I said?* I thought. *I'm putting myself and God on the spot here. What if God doesn't want to reach out to Barry in this way? Am I presuming to know God's will?* I finally settled my interior doubts by reassuring myself that I served a great God who loved me enough to reveal himself to me and save me. He had proved to me that Jesus is alive and well, resurrected from the dead. That same God who could raise Jesus from the dead could easily take away someone's sleep for the cause of salvation. "I'm going to pray you don't get any sleep because you need to know that Jesus is real, that he died on the cross for you too, and that he wants to save you from your sins and give you new life and hope," I finally said.

Barry stared at me for the longest moment, then, with a worried look, replied, "I don't want you to do that."

"Do what?"

"Pray."

"Why not?" I was feeling a bit more courageous. "If Jesus isn't real, then you have nothing to worry about. You won't have any trouble sleeping. If I'm right, though, if Jesus is who I'm saying he is, then you won't be able to sleep until you trust him for your salvation."

Barry seemed stunned, but he didn't say anything else. We both went back to work and eventually talked about other things.

The next day at work, I noticed he appeared tired, so I asked him with concern, "Are you alright?"

"Yeah," he mumbled. "I just couldn't sleep last night."

"Why? Were you at a party or somethin'?" I knew he liked parties, some of which ended up as all-nighters with booze flowing.

"No, no party. I just couldn't sleep."

That day we worked mostly together but spoke no more about sleep.

The following morning, Barry returned to work looking even worse. This time he asked, "Are you praying for me?"

"Yes," I said. "Why?"

"I didn't get any sleep again last night. I tried. I even took some sleeping pills. But nothin's workin'. Would you stop praying?" He looked exasperated.

"Why should I stop praying for you?" I prodded. "God isn't real, right? That's what you told me. Jesus is a myth, a figment of my imagination. If that's so, then my praying won't change anything. Right?"

"Yeah, yeah," he admitted, then we both went on with our work.

On the third day, he looked more exhausted, so I urged, "Listen, just ask Jesus to come into your life and save you, then you can get some sleep again."

He was really put out with me now. "No, I won't. Just leave me alone."

We worked in separate apartments that day.

For the next several days, I didn't see Barry at all; he called the office and said he was sick. I became worried about him, but I didn't stop praying. Each day I asked God to do the same thing: "Father, please take sleep away from Barry until he knows Jesus as I do. Maybe I shouldn't have put you on the spot like this. But I believe in you and your ability to save Barry. If it takes him not getting any sleep until he does, then please make him sleepless. Your reputation is on the line. I know I put it there, but you're the one Barry needs to know is real. Please come through for him. Prove yourself to him—for his sake. In Jesus' name, amen."

After a week of praying like this, having not seen Barry for four days, he finally showed up at work. But this time, he was smiling big. I had never seen

Barry really happy before. He beamed, and he didn't look one bit tired! Naturally, I asked, "What happened?"

"Yesterday I finally got some sleep. It was the best sleep I've had in a long time." He couldn't stop smiling.

"So you accepted Christ, huh?"

"Yes, I did. I was so tired I couldn't stand it any longer. Besides, during all those hours I was awake, I had plenty of time to stop being angry at you and start thinking about God and what you said about him. I realized he was real and that I needed him. So I asked Jesus to take away my sins, and he did. I was so relieved I fell asleep. I didn't wake up for more than fourteen hours."

Barry then found a church home and began growing. I had a new brother in Christ; God had revealed his presence and vindicated his name. "Hallowed be your name" had been fulfilled in front of a young Christian to the benefit of another young man who needed to know Jesus is real.

Second Petition: Reign

"Your kingdom come" (Matt. 6:10), the second petition of the disciples' prayer, goes straight to the heart of the gospel message.

After Jesus was baptized by water and the Spirit, he went about telling the people, "Repent, for the kingdom of heaven is near" (4:17). His message and actions were kingdom-focused. Jesus not only talked about the heavenly kingdom, he also brought the power of the kingdom with him. Emboldened and empowered by the Holy Spirit,

> Jesus went throughout Galilee, teaching in their synagogues, preaching *the good news of the kingdom,* and healing every disease and sickness among the people. News about him spread all over Syria, and people brought to him all who were ill with various diseases, those suffering severe pain, the demon-possessed, those having seizures, and the paralyzed, and he healed them. (vv. 23–24, emphasis added)

Jesus proved the kingdom's imminence by performing miracles, demonstrating with power that he was both its Proclaimer and Bearer; he embodied the message he preached. The kingdom was Christ the King, his authority and power to rule. George Eldon Ladd says, "When the word refers to God's Kingdom, it always refers to His reign, His rule, His sovereignty, and not to the realm in which it is exercised."[10]

What was Jesus' kingdom message? That the rebellion against God, initiated by the angel Lucifer and brought into the human realm through the disobedience of Adam and Eve, was being put down.[11] God's rule was being reestablished through his Son, Jesus Christ, who was working on the Father's behalf through the power of his Spirit. Yahweh was *with* Jesus, *in* Jesus; he *was* Jesus. The same One who preached the coming of the King's rule was, in fact, the King—Yahweh himself. The kingdom is Christ.

During his trials, just prior to his crucifixion, Jesus acknowledged his royalty status before the Jewish Sanhedrin and the Roman governor. To the religious leaders, he said he was indeed the prophesied Messiah, the very Son of God, and told them, "In the future you will see the Son of Man sitting at the right hand of the Mighty One and coming on the clouds of heaven" (Matt. 26:64). They recognized his claim as that of divine kingship, for when they took him to Pilate, they said, "We have found this man subverting our nation. He opposes payment of taxes to Caesar and claims to be Christ, a king" (Luke 23:2). When Pilate asked him, "Are you the king of the Jews?" Jesus responded, "Yes, it is as you say" (v. 3).

Jesus was the King who had come to live among his rebellious subjects.

But he did not come as the King they expected. In his day, the Jews were primarily looking for a Messiah who would either come as a human king to militarily conquer Israel's Gentile rulers (the Romans) and restore political self-rule, or as a supernatural ruler to utterly destroy wickedness and usher in the divine kingdom. In either case, *the Jews anticipated a Messiah who would establish God's rule on earth in power and judgment.*[12]

Jesus upset their expectations. He did come as the sovereign King, but as One who serves and sacrifices himself for his subjects. He did come to defeat his enemies, but he saw his enemies not as the Romans, but Satan, sin, and death—the very opponents we face. These enemies cannot be defeated with military weapons; they require something greater, the greatest force in or beyond the universe. They must be defeated by *agapē*. It is Love who comes to undo the tremendous damage caused by evil. It is our Lover who sends his beloved Son to cast out demons and heal our wounds. It is the Son who cuts the strangleholds of Satan, sin, and death by living a sinless life so he can be the perfect sacrifice, dying in our place and rising from the dead. Through his life, death, and resurrection, Christ overcame the power and penalty of sin (death) and the originator and ultimate promoter of sin (Satan). Jesus triumphed over the enemies of God and man.[13]

Therefore, when we give ourselves to him, when by faith we stop rebelling and submit to him, we receive all that he won for us, including the promise of full victory over the evil trinity—Satan, sin, and death. I say "the *promise* of full victory" because we still do not experience *all* we have in Christ. He defeated Satan, but our "enemy the devil [still] prowls around like a roaring lion looking for someone to devour," so we still must seek to "resist him" by "standing firm in the faith" (1 Peter 5:8–9) and fighting against him with the "armor of God" (Eph. 6:11). Jesus also conquered sin, but we still must choose between letting God or sin be our master, a daily, even moment-by-moment choice, not a once-for-all-time decision.[14] Our Lord likewise overcame death, yet we must still make burial plans, knowing that we will physically die as others have. God's enemies are definitely on their way out—he has promised it—but they are not out yet. Their final end is certain, their full defeat assured, but they still seek to do damage as long as they have any fight at all.

This is why we are to pray to our heavenly Father, " 'Your kingdom come' ": The *fullness* of God's renewed reign and the *full* measure of its wonderful blessings will not be ours to enjoy until death, the "last enemy" (1 Cor. 15:26), is forever vanquished. This will not happen until after Christ's return, which is followed by his thousand-year earthly reign, which is followed by the final resurrection and judgment. Only then will all of God's enemies be *fully* defeated and God be *fully* vindicated.[15] Then, and only then, will all believers enjoy "a new heaven and a new earth," a new order completely devoid of disorder, a place in which we will reign with God "for ever and ever" (Rev. 22:5).

When I was a new Christian, the doctrine of the Second Coming terrified me. I was afraid Jesus would return before I had a chance to live my life. I wanted to do *my* thing before he came back to do *his* thing; the thought of my will getting cut short did not sit well with me at all. I do not feel this way anymore. I have learned that this fallen world, however much beauty and desire it still holds, pales in comparison to what I have "tasted [of] the heavenly gift," to what I "have shared in the Holy Spirit," to what I "have tasted [of] the goodness of the word of God and the powers of the coming age" (Heb. 6:4–5). My imagination is too weak and too limited to comprehend all that awaits me when God's reign finally comes in its magnificence and superabundant fullness. But from the little I *can* imagine, from what I *have* come to understand and experience, I've learned to long for the Lord's return. Now I work to hasten that day. With John, I pray, "Come, Lord Jesus" (Rev. 22:20), and with my Savior, who has taught me more about prayer than anyone else, I often pray to the Father, "Your kingdom come."

Third Petition: Reestablish

The third petition of the disciples' prayer is closely aligned with the second. Jesus teaches us to pray to the Father, "'Your will be done on earth as it is in heaven'" (Matt. 6:10).

While God's rule has not yet been fully reestablished on earth, his rule is furthered with everyone who submits to him:

> One who prays for the coming of the kingdom of God rightly prays that the kingdom of God might be established in himself, that it might bear fruit and be perfected in himself. . . . The Father is present to such a one, and Christ reigns with the Father in the soul that is maturing.[16]

So while we wait for the fullness of his kingdom rule to be realized on earth as it is already realized in heaven, we extend his rule by becoming increasingly obedient to him in our everyday lives. No matter how imperfect our submission may be, in us and through us his rule grows as our loving obedience grows.

Jesus' disciples experienced this. When they were ready, he gave them the "power and authority to drive out all demons and to cure diseases" and even to resurrect the dead (Luke 9:1; cf. Matt. 10:8). Then he sent them out with the same message about the kingdom of heaven that he'd been preaching, and they submitted to Jesus' will, doing what he said.[17] Later, "the seventy-two returned with joy and said, 'Lord, even the demons submit to us in your name.' He replied, 'I saw Satan fall like lightning from heaven'" (Luke 10:17–18). He saw the devil's power broken, not only in his own ministry, but also in his disciples'. Just as Jesus used his kingly power and authority to overcome our enemies, so he granted the royal ability to his followers to accomplish the same. Christ the King furthered his reign through their obedience, and he performs this very task today, granting us the power to break the chains of evil in our lives, calling on us to deliver the same gospel-of-the-kingdom message to a world that desperately needs to hear and heed it.

Every time we resist Satan's temptations, we further God's reign on earth.

Every time we refuse to yield to our lusts—whether for power, prestige, pleasure, or position—we further the Lord's rule.

Every time we reconcile a relationship, we reestablish Love's supremacy.

Every time we forgive a wrong, heal a hurt, or comfort a grieving soul, we show that the greatest power of all is the One loving others through us.

Every time we filter life through God rather than through ourselves, we align ourselves more with him and his loving rule in our lives.

As our heavenly Father's gracious, compassionate will is fulfilled on earth in us and through us, his love for the world is revealed, reaching ever further, conquering evil and, in its place, leaving the incomparable fullness of Christ, the blessed hope of total redemption, and the dynamic growth of everlasting life. Let us keep praying for the full reestablishment of his reign on earth.

Fourth Petition: Provide

To this point in the disciples' prayer, Jesus has laid out spiritual requests specifically regarding the accomplishment of God's purposes on earth. In the fourth petition, Jesus shifts to a request for material need: "'Give us today our daily bread'" (Matt. 6:11).

There is nothing wrong with praying for tangible needs. God created us with physical bodies and provided us with what we need to satisfy our bodies' requirements for water and food. Jesus promised that he knows our needs and tells us not to worry about them:

> "Therefore I tell you, do not worry about your life, what you will eat or drink; or about your body, what you will wear. Is not life more important than food, and the body more important than clothes? Look at the birds of the air; they do not sow or reap or store away in barns, and yet your heavenly Father feeds them. Are you not much more valuable than they? . . .
>
> "So do not worry, saying, 'What shall we eat?' or 'What shall we drink?' or 'What shall we wear?' For the pagans run after all these things, and your heavenly Father knows that you need them. *But seek first his kingdom and his righteousness, and all these things will be given to you as well.* Therefore do not worry about tomorrow, for tomorrow will worry about itself. Each day has enough trouble of its own" (Matt. 6:25–26, 31–34, emphasis added).

The progression of the disciples' prayer follows Jesus' counsel to "'seek first [the Father's] kingdom and his righteousness, and all these [material and physical] things will [also] be given to you.'" The prayer begins with its focus on the Father and his reign over the world, *then* turns to petitioning him for our personal needs, a day at a time: "'Give us *today* our daily bread.'" The

Father knows we need food daily, but Jesus tells us to concern ourselves only with today's need, since the next day will present its own issues. It's the *heavenly* minded who can count on their *earthly* needs being met day by day by day.

During my first five years of married life, I saw God meet our family's needs in a number of ways. I was a full-time college student earning money as a musician. I taught, performed, recorded, and did just about anything else with music that would earn needed funds. Still, no matter what I did, my income rarely rose above the government-declared poverty level. My wife worked part-time, and we were raising two children; we needed more money to meet our daily needs. And God never let us down. Sometimes money or groceries came from family and friends. On other occasions we were blessed anonymously. One particular incident especially stands out in my mind.

We had made a decision to give $25 weekly to our church. This was a big step of faith for us, but we committed the funds to God and were determined to keep our promise. Some months later, our faith was severely tested. Our income had been so low that the household's food total had dropped to one can of beans, and we were in danger of being evicted from our apartment because we couldn't come up with the rent money. All we had between us was $25, already earmarked for the collection plate. Should we use it to buy food or to pay a little on our rent? Or should we follow through with our promise to God and give it to him? With deep concern over our plight but with a deeper conviction of what was right, we decided to keep our pledge. When I offered the money on Sunday morning, I prayed, "Father, we've kept our promise to you. We're counting on you to keep your promise to us to meet our daily needs."

Neither my wife nor I said anything to anyone about our material distress; instead, we persisted in bringing it before God, and, frankly, having some doubts about what we'd done. Would he come through? We desperately hoped, but we agonized over whether he would.

That evening, our telephone rang. I answered it, and on the other end heard the voice of Sam, a friend and fellow church member: "Bill, I want you and your wife to come over this evening. I have some money to give you. The Lord wants me to give it to you. I don't know why—just that he's made it clear to me that you need the money. We owe him some back tithes, and we want them to go to you."

Repeatedly I tried to get out of going to pick up the funds. I knew Sam had eight children of his own, and he was anything but wealthy. However, he would not accept my reluctance, so my wife and I left our two young children with other friends and drove to Sam's home.

Soon after we arrived, Sam handed me a check that took my breath away: It covered all our rent needs, as well as our next church donation commitment. He and his wife also went into their kitchen and loaded some paper sacks with groceries. By the following Sunday, more funds had come in, as well as more groceries; we were flush with money and food. God had met our needs. He had kept his promise, and we continued keeping our promise to him.

God may provide our material needs through our incomes, or through one of his faithful servants, or by intervening in any number of other ways. However he chooses to supply us, we can count on his being faithful to answer the petition, "Give us today our daily bread."

Fifth Petition: Forgive

"'Forgive us our debts, as we also have forgiven our debtors'" (Matt. 6:12). This fifth petition turns us back to spiritual requests. The term translated *debts* refers to our moral (not monetary) account; the petition has to do with our wrongdoing, not with our financial dealings (unless, of course, we have used or gained or lost money immorally). Jesus urges us to pray for the Father's forgiveness of the moral debts we owe him.

The beloved disciple wrote,

> If we claim to be without sin, we deceive ourselves and the truth is not in us. If we confess our sins, he [God] is faithful and just and will forgive us our sins and purify us from all unrighteousness. If we claim we have not sinned, we make him out to be a liar and his word has no place in our lives. (1 John 1:8–10)

That's black-and-white language with no wiggle room. Even we who are sons and daughters of the Father still sin; we do not fully and faithfully do all that we should; we sometimes violate what we believe. When we do wrong, we should seek the Father's forgiveness, and when our confession is honest and true, God promises us that he will forgive. "'Forgive us our debts,'" Jesus told us to pray, and the Father will answer.

But notice that a condition is placed on our petition: Our Father will forgive us our moral debts "as we also have forgiven our debtors." Throughout the disciples' prayer, we are addressing and petitioning the Father, asking him to accomplish his will and to meet our needs. This is the only time in the prayer that anything other than praying is required of us, and it's a specific responsibility: to forgive those who have sinned against us, to cancel the moral debt they have with us just as the Father, through his Son, has canceled the moral debt we have with him and keeps doing so after we enter his family by faith.[18] So that we do not miss this obligation, Jesus further explains the point immediately after giving the disciples' prayer: "'For if you forgive men when they sin against you, your heavenly Father will also forgive you. But if you do not forgive men their sins, your Father will not forgive your sins'" (Matt. 6:14–15).

Only a genuinely penitent spirit can forgive as it has been forgiven. It is only those who approach God with authentically sorrowful and repentant hearts who receive his forgiveness, and it is they who more readily and frequently forgive others who offend them.

Jesus pointed this out in the parable of the unforgiving servant, a man who owed a king several million dollars; he "fell on his knees" before the king and "begged" for more time to repay. The king "took pity on him, canceled the debt and let him go." This same man, however, later roughed up a fellow servant who owed him a few dollars, demanding immediate repayment. When the other servant "fell to his knees and begged" for patience, the first servant "refused" and had the man "thrown into prison until he could pay the debt."

The king learned of this and called the first servant back. He addressed the unforgiving man before him as a "wicked servant" and added, "I canceled all that debt of yours because you begged me to. Shouldn't you have had mercy on your fellow servant just as I had on you?" So the king turned him "over to the jailers to be tortured, until he should pay back all he owed." Jesus made the lesson explicit: "This is how my heavenly Father will treat each of you unless you forgive your brother from your heart" (Matt. 18:23–35).

We are never more *like* God than when we lovingly forgive others as he lovingly forgives us. And we are never more *un*like God than when we refuse to lovingly forgive others as he lovingly forgives us. Forgiveness and forgiving are inseparable, just as are unforgiveness and unforgiving. If we come to the One who has forgiven us so much but inwardly harbor an unforgiving spirit toward others, our petition for our Father to forgive us our sins against him will ring hollow in his ears. He will not honor it until we honor him by forgiving others as he has previously forgiven us. "Like

Father, like son" is never more true than when it comes to the act of forgiveness.

Sixth Petition: Deliver

The final petition of the disciples' prayer singles out the devious allurements of our greatest spiritual adversary and calls for rescue from our Father, to whom Jesus says we should pray, "'Lead us not into temptation, but deliver us from the evil one'" (Matt. 6:13).

The "evil one" is Satan. Scripture refers to him as "the tempter" (4:3), "the accuser of our brothers" (Rev. 12:10), the one "who leads the whole world astray" (v. 9). He is at war with God, striving to undermine and supplant the Lord's rule with his own. Accordingly, he fights against those who align their lives with the Life, working to keep others from yielding themselves to God. He tempts people away from the Way, seeking to deceive them into following paths that do not lead to Christ, accepting "truths" that are not the Truth, and embracing darkness doomed to death.

Jesus faced the evil one throughout his earthly life and was always successful because he remained dedicated to his Father and yielded to the Spirit. Having experienced Satan's enticements, Jesus understands and empathizes with our struggles to withstand demonic assault. The writer of Hebrews is emphatic about this:

> We do not have a high priest who is unable to sympathize with our weaknesses, but we have one [Jesus Christ] who has been tempted in every way, just as we are—yet was without sin. (4:15)

Jesus knew the deceptive power and vicious source of temptation, so he told us to pray to our heavenly Father, "Lead us not into temptation, but deliver us from the evil one."

The first part of this petition might sound as if we're asking the Father not to lure us into committing sin. However, the Bible is clear that God and evil do not mix: He is all-good, and he abhors evil. Moreover, he cannot do anything that contradicts his perfect nature: God "cannot deny Himself" (2 Tim. 2:13 NASB) and "cannot be tempted by evil, nor does he tempt anyone" (James 1:13). This means that only good flows from his infinite goodness; God *does* only good because he *is* only good. The goodness of our Divine Lover assures us that he will never commit evil against us, entice us into evil, or be lured into evil himself. He is eternally evil-free.

Therefore, in asking God not to lead us into temptation, we must realize that the source of sin is not God but Satan: "He who does what is sinful is of the devil, because the devil has been sinning from the beginning. The reason the Son of God appeared was to destroy the devil's work" (1 John 3:8). Satan sinned first and has been sinning ever since, leading others behind him.

Satan is the one we must withstand, but we cannot defeat him apart from the Trinity. The Son showed us how to beat the devil—by submitting to the Father's will through the power of the Spirit. When we pray and live according to the disciples' prayer, we will be committing ourselves to what's needed for standing firm "against the devil's schemes" (Eph. 6:11).

"Lead us not into temptation, and deliver us from the evil one," then, is a petition that God would protect us from and preserve us through the temptations of our shared adversary. Better than seeking forgiveness of sin is not to yield to sin at all. The devil is the tempter of tempters, so we're urged to ask God's help in resisting and overcoming his attempts to entice us into evil.

Jesus prayed this way for the disciples at their last Passover celebration. Judas had already left to carry out his planned betrayal under the influence of Satan,[19] but the other eleven remained. Jesus said, "'Simon, Simon, Satan has asked to sift you as wheat'" (Luke 22:31), and although he addressed Simon Peter by name, his comment was directed to the group. (The Greek word used for *you* is plural, better translated as "all of you.") Thus, the message to them all was that the devil had sought God's permission to challenge their faith so severely that they would either remain standing on God's side or apostatize and switch to Satan's side. In other words, their faith commitment would soon undergo a test of spiritual survival, and, knowing this, Jesus directed his next comments to Peter alone: "'But I have prayed for you [singular], Simon, that your [singular] faith may not fail'" (v. 32). Jesus' focus on Peter indicates that Satan's plan (at least in part) was to bring down the other disciples through Peter; the devil would target Peter and attempt to demolish his faith, which would ostensibly weaken the faith of the rest. So Jesus assured Peter that he had interceded on his behalf, praying to the Father that his faith would not be destroyed, thereby also preserving the faith of the other disciples.

Jesus knew, however, that Peter would soon deny him three times, and told Peter this even after he contended that he would stand at Jesus' side all the way to imprisonment and death (vv. 33–34). Jesus also instructed him, "'When you have turned back, strengthen your brothers'" (v. 32). The Son knew that his intercessory prayer would be answered with a resounding yes, which is why he could say to Peter, "*When* you have turned back,'" not "*if* you turn back." Jesus wanted Peter to know that his serious faith lapse would not lead to its destruction; Peter would confess his sin, receive forgiveness and restoration, and shore up the faith of his fellow disciples.

Simply stated, Jesus saw that the way to fight God's spiritual foe was through the spiritual means of prayer. Furthermore, since the devil had targeted Peter as the key to vanquishing the disciples, Jesus warned them all of Satan's plan while petitioning the Father for special attention to preserving Peter through the coming assault.

After the Passover meal, Jesus led his disciples to Gethsemane, where he urged them to "'pray that you will not fall into temptation'" (v. 40). He wanted them to petition the Father to help them resist sin, to stand firm against Satan's assaults. Then Jesus began praying for himself until his will was fully yielded to the Father's, committed to obeying God's way over Satan's way, thereby withstanding the temptation to avoid the cross.[20]

His disciples failed to heed his warning and counsel. Rather than praying, they slept; when temptation came, they were unprepared. With their spiritual defenses down, they shifted into self-protection and ran from their Savior's side, leaving him alone to face the most horrible rejection, suffering, and death anyone has ever endured.[21]

Within days, however, Jesus rose from the dead, victorious over Satan's plot to destroy him. The Father vindicated his Son, honoring his obedience to the divine will. Through the Son, the Father also began restoring those who had deserted the Son. Except for Judas, who died forever lost because he chose the devil over Jesus, the disciples "turned back" to Christ, received his forgiveness, and went on to Spirit-empowered Christlikeness in life, death, and beyond.[22]

And Peter? After he encountered the resurrected Lord, he experienced restoration at his hand and, like Jesus, became filled with the Holy Spirit, in whose power he walked for the rest of his days.[23] During that time, he obeyed the instruction to strengthen his brothers—not only the apostles, but also many others who by faith embraced Christ and the Spirit-filled life. Indeed, in Peter's first letter, he provides theological rationale, pastoral encouragement, and practical advice for successfully enduring religious persecution. As part of his counsel, he tenderly urges Christians,

> Be self-controlled and alert. Your enemy the devil prowls around like
> a roaring lion looking for someone to devour. Resist him, standing firm

in the faith, because you know that your brothers throughout the world are undergoing the same kind of sufferings. And the God of all grace, who called you to his eternal glory in Christ, after you have suffered a little while, will himself restore you and make you strong, firm and steadfast. (5:8–10)

Peter had learned his lesson well. He knew Satan's power and how to fight it effectively. He also knew that God looks out for his Son's followers, standing ready to protect and preserve them—and, should they fall and then return, promising to restore them and make them spiritually stronger still.

In every way the Father answered Jesus' prayers. If we are to have victory over temptation and the greatest tempter of all, we must heed Christ's teaching to pray that our heavenly Father "'lead us not into temptation, but deliver us from the evil one.'"

SOME LESSONS ABOUT PRAYER

The disciples' prayer reveals much about what and how we should pray to our loving God.

First, our prayers should be *God-centered;* the address and all six petitions have him as their focus. We should be obsessed with his name, his kingdom, and his will. We should rely on him to provide for our spiritual and material needs. We should keep before us that he is our Father-King; we are not only his subjects but his sons and daughters in Christ. In short, God is not tangential to our praying, nor is he merely a means to getting what we want when we want it. Prayer must be consumed with who God is and what he wants, exhibiting the growth of our loving abandonment to him.

Prayer, in other words, exemplifies the other love habits of simplicity and submission; indeed, prayer is a natural and logical outgrowth. When we seek to love God with all we are and have (simplicity), desiring to conform our will to his and to see his will carried out on earth as it is in heaven (submission), we will want to prayerfully commune with him, seeking to better know and serve him. Prayer is an active, effective, and loving way of carrying out our devotion to the Lord. Prayer helps align us to our Divine Lover, revealing how he wants us to cooperate in furthering his benevolent rule. Prayer, at its best, is full of God and therefore full of perfect love.

Second, our prayers should be mostly *petitionary*. God wants us to seek him out and ask him for things. Even intercession (asking on behalf of others) and confession (asking for forgiveness) are forms of petition; thanksgiving and adoration often flow from what God has done (or what we hope he will do) in response to our petitions. It makes sense that our prayer relationship with God is largely petitionary; after all, this *is* our Father's world, and we are his children. He desires to meet our needs. He delights when we come to him, express our needs to him, seek to align our lives with him, and urge him to accomplish all his good pleasure in us, through us, and around us.

Third, our prayers should demonstrate our *love of self*. God cares about us—each one of us—and he wants us to care about ourselves, so he instructs us to bring our concerns to him. Three areas of concern are represented in the last three petitions of the disciples' prayer: *material* needs (daily bread), *spiritual* needs (forgiveness), and *moral* needs (deliverance from evil). Our *relational* needs with God and others are presupposed throughout, for the prayer's address and petitions assume we're seeking a deeper relationship with God and more Christlike relationships with others. God wants each of us to come to him with our relational, material, spiritual, and moral needs so that we can ask him to supply his resources for meeting each and every one of them. This is self-love as expressed in prayer.

Fourth, our prayers should demonstrate our *love of family*. Beyond our self-love, we should reach out to our brothers and sisters in Christ. *Our Father . . . give us . . . forgive us . . . lead us . . . deliver us.* The model prayer's focus is on the family uniting in our petitions to our shared Father. We must mutually care enough to pray for one another; we should pray for *our* church, church leaders, church missionaries, church sins, church victories, church witness. Christians should pray for Christians; family must care for family.

Fifth, our prayers should demonstrate our *love for all others*. Forgiving those who hurt us is a requirement that does not come with any additional qualifier. It does not say, "except for unbelievers." We are to love who God loves, whether or not they treat us well. Since he loves all in his family *and* those who are not, we must love them too, even when they wound us.

Sixth, our prayers should demonstrate our *love of good and hatred of evil*. Hate is not the opposite of love, for God is love, yet he hates sin. The true opposite of love is indifference. Indifference doesn't care; hate does. Hate loves what is being violated or harmed; indifference ignores violation and harm. Hate loves justice; indifference cares for neither justice nor injustice. Hate is protective of what it loves; indifference protects nothing since it loves nothing. Hate fights for what it loves; indifference loves nothing and fights nothing. Hate can be blinded by sin but not by love; indifference is blinded by itself.

The resurrected and transformed Christ confronted the Laodicean church for its indifference:

> "I know your deeds, that you are neither cold nor hot. I wish you were either one or the other! So, because you are lukewarm—neither hot nor cold—I am about to spit you out of my mouth. You say, 'I am rich; I have acquired wealth and do not need a thing.' But you do not realize that you are wretched, pitiful, poor, blind and naked." (Rev. 3:15–17).

It is better to have loved and hated than neither to have loved nor hated. And it is godly to love all that is good while hating all that is evil. God's enemies are ours: Satan, sin, and death. We should pray for their complete demise, praying also for the coming of the full expression of God's universal benevolent rule—in our lives, in the lives of those still rebelling, and in the rest of the created order. Come, Lord Jesus, come! Come and fill up our Father's world with the amazing beauty of goodness, and banish the presence, power, and penalty of evil forever. This is our hope. This is our prayer.

Seventh, our prayers should be *primarily concerned with spiritual matters*. That five of the six petitions in the disciples' prayer have to do with spiritual concerns should emphasize our priority: The Father wants us to place the spiritual above the material. While there's nothing wrong with praying for material needs, they should consume less time and energy. For instance, prayers for physical wholeness, financial health, gainful employment, and the like are perfectly appropriate topics. But if these elements fill our prayers day in and day out—if our spiritual needs and those of others routinely have a small place in our prayers—then our priorities are not God's. We must be more prayerful about the permanent things, which will last beyond the grave. These are all we can take with us.

Finally, our prayers should *take Satan seriously*. A spiritual war rages in and around us; while God is reestablishing his rule in repentant people, Satan is attempting to stop God's progress and thereby hold onto his evil reign. His schemes are unrelenting, powerful, deceitful, and deadly. But as persistent and powerful as Satan is, he is still only a creature limited by his own nature and by the Creator's sovereign will. Even though "the whole world [still] lies in the power of the evil one" (1 John 5:19 NASB), the devil's days are numbered. Jesus has defeated him, and victory over evil is assured, yet until Satan is put away forever, we must seek divinely provided safety and power to withstand his assaults. And stand we can, for "the one who is in [us] is greater than the one who is in the world" (4:4).

Getting Started

Knowing that God wants us to pour out our minds and hearts to him, to seek out his mind and heart for us and all else that concerns him, how can we develop the love habit of prayer? Here are some suggestions.

Commitment

You must choose to make prayer a daily activity. This begins by setting aside time each day to pray. There's no magic formula: You either choose to do it or you don't.

When I was a young Christian, a speaker came to my church and posed a challenge. "Give God just five minutes a day in prayer," he said. "If you do, God will grow your prayer life." That week I began praying five minutes daily. The more I prayed, the more I got to know the Lord. And the more I knew him, the more my eyes were opened to his active, loving presence in my life. Within a few weeks, my prayer time had grown to ten or fifteen minutes a day. By the time several more weeks had passed, I found myself praying sometimes thirty minutes to an hour, as well as during much shorter periods of time most days. Five daily prayerful minutes led to prayer becoming a vital part of my love relationship with God.

Anyone can find five minutes a day to spend with the One who loves them most. Do this, and you will find Love drawing you into its wonderful embrace.

Time

The prayer practice of Jesus shows that he habitually went off alone to pray, and he prayed at various times. His favorite time was early morning, but he also prayed at night and in the afternoon.[24]

We also can pray anytime. However, if we truly want to develop our prayer life to its greatest potential, we need to find a window that will afford us a real quiet time before God. The time of day we choose may fluctuate, but it should be consistent, preferably daily. Some days our alone-time might last for only minutes, but that's fine—duration is not nearly as important as regularity.

Over the years, I've found that morning is the best part of my day for praying. After I exercise, dress, and have breakfast, I go off by myself, usually for anywhere from half an hour to two hours, and occasionally just minutes. Prayer has become like breathing—natural, regular, rarely requiring work— but prayer didn't become like that for me overnight, any more than a parent/ child or husband/wife relationship begins effortlessly. Relationships, espe- cially those with people we love, take much time and cultivation, yielding great rewards if we do not neglect them.

Think about times this week that you can set aside for prayer with your Divine Lover, and then schedule them. Make appointments with God, and strive to guard them from lesser demands and intrusions. If interruptions occur, don't let them frustrate or anger you. Resolve the situation, then set aside another time to pray, for that same day if possible.

Remember that the deepening of any love relationship requires regular time spent between lovers. You can put intimacy on life support by starving it of its needs. When we commit to God even some of our time, he will grow our love—for him, for ourselves, for those we love already, and for those we don't love but should. Give God your time, and he will transform your life.

Place

Jesus routinely found a private place to pray. For him, prayer and solitude went together.[25]

To what place of solitude can you regularly go for prayer? Is there a room in your home where you can post "Do Not Disturb" on the door? A place for retreat in your yard, a nearby park, a chapel or church, a section of beach or spot in the mountains? It doesn't have to be the same place every time, but if possible, try to find a regular spot where you can have uninterrupted alone- time with God.

Consider at least three places you can frequently pray, then try praying in each location during the next few weeks to see which best fit your needs, especially with minimal interruptions or distractions. Use this trial process to help you choose the place(s) that will work well for you.

I've often used all kinds of places for prayer, including my kitchen table, living room, car, and office, as well as libraries, coffeehouses, restaurants, malls, and parks. I've found that I can be alone with God even in public places with a large number of people milling around. As long as no one knows me or interrupts me, I can pray silently and write out my prayers in these settings. Prayers do not have to pass through the lips to speak to God. He knows our thoughts and reads our hearts—he even knows what we will say before we form the words.[26] Silent communion allows me to pray to him anytime, anyplace, apart from or surrounded by people.

Approach

Over the centuries, the church has practiced a wide variety of approaches to prayer—far more than I could explore here. As shown by both study of Scripture and the lives and writings of other Christians, no approach to prayer is higher or more sacred than any other. God cares far more about our actually praying than about the way we choose to do it.

Still, among the numerous valuable ways of praying, I'd like to highlight four and suggest you try them. They will expand your understanding of prayer's incredible effectiveness, enlarge your vision of God, deepen your appreciation of his people, and grow your love so it reaches out increasingly to all he loves. I have used these approaches and often return to them with ongoing benefit.

One approach is *praying through the prayers recorded in Scripture*. I'm not urging you to simply repeat them, though there's nothing wrong with that. What I'm suggesting is that you make the biblical prayers your own—personalize them.

Take, for example, the disciples' prayer. After you say the first line— "'Our Father in heaven'"—you might expand on it by saying something like this:

> *I am so grateful that you, Lord, are my Father. As my Father, you are perfect and unfailing like no earthly parent could ever be. You always seek my best. You always love me. You always discipline me in a way that will make me a more complete person. May you always be exalted and adored by me and the rest of your creation. And may you always help me to come to you as your child and seek your all-good will for my life.*

Do what you can to personalize each line as you lift your voice toward heaven in prayer to the Lord.

The book of Psalms is a magnificent collection of inspired prayers. You could begin praying through them, starting with Psalm 1 and, over a period of months, working your way through all 150 in order. Or you could skip around, praying through psalms that best reflect your own circumstances or needs. The Psalms cover the spectrum of human emotion and an array of situations. They also probe and reflect the nature and activity of God, as well as the glory and corruption of humanity. By praying through them in your interaction with the Lord, you will learn much about yourself and your Lover as you increase your vision of prayer's length, breadth, and depth.

Whether you personalize the psalms, the disciples' prayer, or any of the other prayers in Scripture, when you pray in accordance with God's inspiration, you can be assured he will honor your prayer as he honors his own Word.

A second approach is *praying through the recorded prayers of renowned believers and church traditions.* Collections of prayers abound. Some reflect a specific tradition, such as Anglican, Quaker, Wesleyan, Presbyterian, Benedictine, or Franciscan. Many provide prayers for various occasions. One of the most used and cherished collections in the Protestant tradition is called *The Book of Common Prayer.* Other books contain the prayers of various Christians, such as John and Charles Wesley, Francis of Assisi, Thomas Aquinas, Martin Luther, Augustine of Hippo, Anselm of Canterbury, George MacDonald, Thomas à Kempis, John Chrysostom, C. S. Lewis, John Baillie, Ignatius of Loyola, John of the Cross, Thomas More, Reinhold Niebuhr, Evelyn Underhill, and Patrick of Ireland. Two such collections I've enjoyed are *The Oxford Book of Prayer* and *Disciplines for the Inner Life.*[27] In addition to prayers, the latter book contains selections from authors on almost any imaginable dimension of the spiritual life.

You can learn much about prayer from the church's experience in communing with God over the centuries. By praying through and even personalizing the prayers that have been passed down to us through the ages, you will discover a rich and vibrant spiritual heritage that will profoundly aid the development of your walk with the Lord.

A third approach is *praying the same brief prayer throughout a given day.* You can draw the prayer from Scripture or a collection of prayers, or use a prayer of your own. Repeat it frequently during the day, using it to share your heart with God. Let the words and the spirit they convey sink deeply into your soul, allowing them to impact you and your relationships hour after hour.

One final suggested approach is *praying "flash prayers,"*[28] short prayers offered silently for people we see during the day. They may be standing with us in the checkout line, sitting across from us on the subway, working beside us in a business meeting, or driving next to us in traffic. Whether they're friends, associates, or strangers, intercede on their behalf, asking the Lord to wrap his loving arms around them and draw them closer to himself.

Family Aid

Because we are members of God's family, we should not only pray for each other but *with* each other too. The disciples' prayer encourages this through its use of plural pronouns (such as *us* and *our*). Our Father is delighted when we come together as his children and offer our collective prayers. Of course, he answers the prayers of individual believers, just as he answered his Son's prayers, but he especially enjoys answering those from united groups of believers. Jesus assured, "'If two of you on earth agree about anything you ask for, it will be done for you by my Father in heaven. For where two or three come together in my name, there am I with them'" (Matt. 18:19–20). The God who is a triunity of persons honors the prayers that flow from united followers, so look for opportunities to join with other Christians in prayer. You will see yet another way God works through the prayers of his people to accomplish his perfect will on earth.

THE OTHER SIDE OF PRAYER

Up to this point we've largely explored one side of prayer: *our* side. We've concentrated mostly on whom *we* should pray to, what *we* should pray, and how *we* should pray. The focus has been on us, the pray-ers. But if prayer is communication between God and us, what is *God's* side in this process? Does he speak to us through prayer? And, if so, how may we hear him—indeed, what should we be listening for? It's this other side of prayer that will occupy our attention in the next love habit we'll explore: *guidance*.

7. Guidance:
taking our Lover's hand

Praying to God is one thing. Hearing from God is another.

That God can speak is not the issue. The entire Bible is his Word to us—literally "God-breathed" writings (2 Tim. 3:16). God can and has spoken.

But Scripture was completed two thousand years ago. Did God then stop speaking? More pertinent to us, does he still speak today? If so, how does he communicate and how can we discern his voice? And if we can hear from him, what can we expect him to care about? To what degree will he counsel and guide us through the maze of this earthly life?

From what we've discovered so far, we know that God has not left us alone to fend for ourselves. He actively pursues, seeking to draw us to himself so he can fulfill in us what we so desperately need and want. What we need and want more than anything is him—God in his perfect fullness. To embrace him, to find our fulfillment in him, is to have all that Love has to offer. We cannot find anything better, or have anything better, because nothing better exists.

We can expect our Lover, then, to want to provide direction for us, and his Word clearly tells us that this is an expectation he will meet. The psalmist declares that, for believers, "God is our God for ever and ever; he will be our guide even to the end" (48:14). One of the lessons that the Hebrews learned after God led them out of slavery from Egypt is that his leadership in their lives would continue without fail. "In your unfailing love," they sang in praise, "you will lead the people you have redeemed. In your strength you will guide them to your holy dwelling" (Ex. 15:13). Likewise, we who have been baptized into Christ by the Holy Spirit are "led by the Spirit of God." Indeed, his leading in our lives is one indication that we are truly "sons of God" (Rom. 8:14).

In these passages (just a sampling of the many we could discuss), we see that God guides those who place their trust in him. It's not a question of *whether* he will lead those who choose to follow; if we give ourselves to him, he *will* give us himself, including the incredible advantages of his all-knowing wisdom. Love gives, and infinite love gives infinitely. To receive, all we must do is submit.

> Trust in the LORD with all your heart and lean not on your own understanding; in all your ways acknowledge him, and he *will* make your paths straight. (Prov. 3:5–6, emphasis added)

No hedging here: Our deepening submission will *with certainty* result in our receiving *from* him the direction we need to live *for* him. Divine guidance is assured for the obedient.

This is what we should expect from any love relationship, including one in the strictly human sphere. Lovers care about each other's hopes and dreams. They want each other to be happy and fulfilled, becoming the best each can be and doing the highest each can achieve. Lovers seek to open up opportunities for training, education, networking, spiritual development, and anything else required for the beloved's advancement. Lovers offer each other counsel, proposing different life paths to take and different ways of overcoming obstacles along the chosen way. By doing these things, lovers give each other advantages for finding true and longer-lasting satisfaction.

Nevertheless, human guidance remains finite and fallible. We may sometimes act like know-it-alls, but we are not all-knowing. No matter how much other people love us, they do not know us exhaustively, and we don't even know ourselves that well. Adding our inability to know the future and how little we learn from our past, we can see how much we need the Divine Lover's guiding light. Only he infallibly knows the future as well as the past. Only he knows us fully and perfectly. Only he has the loving power to make us all we can be as he directs us to all he wants us to do, which is where our greatest satisfaction, our everlasting joy resides.

This is the purpose for which he created us and saved us: "It is by grace you have been saved. . . . We are God's workmanship, created in Christ Jesus to do good works, which God prepared in advance for us to do" (Eph. 2:8, 10). We were brought into this world and delivered from evil so we might *become* the people God knows we can be and *do* the good he has prepared for us. Divine Love always acts with purpose, and the purpose always centers on what is best for the beloved.

GOD'S MEANS OF GUIDANCE TODAY

How, though, does God accomplish this loving and knowing direction in our lives? How can we hear him? How can we effectively take our Lover's hand and walk with him wherever he leads? The answer is found in the love habit of *guidance*, which shows us how to discern God's voice in the many ways it comes to us. This habit assumes that we want to hear from God, and, when we hear, that we will want to respond appropriately. Guidance given is guidance wasted if not received as it should be. When divine guidance comes and we choose not to follow it, we spurn our Lover and betray our best interests. The doers of divine guidance reap the benefits, not the hearers who fail to obey.

Of course, we can't do what we can't hear or don't hear. Therefore, let's first consider how God is communicating; we must know the means he uses so we know where to bend our ears. Then we'll look at the telltale signs of his voice so we can distinguish his guidance from that of the merely human or deceptively demonic.

Prayer

One of the most common ways God speaks to us is through prayer. As we pour out ourselves to him, he reaches out to us, meeting our needs and desires according to his benevolent will. This is the testimony of believers throughout recorded history and into our own day. Prayer is a two-way communication between him who loves us and us who love him.

Though Jesus demonstrated this throughout his earthly life, perhaps the most fascinating and insightful instance occurs at the gravesite of one of his dearest friends.

As he was being led to the tomb of Lazarus, "Jesus wept" (John 11:35), and those who witnessed his intense emotional response saw in it his deep love for Lazarus. After he arrived, he ordered that the stone in front of the chamber be removed. Then, standing at the entrance, Jesus prayed, "'Father, I thank you that you have heard me. I knew that you always hear me, but I said this for the benefit of the people standing here, that they may believe that you sent me'" (John 11:41–42). His words indicate that two prayers are in view: the prayer he's now uttering at the tomb, and one he prayed earlier—the one implied by the words "'I thank you that you *have* heard me.'" Commenting on this latter prayer, Curtis Mitchell says,

> This prayer had probably been uttered when Christ *first* heard the news concerning His friend. I say this because at the time that Jesus heard the news, He told His disciples that Lazarus was indeed dead and that he would awaken him (see John 11:11). The reason Christ could assure His disciples that He would awaken Lazarus was that He had already prayed for his resurrection! He knew that His prayers were always answered (see John 11:42). In essence, then, the prayer recorded in these verses [vv. 41–42] was an expression of joyous assurance and thanksgiving for *answered* prayer.[1]

With his second prayer finished—uttered in front of those who were standing near him—"Jesus called in a loud voice, 'Lazarus, come out!'" And Lazarus did, still wrapped in grave clothes (vv. 43–44).

When Jesus prayed, the Father answered, and Jesus knew the Father heard him because the Father *always* responded to him. No exceptions.

How could this be? There's really no mystery: Jesus always heard from the Father because he always prayed according to the Father's will. And how did he know the Father's will? He had cultivated a life of submission to the Father through the work of the Spirit. Jesus, in his humanity, was wholly abandoned to the Father, a depth of abandonment made possible by the baptism and filling of the Spirit; consequently, his Spirit-led prayers always fit the Father's will. Even when he initially wrestled with what the Father wanted, the orientation of his life was single-minded: accomplishing the Father's will was paramount, regardless of the cost.

God always answers prayers that fit his will. This sounds easy enough, but how do we know when we're praying according to his will? We often don't—because of our finite feebleness, "we do not know how to pray as we should" (Rom. 8:26 NASB). This makes the situation sound hopeless, but it isn't. Though our prayers, if left to themselves, would usually miss the divine will, the Spirit comes to our aid and "intercedes for us with groans that words cannot express" (v. 26); he takes our words, even "those emotions, desires, and aspirations which we are unable to clothe in words,"[2] and conveys them to the Father in a way that accords "with God's will" (v. 27). This is just one of many assurances that "in all things God works for the good" of his lovers (v. 28). Even when we do not pray as we should, the Spirit conforms our petitions to the divine will, assuring that they are heard and answered with our well-being in mind as well as the good of those for whom we intercede.

Can we learn more about God's will? Absolutely. And prayer plays a critical role, for through prayer *we,* not just our circumstances, are changed. The more we converse with our Lover, the more we find ourselves conformed to him and thereby to his will.

> Prayer is the central avenue God uses to transform us. . . . In prayer, real prayer, we begin to think God's thoughts after him: to desire the things he desires, to love the things he loves, to will the things he wills. Progressively, we are taught to see things from his point of view.[3]

His point of view is *always* right and *always* the best achievable, not only for us but also for all he loves.

How God's best comes to us—through prayer or otherwise—is what the other modes of communication are about. Love's responses come in a variety of forms; God uses them to speak to us and guide us, whether he's responding to our prayers or to someone else's prayers for us, or seeking our attention apart from prayer. Taken together, all divine communication shows that our Lover is always reaching out to us, speaking to us, striving to guide our steps toward the good that will fulfill and satisfy us here and hereafter. We cannot outtalk him any more than we can outlove him. The following are means through which his talk (and thus his guidance) reaches into our lives.

Action Alone

God's communication frequently comes in direct action rather than words. We ask, and he answers by doing something. We may or may not recognize the act as his response, and we may like or dislike what he does; at any rate, instead of telling us what he's going to do, he simply does it. *God's ways are love in action.* It's not that he disdains conversation; instead, he more highly prizes action, often letting his actions speak for themselves.

For example, during the Last Supper, Jesus told his followers that he would send them "the Spirit of truth," who would give them what belongs to Jesus, which is all that "belongs to the Father" (John 16:13, 15). Then, just before ascending into heaven, Jesus reminded them of the Spirit's coming:

> "Do not leave Jerusalem, but wait for the gift my Father promised, which you have heard me speak about. . . . In a few days you will be baptized with the Holy Spirit. . . . You will receive power when the Holy Spirit comes on you" (Acts 1:4–5, 8).

After Jesus left their sight, the disciples obeyed, returning to Jerusalem, praying and waiting with other followers. Nothing happened until the day of Pentecost; while the disciples and their companions "were all together in one place," a sudden rush of sound "like the blowing of a violent wind . . . from heaven . . . filled the whole house where they were sitting. They saw what seemed to be tongues of fire that separated and came to rest on each of them. All of them were filled with the Holy Spirit and began to speak in other tongues as the Spirit enabled them" (2:1–4). The promised gift came—suddenly, without further announcement. Through Christ, the Father said what he would do. The disciples believed, obeyed, and prayed . . . then the Father delivered on his promise. At that point God was all action.

A contemporary example of God's action-oriented response comes from Richard Foster's *Celebration of Discipline,* in which he tells of a friend who teaches emotionally handicapped children. Believing that God wanted him to pray for these kids, Foster's friend started doing so without letting his students know what he was up to.

> When one of the children would crawl under his desk and assume a fetal position, my teacher friend would take the child in his arms and pray silently that the resurrected Christ would heal the hurt and self-hate within the boy. So as not to embarrass him, the teacher would walk around the room continuing his regular duties while he prayed. After a while the child would relax and was soon back at his desk. Sometimes my friend would ask the boy if he ever remembered what it felt like to win a race. If the boy said yes, he would encourage him to picture himself crossing the finish line with all his friends cheering him on and loving him. In that way the child was able to cooperate in the prayer project as well as reinforce his own self-acceptance. . . . By the end of the school year, every child but two was able to return to a regular classroom.[4]

God answered this man's prayers with actions.

Sometimes when God answers this way we don't see it. Just this morning, my wife and I were talking, and I said to her, "Do you realize how much God has responded to the desires of your heart?"

"What do you mean?" she asked.

"You wanted an affirming place to work, and now you have one. You wanted a better, safer home environment for your children, and now you have that. If you ever remarried, you wanted a man who loved you and your children as a husband and father should, and you got that too. You wanted a church home that demonstrated grace as well as provided for real growth in Christ. That you also have. God has guided you in so many ways by simply giving you your heart's desires."

Tears welled up in her eyes, and she nodded to me an affirming yes. "I had not seen all these things in that way until now."

This is how it is with all of us at one time or another. We seek God's guidance, and he gives it to us without fanfare. But in the demands and struggles of our everyday lives, we can miss what he's already supplied. Actions usually speak louder than words; even so, for us to notice God's work, we must remain aware of what's taking place in and around us.

Action Plus Audible Speech

Sometimes in Scripture God acts and then speaks audibly, or speaks aloud and then acts. For instance, while Jesus was being baptized, he was also praying. In response, "heaven was opened and the Holy Spirit descended on him in bodily form like a dove. And a voice came from heaven: 'You are my Son, whom I love; with you I am well pleased'" (Luke 3:21–22). Jesus prayed and heaven opened—the Spirit acted, and the Father spoke.

During Paul's pre-conversion days (as Saul), he was traveling to Damascus to further his persecution of Christians, when suddenly "a light from heaven flashed around him. He fell to the ground and heard a voice say to him, 'Saul, Saul, why do you persecute me?'" Saul asked who was speaking, and the voice answered, "I am Jesus, whom you are persecuting. . . . Now get up and go into the city, and you will be told what you must do" (Acts 9:3–9). Once again, action accompanied God's words.

Audible Speech

There are times when God shows up just to talk—never for chitchat, but to say something significant.

Long ago he spoke to a young boy named Samuel, calling out to him by name one evening while Samuel rested in bed. When this happened, Samuel believed that Eli, the priest responsible for him, had called, so each time he got out of bed, went to Eli, and said, "Here I am; you called me." Each time Eli told him he had not called. After the third time, "Eli realized that the LORD was calling the boy. So Eli told Samuel, 'Go and lie down, and if he calls you, say, "Speak, LORD, for your servant is listening."'" Samuel obeyed, and sure enough, God spoke to him again—this time, Samuel addressed God as Eli had instructed. God wanted to share with Samuel tough stuff relating to Eli and his family; when morning came, Samuel reluctantly relayed what the Lord had told him.[5]

Centuries later, Paul tells us that he "pleaded with the Lord" on three separate occasions to remove an unidentified "thorn" in his flesh that tormented him. He received this painful problem so that he would not become "conceited" because of the incredible "revelations" God had given him. God had not caused Paul to experience this affliction but had permitted Satan to inflict him with it, ironically using the work of the devil to thwart the sin of conceit, thereby bringing good out of what the evil one meant for evil. Paul recognized that his thorn came from "a messenger of Satan," so he petitioned God to deliver him from the assault.

In other words, Paul prayed according to the disciples' model prayer: "Lead us not into temptation, but deliver us from the evil one" (Matt. 6:13). In this case, however, the persistent, painful thorn was serving a good purpose—a purpose higher than Paul's receiving relief from his suffering. So the divine answer came to him audibly: "'My grace is sufficient for you, for my power is made perfect in weakness.'" Paul accepted God's will for him, seeing that it truly was for his good and that it could be used to help fellow believers likewise see that "when I am weak, then I am strong" (2 Cor. 12:7–9).

Spirit to Soul

One intimate way in which God communicates is from within us. His Spirit speaks "with our spirit," confirming that "we are God's children" (Rom. 8:16) and coming "into our hearts, crying, 'Abba! Father!'" (Gal. 4:6 NASB). His Spirit works in our "inner being [to] strengthen [us] with power" (Eph. 3:16), and he pours his love "into our hearts" (Rom. 5:5). The Holy Spirit "searches all things, even the deep things of God," teaching us so "we may understand what God has freely given us," thereby bringing us to spiritual maturity, which is nothing less than creating within us "the mind of Christ" (1 Cor. 2:11–12, 16).

The Spirit incessantly works to transform us into Christlikeness, and as we cooperate in this deeply intimate process, we find ourselves being guided by and revealing Christlike attitudes and perspectives. Christ's presence in us becomes Christ's life lived through us. More and more we live and breathe Christ, thinking as he thinks, willing as he wills, feeling as he feels.

However, our individual personalities, styles, dreams, and passions are not absorbed into Christ and thereby lost any more than the biblical writers lost theirs as the result of being inspired by the Spirit to convey divine words. Peter and Paul, Matthew and Mark all wrote out of the Christian worldview and all convey the truth, but even a cursory reading of their writings displays different approaches, different concerns, different emphases, even different theological interests and levels of understanding. In his second letter, Peter says of Paul that "his letters contain some things that are hard to understand" (3:16). Peter struggled with Paul's writing style and theological depth, yet he knew that Paul's letters, like his own, were divinely inspired.

The Spirit baptizes each of us into Christ, places us in his body (the church), equips us with spiritual gifts, and fills us with his presence so we have the divine resources to become what each of us was created to be. Day by day we become renewed, transformed creatures who, from the inside out, know the Wounded Healer, the Holy One of God. Increasingly we live out his mind and will in ways that reflect and build upon our uniqueness.

In this Divine-Spirit-to-human-soul relationship, our Lover speaks to us through our thoughts and feelings, through our observations and perceptions. The divine speech may be verbal—articulated in words that come from within us. Or his word to us may be nonverbal—providing us with a sense, an instinct, an intuition that something is right or wrong, that a course of action is good or bad, that a person is being straight or trying to deceive. The Spirit speaks and directs just as surely as if he were physically standing next to us, taking our hand and saying, "Follow me."

Throughout my Christian life I have come to sense God's guidance in this way. At times his counsel has come to me in my thoughts. His discernable words have challenged and chastised me, comforted and healed me. He has guided me to be silent as well as to speak. He has told me to hold a hurting friend, to correct an erring disciple, to request help from a fellow believer. He has given me questions to pose to skeptics that opened the way for defending the faith. He has called on me to be straightforward when I was inclined to be vague. In these situations and countless others, I have heard God's words in my mind, not my thoughts but his.

On perhaps even more occasions, I have not heard distinct words coming from within but still have sensed the Spirit's leading. I've experienced urgings to press a point in conversations. I've felt burdened for someone to such a degree that I found a way to bring him relief. I've been suddenly enlightened to see another side of a truth I thought I knew thoroughly. I've been moved to contact a friend for advice or to seek an employment option I would not have considered if left to my own musings.

All in all, God has demonstrated to me that his guiding presence is as close to me as my own inner life.

The Living Word

Undoubtedly, the greatest single resource for discovering God's will is his Word. The Bible contains timeless counsel about so many elements of life that we would be indescribably foolish to ignore it. Even the incarnate Son steeped himself in the Scriptures, finding strength, wisdom, and direction for his own sojourn on earth. He used them as mighty weapons to counter Satan's temptations and to teach others about himself.[6] If Jesus found so much value in the Scriptures, how much more should we. Besides, regardless of how God guides, he will never lead us to believe or do anything that contradicts or undermines the teaching of his unbreakable, infallible Word.[7] For this reason alone, we should give it our loyal and studious attention.

Biblical study and application is so central to the Christian life that I devote almost the entire next chapter to it. For now, I'd like to say that I've found to be true what Scripture says about itself:

> The word of God is living and active. Sharper than any double-edged sword, it penetrates even to dividing soul and spirit, joints and marrow; it judges the thoughts and attitudes of the heart. (Heb. 4:12)
>
> All Scripture is God-breathed and is useful for teaching, rebuking, correcting and training in righteousness, so that the man[8] of God may be thoroughly equipped for every good work. (2 Tim. 3:16–17)

The same Spirit who inspired the words of the biblical writers works through those words and brings them alive in us as we study them, meditate on them, and apply them. Through our study and the Spirit's illuminating work, the truths of Scripture penetrate the fabric of our minds and hearts, enlightening, reshaping, and redirecting us. The Bible is the Living Word, and in it we find God's will for us on a host of subjects covering a vast range of situations. There our Divine Lover speaks in words meant for all of his beloved.

The Equipping Church

In Ephesians, Paul fleshed out what the church (Christ's body) is all about.

[God] gave some to be apostles, some to be prophets, some to be evangelists, and some to be pastors and teachers, to prepare God's people for works of service, so that the body of Christ may be built up until we all reach unity in the faith and in the knowledge of the Son of God and become mature, attaining to the whole measure of the fullness of Christ. Then we will no longer be infants, tossed back and forth by the waves, and blown here and there by every wind of teaching and by the cunning and craftiness of men in their deceitful scheming. Instead, speaking the truth in love, we will in all things grow up into him who is the Head, that is, Christ. From him the whole body, joined and held together by every supporting ligament, grows and builds itself up in love, as each part does its work. (4:11–16)

I have experienced this in the church. Through her faithful servants, past and present, I have heard Christianity preached and taught, and I have seen it modeled—incarnated in the warp and woof of life. The church has not been perfect, but then neither have I. The church has not acted sinlessly, nor have I. The church has not always been clear or helpful, which has been true of me as well. Still, because of the church, I keep maturing in Christ and receiving valuable guidance. I'd like to tell you about two instances from the mid–1970s that still impact me today.

At the time, I was a musician completely convinced that God's will for me was to play music my entire life. I pursued that end with unrelenting drive and monolithic devotion.

During this period I had gained a friend in my senior pastor, Rick Yohn, a fine teacher and preacher and an insightful counselor. Rick enjoyed music— he played guitar and sang, and he liked the way I played drums. He and the music director often had me perform with the choir during Sunday worship services and other church functions.

One day Rick and I were talking in his office. I don't recall how the subject came up, but he told me he believed God had something other than a musical career in mind for me. I laughed at the suggestion, telling him he was crazy. He didn't get angry with me, however. He calmly reasserted his claim, and I just as casually dismissed it. We talked awhile longer, then parted.

A few months later I went to our associate pastor and told him I thought there needed to be a Sunday school class taught on reasons to believe that

Christianity is true. He listened attentively, then said he thought I should teach it. Since that wasn't my plan, I did everything I could to remove the notion from his head, but he was insistent; I reluctantly gave in. He handed me some books to read, and he oversaw my development of a course outline.

Within four months I was teaching my first class. It began with forty adults, but after four weeks had swelled to more than eighty people, about a dozen of whom were high school and college students. When I started, I was terrified and terribly awkward, even tripping over the chalkboard a couple of times. Yet by the halfway mark of the thirteen weeks, I was in love with teaching.

Before the class drew to a close, I went to Rick and asked to speak with him privately in his office. A bit sheepishly and with teary eyes, I said, "You were right. God does have more in mind for me than simply a career in music. I cannot begin to explain how fulfilling teaching is to me. God is using me to change lives, and he's changing mine in the process. Thanks for guiding me, even in spite of my unwillingness to accept it."

A couple of years and several courses later, Rick advised me again, and this time I listened. He opened his Bible and read this verse: "A man's gift makes room for him and brings him before great men" (Prov. 18:16 NASB). Then he said, "Bill, there's no doubt you are a gifted teacher and a gifted musician. I believe you also have other gifts God will reveal to you in his time. Whatever they are, work at developing them and using them as a faithful servant of God. When the time is right, he will use your gifts to bring you before people you can't imagine right now. Just remain faithful. He will take care of the rest."

I have lived by that counsel and found it to be entirely reliable. It has shaped me consistently, encouraged me when I've been down, and carried me through murky waters. Even more, it has kept me focused on my role and God's, showing me that he is faithful to his Word, and that his church, when she is faithful to him, is a reliable interpreter and applier of that Word. His voice still comes to us through his church, the body of Christ.

Shaping Circumstances

God also uses situations in our lives to guide us.

Paul found that through circumstances he learned contentment:

> I have learned to be content whatever the circumstances. I know what it is to be in need, and I know what it is to have plenty. I have

learned the secret of being content in any and every situation, whether well fed or hungry, whether living in plenty or in want. I can do everything through him who gives me strength. (Phil. 4:11–13)

No matter what Paul faced, he found that Christ led him and gave him the ability to handle it. This is why he could say, "Rejoice in the Lord always. I will say it again: Rejoice!" (v. 4). Paul experienced Immanuel, "God with us" (Matt. 1:23), even in the day-to-day happenings of life.

Sometimes God uses circumstances to discipline us and return us to obedience, for a child occasionally needs parental correction to get back on the right path:

Our fathers disciplined us for a little while as they thought best; but God disciplines us for our good, that we may share in his holiness. No discipline seems pleasant at the time, but painful. Later on, however, it produces a harvest of righteousness and peace for those who have been trained by it. (Heb. 12:10–11)

We must never forget that God's all-encompassing goal for us whom he loves is our full transformation into the image of his most beloved Son. However he can use circumstances to help accomplish this goal, he will, even if it means bringing temporary pain into our lives, including the pain of discipline. He cares for us that much.

God also utilizes circumstances to guide us through confusing choices or troubling voices. An instance of this in the early church occurs in Acts 15, which details a controversy generated by some Christians who believed that Gentiles had to be circumcised and required to obey the Mosaic Law in order to be saved. Church leaders came together in Jerusalem to discuss and debate the matter; along with working through Scripture, they heard Peter, Paul, and Barnabas tell about personally witnessing God's miraculous salvific work among the Gentiles and how all this had happened apart from circumcision and obedience to the law. Taking these reports and positions into account, the leaders rendered a decision that "seemed good to the Holy Spirit and to us" (v. 28). In other words, through the maze of disparate voices, the Spirit used the defining experiences of various Christian workers to guide the early church through a disagreement that threatened to divide her and undermine the doctrine of salvation by faith.

Many times God has worked through circumstances to direct my steps. He has let me suffer consequences of sin so I would follow his will more faithfully. He has allowed me to undergo and witness the unjust hurt of others so I would become more sensitive. He has taught me perseverance through pain, hope through seemingly impossible odds. He has also used my life circumstances to motivate me along the educational and vocational path I've followed.

For instance, while I was in seminary, I grew alarmed and frustrated over the theological ignorance and apathy among my fellow students. So I started two student organizations and published an academic journal to challenge students to take theology and critical thinking more seriously. I received a good deal of help from some faculty members and a handful of students. Our work paid off: Theological awareness among students grew considerably, and the changing atmosphere positively affected even many faculty members.

More specifically, just before I graduated, as a direct result of my work among students, Charles and Cynthia Swindoll offered me a position at Insight for Living that gave me the opportunity to sharpen my editorial and writing skills. This produced in me an even greater desire to get involved in the publishing industry, not only as a writer of my own works but also as an editorial guide to other Christian writers, helping to accomplish a goal to get better material into print for the benefit of the body of Christ.

Now I'm a full-time teacher and part-time writer, fulfilled in career and ministry. My life has taken turns I never planned, much less imagined. Yet through it all I have learned what Scripture declared long ago: "In his heart a man plans his course, but the LORD determines his steps" (Prov. 16:9). His way has always been better than mine, and he has often used circumstances to make that way clear.

Dreams and Visions

The Bible contains numerous examples of God speaking to people through dreams and visions. A dream normally happened during sleep; a vision usually occurred while the recipient was awake.

Jacob dreamt of a stairway to heaven, which led him to make a life-altering vow to God.[9] Joseph had dreams of future prominence over his brothers, which, through a number of trials, eventually came true.[10] King Nebuchadnezzar had a dream that mystified and terrified him; young Daniel interpreted the dream for the king, crediting God with the revelation.[11]

As for visions, Isaiah had one that showed him God's holiness and his own prophetic mission. The Gentile Cornelius had a vision that led him to send for Peter, who likewise had a vision that prepared him for being the first disciple to take the gospel to Gentiles. Paul also had a vision that guided him to take the gospel to Macedonia during a missionary journey.[12]

As far as I know, God has spoken to me once in a dream, but at first I didn't know it was him. Around 1976, when I began researching and praying about seminaries I wanted to attend, I dreamt about riding in a car. The vehicle had four occupants—a driver and three passengers. I was a passenger, sitting in the sedan's backseat, and all of us were wearing dress coats and slacks, dress shirts and ties. We were traveling on a freeway; in fact, we were exiting one freeway and entering another over a rather complicated interchange. The conversation among us was theological, and although all of us were participating, I seemed to be leading it.

Later I mentioned this dream to a few people, commenting on its strangeness. I didn't know anyone in the car, yet I spoke as if I knew them well. Being dressed up on what I perceived as a weekday was unheard of for me and just about everyone else I knew at the time. And our theological discussion seemed odd also, since at that point my mind was mostly filled with thoughts of philosophy and apologetics. I simply couldn't figure out why I would have such a dream or what it meant. It did not arise out of my experience, my thoughts, or anything else that mattered to me at the time.

Two years later, I began attending Dallas Theological Seminary. I almost quit three times during my first year there, thinking I'd made a mistake and should move on to finding a philosophy program elsewhere rather than keeping up with my Bible and theology studies at DTS. However, one of the professors convinced me to stay, informing me that a new teacher was coming whom I'd find challenging and more attuned to my interests.

About a month before my second year began, I found out that this new teacher's name was Dr. Norman Geisler; one of the premier Christian philosophers, apologists, and theologians would be teaching full-time at DTS. Delighted, I met with him before the new school year started, establishing a relationship with him and becoming his teaching assistant. For the next five years we worked together on a variety of topics and projects, and I even substitute-taught his classes when he traveled. In many ways, Norm became like a second father to me, and my association with him made my seminary experience indescribably rich.

It was during that second year at DTS—my first working with Norm—that

I found myself living the dream I'd had three years before. I was riding in the backseat of a car containing three other seminary students. All of us were dressed up for school, on our way to morning classes, talking theology and passing over a freeway interchange. In the middle of that discussion, it hit me that I'd already been at that same place, having that same exchange, with these same people; this identical experience had come years before in a dream. I told my fellow carpoolers about my dream, relating it to the present situation. Until that point, I had not thought about it for three years.

Later that day, while reflecting upon what had happened, I realized why I'd had that dream: God had given it to me, opening up to me a window into my future. I'd not only chosen the right seminary for me, but I had also made the right choice to remain in that seminary's program. My dream confirmed that I was where God wanted me.

When it comes to visions, to my awareness I've also had just one. In the early 1970s, within a year and a half of my conversion to Christ, I went through a terrible experience. I thought, in the depths of my being, that I was going to lose someone close to me. My anguish was intensified by my belief that I was partly to blame for the estrangement in the relationship. I was so distraught by my ominous premonition that I fell prostrate on the floor of my bedroom, sobbing before God and pleading with him to intervene. In near convulsions I begged him to forgive me and show me what to do.

After what may have been a half hour of this intense time of prayer, my cries gave way to a vision. During the experience, I neither saw nor felt anything but what unfolded before me and all around me. Without warning I was high up the side of a mountain, standing on a narrow trail barely wide enough for one person. On my left was a treeless, snowless mountain—dirty, rocky, jutting almost straight up. To my right was a sheer drop, appearing to be tens of thousands of feet down. All around me were primitive and daunting mountains; the sky was an eerie, frightening mixture of black and purple, with tinges of orange and red; a cold wind howled and whipped with such velocity that I was afraid I'd be swept over the edge of the mountain to my death.

Then, the sky far in front of me slowly began to lighten. With the wind still fiercely hurling itself at me, biting at my face, I saw a soft-white glow breaking through the bleakness, gradually engulfing me. I found myself surrounded by light; the treacherous mountains were nowhere to be seen, and the wind was gone. All I saw and felt was this light—incredibly beautiful and pleasant.

Inside it I was warm, loved, safe, forgiven. I knew without question that I was wrapped in God's presence. I heard no verbal messages or counsel, and I saw no forms other than what I have described. They were not needed.

When the vision disappeared and I saw my bedroom again, I knew all would be well. God had come to me. He had answered my prayer. He had shown me that he was with me, and that no matter what I would face, he would be there, protecting, rescuing, forgiving, and guiding. God's direction was clear; I accepted it, and, with renewed hope, I set about to mend the fractured relationship that I'd thought was going to break permanently. By God's grace and wisdom, it healed, and so did I.

Heavenly Messengers

Yet another way our Lover reaches out to us is through angelic emissaries, created spiritual beings who sometimes take on human form to "serve those who will inherit salvation" (Heb. 1:14). Scripture even exhorts us not to "forget to entertain strangers, for by so doing some people have entertained angels without knowing it" (13:2). God can speak through angels, even revealing and carrying out his Word through these "ministering spirits" (1:14).[13]

One of the most dramatic examples of angelic involvement in the early church happened to Peter. He was sleeping in prison, chained between two Roman soldiers, awaiting trial and probably execution the following day. Fellow believers were "earnestly" praying for him (Acts 12:5), and during that night, an angel suddenly appeared in Peter's cell, filling the room with light.

> [The angel] struck Peter on the side and woke him up. "Quick, get up!" he said, and the chains fell off Peter's wrists.
>
> Then the angel said to him, "Put on your clothes and sandals." And Peter did so. "Wrap your cloak around you and follow me," the angel told him. Peter followed him out of the prison, but he had no idea that what the angel was doing was really happening; he thought he was seeing a vision. They passed the first and second guards and came to the iron gate leading to the city. It opened for them by itself, and they went through it. When they had walked the length of one street, suddenly the angel left him.
>
> Then Peter came to himself and said, "Now I know without a doubt that the Lord sent his angel and rescued me from Herod's clutches and from everything the Jewish people were anticipating" (vv. 7–11).

How about you? Could you have been ministered to, freed by, or even entertained angels without being aware of it? You probably have.

The Natural Order

The broadest means God uses to speak to us is the entire universe.

> The heavens declare the glory of God, the skies proclaim the work of his hands. Day after day they pour forth speech; night after night they display knowledge. There is no speech or language where their voice is not heard. Their voice goes out into all the earth, their words to the ends of the world. (Ps. 19:1–4)

Through creation, we learn that God exists, that there are truths about his nature we can know through what he has made, and that there exists a moral order, flowing from God's nature and revealing enough about right and wrong that we are held responsible for disobeying it.[14] Creation provides adequate evidence that One greater than it made it, runs it, and rules over it.

Nature also shows us God's goodness, power, knowledge, beauty, and artistry. "The very creation, by its harmony and ordering, proclaims the majesty of the divine nature," wrote John of Damascus.[15]

Recent scientific findings have likewise confirmed that the world displays dozens of signs of having been made especially for human life. These findings have led to what scientists call *the anthropic principle.*

> [This] principle says that all the seemingly arbitrary and unrelated constants in physics have one strange thing in common—these are precisely the values you need if you want to have a universe capable of producing life. In essence, the anthropic principle came down to the observation that all the myriad laws of physics were fine-tuned from the very beginning of the universe for the creation of man—that the universe we inhabit appeared to be expressly designed for the emergence of human beings.[16]

Our Lover has carefully worked to create an environment well suited for our needs, desires, and amazement. This shows how magnanimously God loves us and that his love "endures forever" (Ps. 136).

God's voice can also be heard in the astonishing wonder that is us, not just in what we see around us. Never forget that even in a huge metropolis covered with concrete and asphalt, images of God walk in and out of buildings, jog along paths, drive cars, shop, and carry on business transactions. *Every* person reveals traits of the Creator; our very being displays his handiwork, and Kathleen Norris points out, his handiwork "invites us to share in God's love."[17]

When I sit on a beach and look out at the ocean, marveling at its rhythmic vastness, picturing all the life teeming under its surface, I hear it proclaim the Creator. I hear it speak of how small and weak I am in comparison to its size and strength, and yet, nevertheless, the ocean also reminds me of the majesty of humanity. *We* can think God's thoughts after him, receiving and enjoying his boundless love; oceans ebb and flow, mindlessly and emotionlessly. You and I feel, reason, and choose on a higher plane—one impressed upon us by the same Creator who made the oceans and mountains, trees and clouds, flora and fauna. *We* are made in his image; nothing else is.

We have been uniquely made to see and hear and respond to our Creator. But we too often scurry about to and fro, "getting things done," while ignoring his presence. We would do better, both for ourselves and others, to slow our pace and listen to our Lover speak through the wonder of his creation, including through those who, like us, bear his special mark.

The Convicting Conscience

Still another way God speaks is through the moral witness within us. *Conscience* defends us when we do what's right and accuses us when we do what's wrong. Our conscience bears—and sensitizes us to—God's moral law.[18] Though the Bible gives us specific, written, moral commands, morality is even closer to us. *We ourselves are moral beings;* we have the rational and volitional ability to choose between right and wrong. Moral consciousness leads us to feel good when we choose well and feel bad when we choose poorly. It enables us to analyze situations and actions from a moral viewpoint and to respond appropriately. It empowers us to discern good as good and evil as evil. In other words, God has placed within us a moral guide, a compass that can help us stay on the right ethical path if we will but listen to it.[19]

Our conscience, however, is tender. It can be weakened, defiled, and even seared.[20] By ignoring it, we can weaken its effectiveness, and by constantly violating it, we can render it virtually inoperative. To be the best guide it can be, our conscience requires fine-tuning and strengthening, which come as we better understand and more consistently apply God's written moral law.[21]

As I have learned and applied God's Word, my sense of right and wrong has matured. Options and actions I once may have had a vague idea were wrong, I now know without doubt are wrong. Moral specifics I never grasped now loom large and clear. Direction I once sought I now have—even when I don't want it. On more occasions than I care to remember, I have arm-wrestled my more informed, sensitized conscience over what it was convinced was the right course of action. I attempted to get my moral sense to offer me another option, one I saw as easier; thankfully, it would not let me budge without my being immersed in moral agony. "You know what's right!" it shouted within, "so do it!" I would offer excuses—"reasons," I told myself—to take a different course. But my conscience, with teeth sharpened on the instruction of Scripture, bit deeper into my being until I chose to relent. On those occasions when I did violate my conscience, its indictment hung in my soul, urging me to seek divine cleansing for my guilt and return to the path I knew was right.

Intellectual Exercise

Finally, God speaks to us through our most phenomenal faculty: our mind. Indeed, every means of speech we've covered requires a working mind to be received, understood, and followed. We cannot discern our Lover's voice, from inside or outside, apart from our mind perceiving what we see and hear and analyzing it clearly and accurately. God encourages us to engage him with our mind: "'Come now, let us reason together,' says the Lord" (Isa. 1:18). He expects us to use our head, to process issues and options. Thinking is a good human activity, and thinking well is godly; as we saw earlier, even the act of loving God requires our mind (Matt. 22:37). Love is guided by reason.

Even so, our reason must be trained. We do not begin in Christ with a spiritually mature mind. We are immature, mere spiritual infants requiring "milk, not solid food" (1 Cor. 3:2). We spit up, burp, and soil our diapers with amazing frequency. This is when we need much training and care from other Christians, simple instruction in the "elementary teachings" of the faith (Heb. 6:1). We need help in understanding the nature of our new relationship with Christ, including how to grow it through the habits of love.

As we mature in Christ, we move from bottle-feeding to eating solid food. We can be served meals that require chewing; intellectually speaking, this is nourishment that takes us beyond the easier consumption of Christian basics and provides us with the challenges of deeper truths. These realities include more complex doctrines, the church's history, and knowledge about her time-honored, proven practices. Through all this, we need mature believers walking beside us and ahead of us, urging us on, inspiring us by word and example, guiding us, showing us how to renew and best use our mind.

I am the grateful recipient of this tried-and-true approach to spiritual growth. It has matured every aspect of me, including my ability to reason through the countless choices life brings. Using all the resources God and his church provide, many life decisions have become automatic. Options that lead to what I know is wrong (or at least wrong for me), I refuse to embrace (not always, I confess, but far more often than not). I don't normally need to grapple with or pray over these choices—for me they are wrong, and that's the end of the decision-making process. This has greatly simplified my life.

Those choices that I know would lead to what's good are the ones I pursue, sorting out with my mind the ones that are best. I take into consideration a host of factors, such as my spiritual giftedness, my family's and friends' needs, my financial goals, my church's ministries, and my vocational aspirations. The options that best meet and further the other pertinent life factors rise to the top of my list and get my most serious attention. As I continue reasoning, I bathe the entire process in prayer, asking the Lord to guide my mind so I will end up choosing the best. I may decide to engage in more research and even deeper analysis; I may also seek the counsel of others who can fill gaps in my knowledge base. Through it all, I know I'm operating within God's will, for I'm reasoning through good options, not evil ones, and I'm using the discernment he has built up in me through the maturing process. No matter which option I take, I rest assured that it will be a good one for me and for those it impacts.

KNOWING GOD'S VOICE

Considering the many and diverse ways God speaks, we can see how much our Divine Lover is communicating to us. He is there, and he is not silent. All around us and in us and through us he talks. His communication may not always come in words, but it is always coming.

Of course, his speech—verbal or nonverbal—is not the only communication we hear. Other voices enter our personal space. Because we live in a world suffering corruption, sometimes nature seems to mock us, making us feel insignificant, worthless, and without meaning. Parents who should have loved us may have instead handed us a legacy of self-condemnation and bitterness. Teachers who could have inspired in us the joy of learning instead bored and frustrated us, perhaps leaving us convinced that the academic world offers nothing of value. For some, clergy trained to shepherd instead preyed on us, feeding themselves at our expense. Employers may have used us and then tossed us aside, gaining from our talents before robbing us of our dreams. Then the demonic voices of Satan and his cohorts attempt to turn us against God, against ourselves, against our loved ones, and against anything else that's good. Just as God is not silent, neither are his rivals.

How, then, can we discern the voice of our most devoted Lover from the cacophony of others competing for our attention and obedience? What must we do to identify his voice and receive his guidance? There are three crucial tests that the historical church has repeatedly used and preserved for us: (1) the weight of divine authority, (2) the Spirit of Christ, and (3) conformity to Scripture.

The Weight of Divine Authority

When Jesus spoke, people sat up and listened. Luke records that those who heard Jesus "were amazed at his teaching, because his message had authority" (4:32). From the religious leaders, the people were used to hearing large heaps of hedging ("It could be the case that . . ." or "It seems to me . . ."), scholarly opinion ("In my reading . . ." or "As a result of my study . . ."), and references to other authorities ("According to Rabbi Gamaliel . . ." or "As Moses said . . ."). From politicians, the people heard promises that went unfulfilled, decrees that were issued only to later be subject to change at expedient whim. When Jesus spoke, people immediately heard the difference.

Jesus did not hedge; instead, he contrasted what he knew was the full truth with what he knew was part of the truth.

> You have heard that it was said to the people long ago, "Do not murder, and anyone who murders will be subject to judgment." But I tell you that anyone who is angry with his brother will be subject to judgment. . . .
> You have heard that it was said, "Do not commit adultery." But I tell you that anyone who looks at a woman lustfully has already committed adultery with her in his heart. (Matt. 5:21–22, 27–28)

Nor did Jesus simply voice scholarly opinion. Instead, he spoke divine fact, speaking God's words rather than human commentary on what God said:

> My teaching is not my own. It comes from him who sent me. If anyone chooses to do God's will, he will find out whether my teaching comes from God or whether I speak on my own. . . .
> I did not speak of my own accord, but the Father who sent me commanded me what to say and how to say it. . . . So whatever I say is just what the Father has told me to say. (John 7:16–17; 12:49–50)

Jesus spoke with the full authority of his heavenly Father. What the Father told Jesus to say, he said. Therefore, Jesus' words carried the weight and power of God. They were definitive and effective, just as God is.

Likewise, when God speaks to us, we will not hear any hedging or opinion or references to higher authorities—none exist. Nor will we hear promises that will go unfulfilled or commands subject to change with the wind. God's words will come with the authority of the One from whom all other rightful authority comes. His words will come with indisputable veracity. His commands will come as orders requiring nothing less than absolute obedience. His assurances will marshal trust, his promises hope. We will not hear anything like what Satan said to Eve in Eden, "Did God really say . . . ?" (Gen. 3:1). Instead, we will hear, "Do . . ." and "Go . . ." and "Learn . . ." and "Say . . ." and "I will be with you . . ." and "Do not fear. . . ." The words will be certain and compelling, able to persuade on their own, bearing the full weight of divine authority.

There are times when I'm writing down my prayers (journaling) and God speaks to me. I put quote marks around those words and usually set them in their own paragraphs, for I know they are his words and not mine. They shine light on darkness and provide direction through fog beyond which I cannot see. They bring insight to familiar truths I thought I'd already mastered. They wrap me with comfort when I'm scared and confused, and they push me out of my comfort zone when I'm clutching it too tightly. I know they are his words because I would not have thought of them; they have within them the fiat that can only belong to the words of God.

Jesus said, "I know my sheep and my sheep know me—just as the Father knows me and I know the Father. . . . My sheep listen to my voice; I know them, and they follow me" (John 10:14–15, 27). The Shepherd's voice bears the weight of divine authority and, consequently, is like no other voice you hear.

The Spirit of Christ

God's voice will also be marked by the Spirit of Christ. Jesus was filled with the Holy Spirit, which is why his words and actions bore all the marks of the Spirit at work. When the Spirit works in the believer's mind and heart, his fruit shows up: "The fruit of the Spirit is love, joy, peace, patience, kindness, goodness, faithfulness, gentleness and self-control" (Gal. 5:22–23). Anything that opposes these virtues is not from God.

James, the half brother of Jesus, builds on this fact in the letter that bears his name: "If any of you lacks wisdom, he should ask God, who gives generously to all without finding fault, and it will be given to him" (1:5). What exactly should we look for when we request divine wisdom? What traits will it have? What will it not be like? James later contrasts divine wisdom with its demonic counterfeit so we will not confuse them:

> Who is wise and understanding among you? Let him show it by his good life, by deeds done in the humility that comes from wisdom. But if you harbor bitter envy and selfish ambition in your hearts, do not boast about it or deny the truth. Such "wisdom" does not come down from heaven but is earthly, unspiritual, of the devil. For where you have envy and selfish ambition, there you find disorder and every evil practice.
>
> But the wisdom that comes from heaven is first of all pure; then peace-loving, considerate, submissive, full of mercy and good fruit, impartial and sincere. (3:13–17)

God's voice is life-giving and life-sustaining, flowing from who he is—Eternal Life. All other voices may promise life but, in fact, lead away from it. Instead of consoling us, they desolate us; rather than uplifting us and giving us a renewed sense of order and purpose, they pull us down into ever more despairing degrees of disorder and insignificance. God's voice is full of goodness, mercy, love, and grace; contrary voices seek to tempt us to evil, to self-condemnation, and to paralyzing guilt. Sometimes what God says may be painful to hear, but it is always meant for our good, not for our destruction.

In Ignatius of Loyola's *Spiritual Exercises,* he rightly observes,

> [The] characteristic of the evil spirit [is] to harass with anxiety, to afflict with sadness, to raise obstacles backed by fallacious reasonings that disturb the soul. It is characteristic of the good spirit, however, to give courage and strength, consolations, tears, inspirations, and peace.[22]

You will know God's voice by what it produces inside of you as you hear it and outside of you as you live it. If it leads you into greater Christlikeness, it is from God. If it hinders your growth into Christlikeness, it is not from God. The Holy Spirit always directs us toward Jesus and seeks to create in us his life. Any voice opposing this, however subtle and indirect, is not God's.

Conformity to Scripture

God's Word is his bond—he will never violate it. Scripture reveals who he is and what he is like, how he behaves and how he desires that we respond. The Bible unveils God's mind and will; therefore, when we hear anything that undermines or contradicts what he has revealed, we know it is not from him.

When people came to Jesus and voiced opinions or posed questions that demonstrated their misunderstanding or ignorance of biblical truth, he pointed them back to God's Word: "Have you not read?" After posing the question, he would direct attention to what Scripture said, then accurately draw out the meaning of the text and apply it to the situation at hand. Even when he was confronted by Satan, Jesus countered with the Word of God, resting upon it his authority to battle the enemy. Scripture was central to Jesus' life, and he reiterated its centrality for us when, in his confrontation with Satan, he quoted these words from Deuteronomy: "It is written: 'Man does not live on bread alone, but on every word that comes from the mouth of God'" (Matt. 4:4). Nothing is more important to our lives than the food that comes to us as God's Word.

When we want to know the Lord's will, the best place to look is in the Bible. Scripture has answers well worth our time to find, learn, and apply. There we will discover our Lover's answers to our most important questions and needs.

In that Word, he also warns us that other voices will attempt to lure us away from him and what he tells us. The voice can come from what appears to be "an angel from heaven" (Gal. 1:8) or a "prophet" claiming to speak for God (Deut. 13:1–5). The voice can come from the "world system," which, in our day, seeks to paralyze minds, squelching and reshaping speech through such postmodern viruses as political correctness, tolerance, and relativism.[23] Whatever the source and message of such voices, if what they are telling us is inconsistent with Scripture, we should not heed what they say, for they are not speaking with divine authority or with the Spirit of Christ. They are, in effect, denying God, sometimes even in his name. Again, God "cannot deny Himself" (2 Tim. 2:13 NASB), and anyone who contradicts him speaks falsely.[24] Our Lover is faithful to his Word. When we are faithful to his Word as well, we will live in faithfulness to him, for there is no difference between what he says and who he is.

IN THE MEANTIME . . .

In all the ways we seek God's guidance, we must "test everything, hold on to the good, [and] avoid every kind of evil" (1 Thess. 5:21–22). The better we know what God reveals to us in his Word, the better we'll be able to test for truth, embrace all that's good, and turn away from the evils that entice. In other words, we will grow in our likeness to the Son. The more Christlike we become, the more we'll follow God's lead subconsciously, automatically. His ways will become our ways; His thoughts will become our thoughts; His plan will become our plan; His call will become our obedient response.

In the final analysis, guidance is not as much about what we should do as about who we are to become. God is laboring alongside us to transform us into the magnificent image of his beloved Son. As we cooperate, we become more like him and thereby express his will through our own. Our *doing* will become more Christlike as our *being* becomes more Christlike. We won't have to ask, "What would Jesus do?" We will already know.

8. Study:
depth between lovers

I know a man who loved his wife so much that he set out to learn everything he could about her. He believed the better he knew her, the better he would know how to love her, so he began studying her. It was only then that he learned things he may never have otherwise discovered.

He noticed that when she was under a great deal of stress, she would still be kind and considerate to others, but she would clench her fists, often holding them tightly to her side when she stood or pressing them into her lap when she sat. When she was afraid or nervous, she withdrew from him. However, he learned that she didn't want him to pull away from her; on the contrary, she wanted him to come closer, to hold her quietly and firmly, to help her feel safe.

For the first time in their nearly decade-long marriage, he also observed that she rarely shared with him from her heart, and on those few times when she did, she would often shut down. Carefully reflecting on the incidents, he came to see that he was part of the problem. She wanted someone to talk to; he was looking for a problem to solve. She wanted to share her feelings and thoughts; he wanted to analyze them and show her where she was being "illogical" or "ridiculous."

So he started changing the way he related to her. He listened with his heart. He asked more questions, seeking understanding, leaving behind words that bespoke criticism. He became intent on coming alongside her rather than instructing her.

The more he learned about her, the more he appreciated her. He began to see her as a woman of depth and strength. He saw her courage, her ability to overcome her fears and act for her own good as well as the good of others. He saw how much she gave to those she loved, and how much more she could achieve with support and encouragement. He even noticed some weaknesses he had never seen before, such as how her physical reaction to stress was tearing down her body, and how her tendency to withdraw from people when afraid often left her feeling alone and abandoned.

After just a year of studying his wife, he wrote in his journal:

> I have married a woman I didn't really know until now. She's not the woman I thought I had married. She's so much better, richer, real, alive. I can truly say that I love her more now than I ever have. I am anxious to learn even more about this beautiful, mysterious creature I call my wife.

> I have also found that my learning experience has changed me. I am not the man my wife married. I have grown. I understand more, notice more, appreciate more, and love more deeply than I ever have at any time in my life. I have also come to see my own strengths and weaknesses, in some cases for the very first time, and in almost all cases more clearly and realistically than ever. My study has certainly enriched me as a person and as a lover. I would never have imagined that becoming so focused on someone else would have benefited me so much.

The best lovers are the best students of those they love. They are so struck by the objects of their passion that they devote themselves to learning all they can about them. Their desire is to please them, to grant their wishes and satisfy their needs. They want all the best for their beloved, so they seek to learn what will benefit them the most, then strive to meet the need. In the process, the students change as their ability to love expands and matures. Study can be a remarkably loving act for lover and loved one alike.

The spiritual habit of study ushers us into this deeper aspect of love. Incarnate Love told us that we are to love God with our whole self, including our mind; on the heels of this greatest commandment, he told us the second-greatest, which is "like" the first: "Love your neighbor as yourself"

(Matt. 22:39). Love requires study, the work of the mind. We cannot love what we do not know, and we cannot love deeply what we know superficially. If we're going to love God with our *whole* being, we must come to truly *know* him. And if we're going to love others as we love ourselves, we must become students of their lives. The more we study God and others, the more we will learn about ourselves, and the more our love for them and ourselves will grow.

WHAT IS STUDY?

Richard Foster defines study as "a specific kind of experience in which through careful attention to reality the mind is enabled to move in a certain direction."[1] This direction is toward truth that corresponds to reality, to what fits with what actually is. Jesus made it clear that the knowledge of the truth will set us free;[2] nothing short of it will liberate us. We must align ourselves with what *is* and, therefore, *will certainly be*. Study is essential to achieving this goal, and the study experience has three key elements: focus, exploration, and analysis.

By *focus* I mean that study hones in on finding the truth. Whatever the subject, whatever the reason for picking that subject, whatever the hoped-for application of what is discovered about that subject, the focus of the study remains constant—to discover the truth of the matter.

When Paul and Silas arrived in Berea and began presenting the gospel, the Jews there didn't stand up, clap their hands, and yell, "Preach it, brothers!" While excited about the truth of Jesus Christ, they kept their heads, knowing that something isn't made true simply by sounding good or by generating desirable emotions. Rather than allowing themselves to be "blown here and there by every wind of teaching" (Eph. 4:14) that passed through their city, they applied their minds to "examin[ing] the Scriptures every day to see if what Paul said was true" (Acts 17:11). The Bereans searched what we now call the Old Testament—the Word they already had—and measured what Paul told them against what they already knew was true. The result? Exactly what we'd expect from such focused purpose: "Many of the Jews believed, as did also a number of prominent Greek women and many Greek men" (v. 12). Seekers of the truth will find the truth.

In the Christian worldview, all truth leads to God. All truth in some way points back to him because he is Truth personified. He is also the ultimate Reality—the One who existed before all else. He made everything that exists, so all created reality exhibits itself as his workmanship, and since truth accords with reality—with what *is*—all truth directs us beyond creation to the Creator. Seek the truth, and you will find the Truth in every truth you discover.

The second key aspect of study is *exploration*—the process of seeking out information pertaining to one's chosen object of study. When I decided to learn everything I could about the Christian doctrine of God, I began rereading books of the Bible and taking notes on what they say about who God is, what he's like, and what he does. I also researched through books and creeds that directly concerned themselves with what I wanted to learn about God. This led me into seeking out a host of academic essays and popular articles on the topic. The whole process helped me see, with a more discerning eye, how God reveals himself outside of Scripture as well as in and through Scripture.

This idea of discernment leads to the third essential facet of study: *analysis.* Study requires intricate examination, which can mean taking something apart, paying attention to the nature and interaction of its components, and applying logical rigor to the proposed evidence in assessing what's genuinely true and what isn't. You can do this, for example, with sports, recipes, cars, friendships, and books. Anything and anyone can be carefully analyzed and thus better understood and appreciated.

Analysis forms the basis of discernment. For instance, I cannot discern between good and evil until I comprehend what is good and what is evil. I must know what these categories mean and what exemplifies them before I can see what's good and then choose it.

WHAT SHOULD WE STUDY?

For Christians, the arena of study is wide open. History, geology, philosophy, ethics, theology, biology, psychology, medicine, sociology, politics, art, economics, music, sports, business, agriculture, technology, architecture, education, literature . . . all fields are appropriate to pursue. Since all truth is God's truth, truth coming from any discipline is worth discovering, learning, and applying.

For some believers, however, certain topics may need to be put aside or never tackled to any significant degree. This is not because the subject has been made biblically (or is inherently) taboo, but because it may lead some to compromise themselves morally, intellectually, and/or spiritually.

When I began studying non-Christian religions in the late 1970s, I wanted to explore the occult; I knew Satan was the adversary and that Scripture encouraged knowledge of his ways,[3] so I concluded that one of the best means was the study of occultic religions and practices. I bought a number of books with this purpose in mind, and among the resources I sought was *The Satanic Bible,* one of the movement's most significant books. One day while perusing a bookstore in San Francisco, I finally came across it. I picked it up, thumbed through it, and read numerous paragraphs from several pages scattered throughout. The more I read, the more I realized I was not ready for such irrational, immoral, blasphemous material. I even felt as if a dark presence was pressing in on me, seeking to pull me away from truth. I shut and reshelved the book, leaving the store without buying anything. I wanted to get out of the building and away from that book; I simply couldn't handle what confronted me.

Since that time, I've studied what Scripture teaches about fallen angels, I've read other books on the occult, I've talked with people in the occult, and I've conversed with others who've left it and become Christians. While I have not purchased or fully read *The Satanic Bible,* I have come across it several times and occasionally read more portions from it. While I still see and sense in it a clear demonic influence, it no longer disturbs me as before. I am now more equipped for it; *even so,* I still have no desire to fill my mind with its diabolical distortions; I know all I want to know about it, and I do not wish to push myself further to see how well I could deal with the evil that emanates from its pages. I'm deeply grateful that other Christians have waded through the bogs of the occult and reported their findings to us, but for me, it's not an arena in which I can linger for long.

Many years ago, when I first read C. S. Lewis's *Screwtape Letters,* I was encouraged to find this literary giant expressing how oppressive it was for him to enter into the mindset of writing fictitious correspondence from a senior demon to a subordinate:

> Though I had never written anything more easily, I never wrote with less enjoyment. The ease came, no doubt, from the fact that the device of diabolical letters, once you have thought of it, exploits itself spontaneously. . . . But though it was easy to twist one's mind into the diabolical attitude, it was not fun, or not for long. The strain produced a sort of spiritual cramp. The work into which I had to project myself while I spoke through Screwtape was all dust, grit, thirst, and itch. Every trace of beauty, freshness, and geniality had to be excluded. It almost

smothered me before I was done. It would have smothered my readers if I had prolonged it.[4]

Demons entice people to evil by offering counterfeit goods and pleasures; their desire is to manipulate and destroy. So when I study their perverted world, I cannot long remain in it without feeling like I'm suffocating. I must leave it to breathe the pure oxygen of Christ.

The world is open to believers for study. But we must remain aware that *in* this fallen world we will encounter pockets of densely polluted (even poisoned) air. If we do not have the proper tools or matured abilities to move safely through those areas, then we'd best move on to other vistas.

THE STUDY OF SCRIPTURE

Among all the areas worth our study, the best is the Bible.

In the last chapter (on the love habit of guidance), we saw the ways God reveals himself and his will. Among those, *one* source of revelation holds supremacy: his Word. Scripture alone gives us "God-breathed" written words (2 Tim. 3:16).[5] Through sixty-six books, our Creator speaks to us in human language, unveiling truths about himself, us, and the rest of what he's created. He shows us how much he's willing to sacrifice so we can have all the good he longs to give us. In Scripture are love and knowledge, direction and wisdom, through the definitiveness of language, stamped with God's error-free omniscience.

It's no wonder that his people have always regarded the Word as the lens through which all truth claims must be examined. If someone comes along and says human beings have no more value than driftwood, Christians point to the Bible, which reveals that we are uniquely created as God's image-bearers, and that, despite our rebellion, God sent his Son to live, serve, and teach among us and to sacrifice his life for us. These biblical realities, along with many others, inform us that we are specially loved, God's most prized possession, preciously high on the value meter.

The Bible comes to our aid, helping us to sort out what's true and right from what's false and wrong. We can call on Scripture's help because what it says, God says, and God is always correct in his unlimited understanding. On any matter that he has spoken, his Word settles the matter. Period. We may not always like or agree with what he says; his Word may even discomfort us. But truth is not primarily concerned with our preferences or comfort levels:

Truth is about reality, and sometimes reality is hard.

Failure to conform to reality can lead to much more than minor discomfort and a sour disposition. It can lead to serious illnesses, shattered relationships, missing limbs, dashed dreams, and loss of life. Fight reality and you will lose every time. Discover its secrets, conform to its truths, and you can traverse the oceans, fly through the sky, orbit the moon, and follow Love's lead to heights that soar beyond imagination. Both the choice and the consequences are ours.

The Bible must be the centerpiece of our reality study. Like the Bereans, we must examine the Scriptures to find out what it is, and when we learn what God's Word teaches, we must conform our lives to it. The Bible is our primary and preeminent authority; therefore, when it tells us that all human life is sacred, we must treat all human life accordingly. When it reveals that God's creation is good and that we are its earthly stewards, we must care for it—including ourselves, for we are part of the created order.

Granting, then, the centrality and authority of Scripture, we must learn *how* to study it. While the Bible is a special library, its books can be read, understood, and applied through a three-step process common to learning any literary work: observation, interpretation, and application.[6] All three elements of general study—focus, exploration, and analysis—are involved in these three steps of Bible study. We'll walk through them, providing a brief overview of each and then showing how each works. I'll illustrate the process by applying it to Genesis 1:26–28, focusing on the phrase "the image of God."

Step One: Observation

The first step in the Bible study process is *observation,* whereby you are seeking to answer, What do I see? You want to learn what the text *says,* not what it means or how it might apply to you. You're not trying to interpret the message but simply read it correctly. Like a detective looking for clues, nothing is too small or insignificant for your eyes to notice and your mind to ponder.

The initial order of business is to get the lay of the land. You accomplish this by reading, rereading, and reading again. Whether you are dealing with an entire book, a few chapters, or a couple of verses, read the material several times so it will become familiar territory.

After several readings, start delving into the details. In this phase, you're looking for the facts, including how the facts relate to each other, and you're raising questions about what you see. Many times the facts will answer your questions during the observation phase of your study. At other times, answers will not surface until you enter the interpretation stage.

Among the facts to search for and identify are these:

- *Grammar:* subjects (nouns and pronouns), verbs, objects, prepositions, connectives, adversatives, adverbs, adjectives, etc. (There's rarely a need to put a grammatical label on every word in a biblical passage. I recommend doing it with the words that appear to play a key role.)

- *Terms:* repeated, unusual, or emphasized words and phrases; terms that require clarification; terms contrasted or compared.

- *Genre:* the kind of literature—poetry, parable (fictional story), narrative (historical story), biography, autobiography, dialogue, correspondence, apocalyptic (futuristic or prophetic), satire, tragedy, allegory, comedy, exhortation, explanation, instruction, argumentation.

- *Historical details:* the writer or speaker, the audience, the setting (e.g., city or country, indoors or outdoors, home or synagogue, peacetime or wartime, Rome or Jerusalem), related events, chronology.

- *Atmosphere:* the mood (happy or sad, restful or fearful), the smells (sweet or foul), the sounds (soothing or grating, whispers or shouts).

- *Context:* what precedes and what follows the text; how this relates to the text at hand.

- *Structure:* how the text and its details are organized.

In addition, you want to pose these questions along the observational trail: who, what, where, when, why, and how.

- *Who?* is concerned with the divine, angelic, demonic, and human characters in the text, as well as with the text's human writer and first readers.

- *What?* identifies the content of the text. What is the series of events conveyed? What happens to the people involved? What is the flow of the writer's argument? What are his main points and the evidence he provides?

- *Where?* deals with place. Where do the text's happenings occur? Where was the writer when he wrote his book? Where were his initial readers?

- *When?* takes you to the matter of time, especially identifying when the passage was written and when its events took place.

- *Why?* gets at purpose, goal, and significance. Why did this person say or do that? Why are these events recorded in this particular sequence? Why did the author write this book? Why is its message important?

- *How?* is concerned with method, process, development, movement, and structure. How was the book written? How does the story unfold? How do the key characters interact? How is the material configured?

This may seem like a lot of things to note, but the more time you spend discovering the facts of a text and seeking answers to your questions in it, the less time you will spend interpreting. Well-done observation is the key to arriving at sound interpretation; you can visualize the truth of this by reflecting on times when you've misunderstood someone's words or vice versa. We must first hear what our Divine Lover really says before we can correctly interpret what he's teaching us.

Now let's see how the observation step works. I have reproduced Genesis 1:26–28 below, using the *New American Standard Bible* (NASB). I have also quoted it in such a way that the relationships between the facts presented are more clearly shown; that is, the layout displays *structural* aspects.

Then God said,
"Let Us make man
in Our image,
according to Our likeness;
and let them rule
over the fish of the sea
and over the birds of the sky

        and over the cattle
        and over all the earth,
        and over every creeping thing that creeps on the earth."
    God created man
        in His own image,
        in the image of God
            He created him;
        male and female
            He created them.
    God blessed them;
    and God said to them,
        "Be fruitful
        and multiply,
        and fill
            the earth,
        and subdue
            it;
        and rule
            over the fish of the sea
            and over the birds of the sky
            and over every living thing that moves on the earth."

Now we can make further observations.

Look first at the *grammar*. In these verses, we find that the subject, who performs the action, is described as "God" five times, "Our" twice, "Us" once, "His" once, and "He" twice. "Our" and "Us" are plural, while "His" and "He" are singular, yet all these terms refer to the same subject—the Creator God.

The introductory material in the front of your Bible likely tells you that *Elohim,* the most common Hebrew word used to designate God, is translated "God." In fact, *Elohim* is the only word used for God from Genesis 1:1 until the latter half of 2:4, where the word *Yahweh* (translated LORD) first appears. More exploration reveals that *Elohim* is plural, not singular—*literally* translated "Gods," not "God." So how do we know that in 1:26–28 the word should be translated "God" (singular) rather than "Gods" (plural)? By noting that although God refers to himself as "Us" and "Our," he also refers to himself as "His" and "He." In these three verses, God uncovers himself as somehow *both* plural and singular. How can God simultaneously be both one and yet more than one? This issue will have to be resolved under the interpretation step, because Genesis 1 does not provide an answer.

Still pursuing the grammar aspect of observation, we can see that God (the subject) performs various actions. He speaks, makes, creates, blesses, and commands. He speaks to himself ("Let Us") and to the humans he creates ("blessed them," "said to them"). He calls once on himself to "make man," then three times uses the word *created* to describe his making activity. And he doesn't create human beings just any old way; he creates man "in His own image, in the image of God He created him." Notice that "man" and "him" are singular, but then the text says, "male and female He created them." God did not create just one gender but two. Then he blessed "them" and commanded "them." In other words, the text recognizes that somehow God is singular yet plural, and the humans he creates "in His image" are also singular yet plural.

Moving to observations about key *terms,* the text first says that God will "make" man, then three times it says he "created" man. "Make" and "create" are two different Hebrew words—you can discover this by looking them up in a Bible concordance or Bible dictionary. The term for "make" is the most common Old Testament word for fashioning or crafting something, while the word for "create" (*bārā*) is used sparingly. An Old Testament word study of *bārā* shows that it always refers to God and his activity, never to human beings and what they accomplish.

Also, *bārā* emphasizes the occurrence of an amazing new thing that only God can do.[7] Therefore, the triple emphasis on God having created the first humans affirms that humanity was God's work alone and that the creation of humanity was stunningly different than anything he had made up to that point. Indeed, the Genesis account says that only human beings have been created in the image of God; no other creatures are the divine image-bearers.

Continuing with terms, observe as well that when God speaks to himself about what he will do, he first talks about making man "in Our image," then adds, "according to Our likeness." And yet, when he actually creates the first humans, the word *likeness* doesn't appear again, only the term *image*. In verses 26–28, *image* occurs three times and *likeness* only once. The emphasis on *image,* along with the absence of *likeness* after its first appearance, suggests that the words are at least roughly synonymous and that *image* is the more critical term.[8]

What, then, does *image* mean? Once again, research using a dictionary or concordance would show that the Hebrew *selem,* translated *image,* means "resemblance" or "representative figure," like a statue or an imprint of someone's face. In the Old Testament, *image* most commonly refers to idols. How do we resemble God? How do we represent him? What, if anything, do idols have to do with all this? Great questions to ask in the observation phase, but we still have to wait for the interpretation phase to answer them.

One more observation of Genesis 1:26–28. Before God creates the first humans, he says what he wants them to do: exercise a degree of sovereignty over the earth. After God creates humans, he commands them to be "fruitful and multiply, and fill the earth, and subdue it" and "rule over . . . every living thing that moves on the earth." The command to be fruitful and to multiply and to fill was also given to sea and sky creatures (v. 22), so, in this respect, they share a common purpose with humans. However, when it comes to subduing and ruling over the earth, only people receive this command. Does this indicate that our unique purpose is enmeshed with our unique image-bearing status? Interpretation will answer this for us also.

We could go on with the observation of Genesis 1:26–28, but we've sufficiently demonstrated what's involved in this first Bible study step.

Step Two: Interpretation

Interpretation seeks to answer, What does the text mean? You're not trying to determine what the text means to you; rather, you want to get at what the writer meant by what he wrote.

For example, someone who rejects the possibility of miracles might interpret the biblical accounts of the Resurrection as mythical stories intended to inspire us to persevere even through the toughest forms of adversity; when we do, we'll find that, like Jesus, we rise to the top as stronger, better persons and finally receive the recognition we deserve. This is interpreting the Bible according to what it means to the interpreter.

To the authors who wrote about Jesus rising alive from the grave, the Resurrection was proof that he is the incarnate Son of God, the prophesied Messiah, the victorious Savior of the world.[9] They did not believe the Resurrection was a myth or inspirational fiction. They knew it occurred in history, in their lifetimes, and they concluded that this miracle authenticated Jesus' teachings and claims about himself. This interpretation arises out of the biblical text; the interpreter does not impose it onto the text.

We must let the Bible speak for itself. If we don't, we will only get back what we think it teaches or what we want it to teach, not what God is actually teaching through the words he inspired.

Moreover, interpreting the biblical text objectively and accurately is critical to applying it well. We cannot rightly apply a passage to our life unless we correctly understand what it means. A mistaken interpretation will inevitably lead to an erroneous and often harmful application.

The critical importance of interpretation first impressed me even before I became a Christian and began studying Scripture. When I was a high school student in the late 1960s, my parents surprised me with an incredible Christmas present: a six-week trip to Europe. The excursion was with the Foreign Study League, and its purpose was to tour several countries while learning about their history, customs, and languages. About one hundred seventy students, accompanied by about twenty adult teachers, went on the tour.

Our first stop was London, where we began what would become routine throughout the tour. We spent four or five mornings per week in classroom settings, learning about our current country and city. In the afternoons and evenings, we would get out in our surroundings, visiting important historical spots, sightseeing, shopping, and simply experiencing a new culture firsthand. Our classes were taught by our teacher chaperons, local university students, or, on occasion, local professors or government officials.

During one of our sessions in London, a university student came to orient us to the local customs and advise us on the best places to visit. Before he left, he gave the females in our group a warning: Avoid going out at night in a red dress, especially if unaccompanied by a man. At that time (I don't know if it's still true), a woman wearing a red dress around London in the evening hours marked her as a prostitute; if a woman didn't want to be propositioned, she must wear a dress of a different color.

That night, one of our chaperons left to attend a play across town. She went out alone, and she wore a red dress. She had not heard about the warning we'd received.

On her way to the performance, she took a taxi and didn't encounter any problems. Afterward, she decided to return on London's subway system, which at that time was quite safe, day or night. While on the train, she noticed a couple of men leering at her.

When she got off at her stop, one of them came up and began making advances. Another man joined in and began doing the same.

Understandably, she was confused and afraid, and she tried to put the men straight. But they thought she was just playing hard to get, so they became more direct and vocal about their intentions. At this she turned away from them and began to run. A broken heel, a lost shoe, and two long city blocks later, she had managed to outrun her pursuers. It wasn't until she got back to our tour group and relayed her awful experience that she learned that the color of her dress had been the cause of her distress.

This teacher had an encounter with interpretation, even though during the experience she did not understand why it was happening. For her, the red dress was appropriate attire for attending a theatre performance; for London's men, the red dress indicated a desire for an evening of sexual play with a performer of a different sort. Different cultures with different customs meant different interpretations of the same attire.

The same thing happens when people approach the Bible and attempt to discover its meaning; they frequently interpret it in various ways because they view it through various interpretive glasses. Different backgrounds influence people to view the same facts differently: upbringing, education, profession, religious instruction, local custom, and a number of other factors will affect the meaning attached to what people observe or read. What they see may be the same, but what they think it means is not.

Therefore, after we have come to know what a biblical text says, we need to learn what it *means* by what it says. This requires getting to know the writer's time, culture, customs, land, and, to some degree, their language. We also need to learn about the audience the writer sought to reach. Like the chaperon wearing a red dress, we don't want to go out into the world with one interpretation in mind, only to find out, perhaps in an embarrassing or even frightening way, that we are unprepared.

To learn such things, we must draw on additional resources. When you study the Bible, you are studying cultures and peoples from thousands of years ago. Just like my tour group needed guides to help us understand the lands and peoples we visited, so do you in your study of Scripture. As I provide an interpretation of "the image of God" in Genesis 1:26–28, I will mention some of the resources I've used in the interpretive process. The endnotes at the back of this book contain references to many good Bible resources as well.

From the structure of Genesis and other telltale signs found within its pages, we know that the book's *genre* is historical narrative.[10] When we add to this that the book is God-inspired, we can conclude that what it says about humans *created* as divine image-bearers is true—that is, it accords with reality. But can we say that this is *still* true? After all, Genesis 3 records the entrance of sin into the world; did humans lose the image after the Fall?

No, we did not. Genesis 9:6 bases capital punishment (for the crime of murder) on the fact that God created us as his image-bearers, thereby assuming that we still bear his image. The New Testament affirms likewise; in James 3:9, we're told that with our tongues "we bless our Lord and Father, and with it we curse men, who have been made in the likeness of God" (NASB). When we verbally lash out against others, we are using our tongues to whip fellow image-bearers. We were *created* in God's image and *still bear* it.

This reality suggests that the image exists as long as we do; in other words, the image is either part or all of what makes us human. Is there anything in Genesis 1:26–28 that would lead us to this interpretive conclusion? Yes. In the phrases "in Our image," "in His own image," and "in the image of God," the Hebrew word translated *in* is better translated *as*.[11] We are, therefore, images of God. You are his image. I am his image. Your neighbor is his image. Each human being is God's image. There's not *something* in me—such as my soul, mind, heart, or will—that is the image of God. It's *me in all that I am as God's creation* that is his image. Paul clearly understood Genesis 1 this way, for he said an individual human being "*is* the image and glory of God" (1 Cor. 11:7, emphasis added), not "contains" the image or "is partially" the image. In short, our human nature and personhood is the image of God; if we "lost" the image, we would cease to be human.

Furthermore, an image is *not* the original. When I look in a mirror, the image in the mirror is not me but a reflection. I could not reach out to the surface of the mirror and touch myself; instead, I would touch the mirror that is presenting an image of me. Likewise, if I came across a drawing of the sun, I would see an image of the sun, not the sun itself. The drawing represents the sun and resembles it enough that I can recognize it as standing for the sun instead of something else. An image, then, is *like* what it resembles and represents, but the original is not comparable to the image.

Consider my image in a mirror: I am flesh and bone, but my mirror image is not. I continue to exist even when I pass out of the mirror's view and my image vanishes. The mirror can also distort the true dimensions of my features, making me appear larger or smaller than I really am.

Consider also the drawing of the sun, which provides no heat or light, even though what it depicts provides both. The drawing, no matter how detailed and accurate, does not move while the sun itself is explosively and continually active. Likewise, the drawing is miniscule compared to the immensity of the sun. Images reflect the originals, but the originals are not like the images.

How, then, do you and I resemble and represent God? How are we like him, and how do we stand for him? Let's return to some of the observations we made and see what will help us answer these questions of interpretation. We'll begin with the matter of *resemblance.*

When we observed Genesis 1:26–28, we saw that just as God is one and yet more than one, so are we; we are like God in singularity and in plurality. God is singular in at least two ways. First, he is singular in that he is the only God. Just one God actually exists, not two or more. Second, he is singular in that he is a unity of persons: Father, Son, and Spirit exist in perfect harmony within the same divine nature. God is also a plurality, three distinct persons: Lover, Loved One, and Bond of Love. He is one divine, eternal, triune, personal community of love.

We can see ways in which we resemble God's singularity. For instance, our humanity is the image; humanity is singular. There are not two humanities, much less three or four. There is but one human race, one human nature. Moreover, each human being is a unity: a person existing in a united nature of body and soul. I am one "who" (person) in one "what" (nature). This one "what" has two aspects—a physical side (body) and a spiritual side (soul)—but I am a unity.[12]

How about God's plurality—how do we resemble that? Here's one way: community. Before God created Adam, he said, "It is not good for the man to be alone; I will make him a helper suitable for him" (Gen. 2:18). This "helper" was Eve, the first woman. God, then, brought Eve to Adam, and Adam recognized the similarity between him and Eve, as well as the difference between them and the wonderful fit they were for each other (vv. 22–25). While Adam and Eve *individually* were full-blown image-bearers, *together* they resembled God in at least one way they could not separately: they formed a community of persons that began in perfect relationship with each other and with their Creator. Just as God is a community of persons, so are humans to be in community with one another.

Yet another way we resemble God is that we are living as he is. He is not dead, nor is he imaginary; he is alive, and he made us. When he breathed into Adam "the breath of life," Adam "became a living being" (v. 7). Only a living, personal being can resemble the living, personal God. Humans are thereby suited to bear God's image. Idols, on the other hand, fail at this; because they are the nonliving artwork of human beings, they cannot possibly resemble or represent the true God. He created us to do what no craft coming from our creativity could ever accomplish.

As living images, we also resemble God in many of our activities. In our limited way, we copy what he does. At points during creation, God names certain things. He calls "the light day, and the darkness . . . night" (1:5 NASB). He names the expanse "heaven," the dry land "earth," and the gathered waters "seas" (v. 10 NASB). Likewise, after Adam is created, he does this, imitating God by naming the animals as well as the woman. Concerning Eve, Adam first distinguishes her from himself by naming her "Woman" (2:23 NASB), then later he calls her "Eve, because she was the mother of all the living" (3:20 NASB). Likewise, whenever we name, love, create, procreate, work, serve, and fellowship, we are copying our Creator, fulfilling what he made us to do.

Now that we see some ways we resemble God, how do we *represent* him? An image, like an idol, stands for the original, perhaps for the original's *authority*. In Genesis 1, the sovereign God commands his image-bearers to subdue and rule over the earth. He grants them the authority to represent him before the other things he has made.

An image may also stand for the original's *creativity*. God commands human beings to be fruitful and multiply. Just as he creates, he gives us the ability and responsibility to procreate.

An image can also stand for the *presence* of the original. God is Spirit and therefore invisible—he cannot be seen. Humans, however, have a physical side to their nature; our bodies visibly represent the invisible God. The incarnate Son did the same: When he took on a human nature, he became visible. It was as an embodied man that the Son could be described as "the image of the invisible God" (Col. 1:15).

This interpretation of "the image of God" is far from exhaustive, but it's enough to show that what a text *means* is dependent on what a text *says*. Apart from observation, interpretation has no anchor, but is left drifting on the sea of poorly informed personal opinion and group pressure. On the other hand, observation void of interpretation gives a mere set of facts lacking significance and purpose. Observation and interpretation are critical to understanding what God teaches us in the Bible.

Step Three: Application

Once we understand a passage's meaning, we are ready to consider its applications. "All Scripture," says Paul, "is useful for teaching, rebuking, correcting and training in righteousness" (2 Tim. 3:16). God's Word is alive, still speaking. Application, the third step in the study process, seeks to discover a text's enduring relevance to contemporary people and their times.

Biblical application can cover anything from the most personal, intimate issues of someone's life to matters of broader ecclesiastical or social concern. In some passages, the application will be clear and straightforward. In others you will need to ponder the text's meaning for a while before application ideas come to mind. No matter what Bible text is your focus, there are several questions you can pose that will help you glean applications for your life.[13]

- *Is there an example to follow?* Many people in Scripture are worthy of emulation. We can learn from the way they face trial and temptation, or stand up to demanding people, or articulate their faith, or offer praise to God, or provide leadership, or parent their children, or love their spouse.

- *Is there an example to avoid?* Not all examples are worth modeling. The Bible tells about believers and unbelievers making mistakes, some serious, even fatal. By learning from their errors, we can avoid much pain.

- *Is there sin to confess?* Better than any other book in the world, the Bible reveals our sin, judging "the thoughts and attitudes of the heart" (Heb. 4:12). When it convicts us, we should fall to our knees and turn our eyes toward heaven in repentance, remembering that God is quick to forgive those who humbly seek his mercy and grace.

- *Is there a promise to trust?* The Bible is full of God's promises. While some were only for specific individuals and others for certain groups or nations, many are timeless. John 3:16 is one of these: "God so loved the world that he gave his one and only Son, that whoever believes in him shall not perish but have eternal life." When you find such promises in Scripture, embrace them. God always honors his promises.

- *Is there a prayer to repeat or model?* The Bible is a gold mine of prayers: praise and confession, petition and thanksgiving, confidence and confusion, joy and depression, anger and reconciliation, anxiety and trust. We can learn about prayer from the prayers of others. In fact, as we have seen, many prayers in Scripture can be spoken as our own.

- *Is there a command to obey?* Loving Jesus involves following him: "If you love me, you will obey what I command" (John 14:15). John intertwined love and obedience when he stated, "This is love for God: to obey his commands. And his commands are not burdensome" (1 John 5:3). If you ever wonder about God's will for your life, consider his commands; they will give you plenty of guidance.

- *Is there a condition to meet?* Many of God's promises depend on our doing something first. For example, when Jesus says, "Come to me, all you who are weary and burdened, and I will give you rest" (Matt. 11:28), the condition is wrapped up in the call "Come to me." If we don't turn to him, we will not find the rest that only he can give. God always delivers on his promises, but frequently we have to act before he will.

- *Is there a doctrine to accept and understand?* Doctrinal riches abound in Scripture. Teachings about God, nature, people, angels, demons, morality, relationships, salvation, the church, heaven, hell, and many other subjects are numerous and frequently detailed. But the Bible is not a systematic presentation of theology; rather, within the context of God's work in human history, doctrine slowly unfolds. To learn all the Bible has to say about a particular subject, you will have a good deal of ground to cover. You won't be able to go to only one chapter or one book to find all the pertinent information. Even so, what you will unearth in just one book will usually give you plenty to contemplate and implement in your life.

- *Is there a belief to reject?* Not all beliefs are true. The Bible talks about those who believe in false gods or pursue dead-end paths to salvation. It tells of earthly rulers who command their subjects to worship them as divine. It shows people following false messiahs, believing that the stars and planets determine their destiny, and accepting the lie that wealth will bring them happiness. It warns us about devious teachers who distort the truth about Christ. Jesus said the truth would make us free; truth liberates, error enslaves. When Scripture exposes errors, take note so as to avoid falling prey to them.

- *Is there a social challenge to face?* The Bible calls on us to clothe the naked, feed the hungry, defend the vulnerable, right wrongs, and engage in other challenging activities.[14] When a passage speaks to social concerns, consider how God might want to draw on your resources to help meet one or more of those needs.

- *Is there a personal difficulty to confront?* Studying Scripture may invoke deep-seated hurts that have never healed. It may put you face to face with a character flaw you've tried to ignore or rationalize. It may even uncover poor attitudes or bad habits. Whatever personal issue it touches, and no matter how deeply its touch penetrates, accept the pain as the work of a caring surgeon. The Bible's work at times may feel like a sword thrust, but its design is to cut out only what is harmful. Bear the wounds and stay on the operating table until the Surgeon has completed his work. You'll be a healthier person for it.

- *Is there a relationship to improve?* Marriage, parenting, friendship, employer/employee, citizenship, church ministry . . . the Bible covers these relationships and more. It tells us the pitfalls to avoid, the habits to cultivate, the characteristics to seek, the values to prize, and the fractures to heal. No source teaches more about improving our relationships than the Bible.

- *Is there a reason to offer thanks to God?* At the heart of all that the Bible teaches is the attitude of gratitude. Its absence leads to corruption and idolatry;[15] its cultivation brings God's peace and blessing, placing us in his revealed will and paving the way for enjoyment of his creation.[16] God has given us so much for which to be grateful. Even if he never did anything more, he still deserves our thanks.

- *Are there questions to pursue?* Sometimes your interpretation of a passage will raise questions, even troubling ones. God's dealings may appear overly harsh or excessively lenient. You may be disturbed reading about a prophet who obeys and suffers for it. Perhaps you will come across two accounts of the same event that seem to differ. Or maybe a text will describe something that strikes you as dubious or preposterous. Whenever such issues arise, write them down and commit yourself to seeking answers. Over my three-plus decades of studying Scripture, I have raised hundreds of such questions and have found good answers to almost all of them. In most cases, other texts have supplied the missing pieces. Frequently I've found invaluable help in secondary sources, such as Bible commentaries and dictionaries, lexical aids, and theology books. Never suppress or ignore your questions. Only by asking them and looking for answers to them will you resolve them.

Now let's take some of these questions and pose them in light of our understanding of Genesis 1:26–28.

Is there an example to follow? Absolutely. It's the best example of all—the one and only living, personal God. He created us to image him, which involves following his example. While we cannot do what God does infinitely and perfectly, we can follow his lead finitely and imperfectly. We cannot be or do all good, but we can become increasingly better through the Spirit's work in our lives until he completes and perfects our moral nature and behavior.

Is there a doctrine to accept and understand? There are many in these few verses. Take, for example, the doctrine of God. One hears rumblings of the Trinity, which is wrapped up in God's plurality and unity. Genesis 1:26–28 does not tell us that God is three persons in one nature, but it does affirm that there is a plurality in the one God and that we image the divine plurality and unity. For the sake of application, this should lead us to want to understand the Trinity; the better we understand it, the better opportunity we have to understand ourselves and how we should live. For instance, since God is a community of persons, and since he has created us to form and live in community with one another, I should not seek to live in isolation from other people. I need them and they need me. Loners should not be romanticized or idealized but prayed for and befriended.

Is there a relationship to improve? That depends. Are you harboring prejudicial opinions about another person? She is God's image-bearer. In that sense—the full human sense—she is your equal. She bears the image as much as you do. It makes no difference what color she is, where she lives or comes from, who her parents are, what her political views are, how much money she makes, or even how she treats you. As a human being, she is God's image and therefore has intrinsic dignity and worth. That is enough for you to treat her with respect and reach out to her in love. This may be extremely difficult to do, and she may even spurn you in the process. But this is precisely what the Son of God did while embodied on earth. He reached out to the greedy, the heretics, the promiscuous, the legalists, the drunkards, the gluttons, the poor, the wealthy, the average, the traders, and the traitors. He ignored no one, not even his critics. The Perfect Image loved all the other images living in God's world, so much so that he died for them. How can we then turn away from loving others?

Are there questions to pursue? Without a doubt. Here are a few: Does "the image of God" mean more than we've spelled out here? In what other ways might we be different from the animals? Why don't angels image God, since they are invisible spirit beings as God is? How was the image affected when sin entered the world? Pursuing answers to these questions alone would keep you busy for some time to come.

We could easily generate many more applications. Indeed, I've found that almost any passage yields far more applications than I could ever tackle at once. If you face this problem, here are a couple of ways you can handle it.

First, you could choose one or two of your application conclusions and make those your focus until they become second nature. *Then* go back and choose another application point or two, and work on those until they also become routine. Like the Energizer Bunny, keep going and going and going until you run out of applications. Over the years, I have often used this beneficial approach; it keeps applications to a manageable number and allows me time to incorporate them into my experience until they become habitual.

Second, at times, no matter how many applications I pull out of a text, one stands out above the rest, striking me in a way the others don't. I just know that if I do not accomplish anything else that passage teaches, I must work on this one thing. In those instances, I take that application and concentrate on it to the exclusion of the rest. I may not return to my application list for many months or even years. However, I will give my attention to that single application until I am confident in my practice of it.

Whatever approach you choose, whether one of these or another, make sure you do at least two things: (1) keep your plan flexible, realizing your individuality and life situations may require you to make adjustments along the way; and (2) continually and prayerfully rely on God to guide you in your application decisions and enable you to take the steps necessary to bring them to fruition. Remember what Jesus said: "I am the vine; you are the branches. If a man remains in me and I in him, he will bear much fruit; apart from me you can do nothing" (John 15:5). Separated from the vine, branches wither and die. As long as we stay connected to Christ, which the love habits help us do, we will bear fruit. That's a promise from the Son of God.

GETTING STARTED

After reading through these steps of Bible study, I hope you feel intrigued and inspired—even excited that so much can be gleaned from just one biblical phrase. Augustine certainly felt this way:

> The depth of the Christian Scriptures is boundless. Even if I were attempting to study them and nothing else, from boyhood to decrepit old age, with the utmost leisure, the most unwearied zeal, and with talents greater than I possess, I would still be making progress in discovering their treasure.[17]

Countless Christians throughout the centuries have also found this to be true.

On the other hand, you may feel you just don't have the time to devote this kind of study to the Bible. You may think you are not smart enough or talented enough to do anything more than read it, and even that may be pushing things. If so, I know just how you feel. I too stayed away from the study of Scripture for these reasons. But with some help from others, I learned what I was missing and began stumbling through the study of God's Word on my own and in small groups. I picked up a couple of books that taught me how to study Scripture, I noticed how some believing friends worked through it, and I set aside fifteen to thirty minutes a few days a week for my own study. Slowly my skills improved, and along the way I changed. The more I studied my Lover's words, the more they reshaped me. Now I can honestly say from an informed perspective that no book matters more to me than the Bible.

You *can* study God's Word and mine its riches. Do not let anyone—even yourself—keep you from the boundless riches awaiting you in our Lover's Word. God has words of love and truth for you between the covers of the Bible. Left unwrapped, they will not benefit you. But when tasted and digested through study, you will find them "sweeter than honey" (Ps. 119:103), able to nourish you through the Spirit's work into the fullness of the image of Christ.

9. Meditation and Journaling:
lingering in his presence

By his own admission he was a thieving, sexually immoral, pleasure-seeking demon-worshiper. Raised by a devout Christian mother, he turned away from the moral truths of the faith as a teenager. He had an illegitimate son by a mistress, whom he lived with for more than ten years.

He pursued a non-Christian religious system that allowed him to indulge in the many sensual and material pleasures that excited his interests. As he grew older, he eventually abandoned this set of beliefs and became a skeptic, but his sinful escapades went unabated as he studied persuasion and public speaking in his search for fame and fortune.

He also ran with a group called the Wreckers, known for their outbursts of violence and perverted sense of humor. The Wreckers liked nothing more than cornering unsuspecting individuals and violating their sense of decency, then deriding and debasing them for becoming upset or embarrassed. He envied and wanted to emulate the Wreckers, but he felt ashamed because at times their malice horrified him.

He longed to be loved and to love, and he searched relentlessly for answers to his many questions. In time he found someone who could satisfy his every need, who offered matchless love and undeniable solutions. The new relationship revolutionized his life and dramatically shaped human history; the Someone who saved his soul was God as revealed in Jesus Christ. This seeker committed his life to the Lord and through no ambition of his own became one of history's premier church leaders and theologians. His name was Aurelius Augustine, and he lived from A.D. 354 to 430.

To most Protestants, Augustine is the father of classical theology. To the Eastern Orthodox, he is the greatest of the church fathers. To Roman Catholics, he is the patron saint of theologians. To philosophers, he is the dominant thinker between Plotinus in the third century and Aquinas in the twelfth. To all who study the history of Western civilization, Augustine is the primary shaper of what would become known as the Middle Ages. One would be hard pressed to find any ancient follower of Christ more highly regarded or thoroughly studied than Augustine of Hippo.

Sixteen hundred years ago, Augustine wrote a moving and profound series of meditations, simply called *Confessions*. It is a classic piece of devotional literature, a proven perennial seller. Every time I read it, I feel as if I've been invited into the inner sanctum of a man's spiritual journal. Written as a prayer addressed to God, *Confessions* shows Augustine recounting his struggle with sin and searching for the truth. His ruminations are deeply personal and astonishingly honest, readily revealing his errors and judging them severely.

When he reflects on God and his ways, Augustine probes the mysteries that abound, always with reverence and awe. Like the lighthouse beacon piercing dense fog to ensure sea-vessel guidance, *Confessions* has lighted the return voyage to the Source of all light for believers and unbelievers alike. Augustine's work also magnificently illustrates the power of the love habits called *meditation* and *journaling*.

MEDITATION: PONDERING THE UNFATHOMABLE

When the word *meditation* is mentioned, some people conjure up images of burning incense and candles, eerie rooms with head-shaven worshipers sitting cross-legged on the floor in loose-fitting robes, facing depictions of Eastern gods or gurus illuminated by the flickering flames. The worshipers' eyes are closed, their hands resting on their knees, palms face up, the tips of thumb and index finger of each hand touching. Strange, repetitive, monosyllabic sounds flow from their mouths.

This is certainly one form of meditation, with different manifestations in

Hinduism, Buddhism, Taoism, and other Eastern religions, as well as Western New Age expressions. Its goal is usually to empty the mind of all conscious thought and calm the body so it experiences nothing. Through this method, practitioners attempt to go beyond reason, emotion, sensation, morality, and the rest of this world of supposed shadows and illusion. They desire to achieve a state of nothingness, allegedly becoming one with the all-encompassing Reality. This Reality, they believe, is the only reality—all else is nonexistent, except in our mind, and our mind does not really exist either. Neither do we, for that matter. All that is, is the One—the It that transcends all categories.

This, however, is *not* the kind of meditation Christianity teaches, nor does it even remotely resemble the meditations of Augustine in his *Confessions*. Christian meditation is

- *contentful*—its focus is not on *nothing* but on the Creator and his creation;

- *mindful*—it does not attempt to escape the mind but uses it to its fullest capacity;

- *sensual*—it frequently draws on the senses, even delights in them;

- *emotional*—it can involve all human emotion, from riotous laughter to remorseful sobs;

- *moral*—it dwells on the good and how good can be increased;

- *position-free*—like prayer, it demands no preset position of the body;

- *personal*—it helps us to understand our uniqueness, identity, and personality, the richness of our humanity, and how we can become even more fully human.

In every important way, Christian meditation is virtually the opposite of Eastern meditation. Christians might use candles and incense. Christians might use paintings or sculptures to facilitate their contemplation of the realities they represent. Christians might even sit cross-legged with their eyes closed. But these practices are not essential to what Christian meditation is, how it is done, and what it's designed to achieve.

In short, Christian meditation is "getting to the middle of a thing, pinning yourself down to a certain thing and concentratedly brooding upon it."[1] J. I. Packer expresses it this way:

> Meditation is the activity of calling to mind, and thinking over, and dwelling on, and applying to oneself, the various things that one knows about the works and ways and purposes and promises of God. It is an activity of holy thought, consciously performed in the presence of God, under the eye of God, by the help of God, as a means of communion with God.[2]

Christian meditation leads us to fill our minds, and therefore ourselves, with God. Even when our meditations begin with angels, people, animals, or events, they still lead us to him. We can zero in on Scripture, other literature, art, or music. We can give our attention to ideas and to truths about virtues and vices. In fact, our meditations can encompass everything from the Creator to the creation, from eternity to any period in time past, present, or future. The subject matter of meditation is vast and changeable, but it will always take us to God because he is the beginning and end of all things. Meditation's goal always remains the same: to open ourselves more thoroughly to God, to his perspective and ways, to his direction for our lives, to his unwavering love for us, so we might be filled with him and become more like Christ.

Meditation and Love: The Quiet Revolution

The connection between meditation and love is this: in meditation, we lovingly ponder our unfathomable Lover and his wonderful works and ways.

Consider his work of Scripture. Thousands of years ago, one of the psalmists wrote in devotional praise of God's law, saying to the Lord:

Oh, how I love your law!
    I meditate on it all day long.
Your commands make me wiser than my enemies,
    for they are ever with me.
I have more insight than all my teachers,
    for I meditate on your statutes.
I have more understanding than the elders,
    for I obey your precepts. . . .
How sweet are your words to my taste,
    sweeter than honey to my mouth!
I gain understanding from your precepts;
    therefore I hate every wrong path.
    —Psalm 119:97–100, 103–104

Notice that love and meditation go hand in hand. Mulling over God's Word deepens one's love for it, and the more one loves it, the more one ponders it. The psalmist also connects his growth in wisdom to his loving meditation on Scripture. How does he understand more than his teachers? Through the time he spends thinking over what the Divine Teacher has already said. By the Word of God, the Lord has "taught" the psalmist.

All this has led the human author away from paths of evil and toward a long obedience in the same direction. His love for the ultimate Good has been enriched through the delectable, nourishing path laid out in God's Word. Meditation on Scripture was the love habit that deeply ingrained Love's way in the psalmist's mind and will.

In another psalm, we're told that the blessed man is the one whose "delight is in the law of the LORD, and on his law he meditates day and night." This person is "like a tree planted by streams of water, which yields its fruit in season and whose leaf does not wither. Whatever he does prospers" (Psalm 1:2–3). Clearly the quality of our lives is directly related to the time and effort we put into dwelling on our Lover's written revelation.

Jesus exemplified this. Even as young as twelve, he amazed the Jewish religious leaders and all others who heard him with "his understanding and his answers" (Luke 2:47); his knowledge of Scripture and Jewish tradition stunned the Bible teachers of his day. After surveying some of the evidence in the four Gospels concerning Jesus' use of Scripture, John Wenham concludes:

> The total impression that these and many other allusions in the Gospels give is that the mind of Christ is saturated with the Old Testament. . . . His mind is so steeped in both the words and principles of Scripture that quotation and allusion spring to his lips naturally and appositely in all sorts of different circumstances.[3]

How does it come about that Scripture penetrates the depths of *anyone's* mind? The cause is not a secret: (1) intensive, consistent study and (2) regular meditation on Scripture done under the guidance of the Spirit and in submission to the Father. Citing Wenham again:

> Jesus condemns neither minuteness of study nor the exercise of reason. His condemnation comes when the wickedness of men so perverts their reason or their methods of study that they become blind to the inner principles of the divine revelation. He himself knew how to stimulate the exercise of reason, and repeatedly he encouraged his hearers to go beneath the externals of Scripture language and think out its

underlying principles. . . . He demands more thought, not less; but it must be thought conducted in a humble and teachable spirit directed by God himself.[4]

As a result of his love-motivated commitment to studying, meditating on, and applying Scripture, Jesus "grew in wisdom and stature, and in favor with God and men" (Luke 2:52), becoming the most authoritative and effective teacher in history, living a sinless life, and always doing his Father's will until he was able to say from the cross that he had fully accomplished what he'd been sent to do.[5]

The amazing, life-changing results of Christ's devotion perfectly illustrate the revolutionary impact God can have on us if we will simply treat his Word as love letters to us. When people receive correspondence from those they love, they pore over every word, reading and rereading, picking up shades of meaning, carefully deciphering all that is said, even noting what is left unsaid. They savor each sentence and phrase, taking everything to heart. They look for reaffirmations of loyalty and cringe over expressions that hurt or disappoint. They exult in thanksgiving when their beloved brings good news, and they shed tears when there is news of deep loss. They enter into their lover's mind and heart. They identify with the loved one, laugh and weep with him or her, and become more united to them.

Our Divine Lover has written to each of us. He has opened himself up to us, sharing his all-knowing mind and unending love through his words. The many books of the Bible are his love letters to us; when we read them, study them, and repeatedly mull over them—story by story, chapter by chapter, verse by verse, word by word—we get inside our Lover's mind and heart. We move beyond lectures and sermons and delve beneath secondhand presentations. We hear him speak our name. We sense him walking alongside us. We see the world as he does and see him at work in it. We find him tugging at us, wooing us, correcting us, and all the while unveiling to us the innumerable ways he has always loved us even when we were too blind to notice.

Through meditation we are illumined about Love and impassioned to love. *Agapē* seeks to fill every crevice and overflow every pore. The more *Agapē* fills us and floods through us, the more we change and influence others to change.

Coupling meditation with the other love habits can incite a quiet inner revolution that will break down walls to change as it unleashes the convicting and transforming power of divine love. I use the word *incite* for a reason:

Although meditation does not *cause* change, it does help create an interior environment that God uses to change us from within. Richard Foster explains:

> What happens in meditation is that we create the emotional and spiritual space which allows Christ to construct an inner sanctuary in the heart. . . .
> Inward fellowship of this kind transforms the inner personality. We cannot burn the eternal flame of the inner sanctuary and remain the same, for the Divine Fire will consume everything that is impure. Our ever-present Teacher will always be leading us into "righteousness and peace and joy in the Holy Spirit" (Rom. 14:17). Everything that is foreign to his way we will have to let go. No, not "have to" but "want to," for our desires and aspirations will be more and more conformed to his way. Increasingly, everything within us will swing like a needle to the polestar of the Spirit.[6]

God doesn't just buff his corrupted image-bearers, polishing without repairing. He restores us by purifying us, removing from us all that fails to mirror him fully. Meditation is one of the means he uses to bring about our complete restoration.

Meditation is so important in this process that Paul highlights it in his letter of joy to the Philippian Christians:

> *Practice thinking* on what is true, what is honorable, what is right, what is pure, what is lovable, what is high-toned, yes, on everything that is excellent or praiseworthy. [When this is done and joined with practicing] the things you learned, received, and heard from me, things that you saw me do . . . *then* the God who gives us peace will be with you.[7]

Meditation on what is good, beautiful, and true—along with its application to our lives—will bring the God of peace alongside us. After all, he *is* good and beautiful and true. When we dwell on what is praiseworthy, we soon find ourselves dwelling on him.

Meditation, then, like all the other love habits, directs us back to *simplicity* (the most foundational love habit of all). Through meditation, we soak in the Center of life and love, truth and goodness, beauty and purity. Meditation is one way of loving God with all we are.

This is clearly seen in Augustine's *Confessions,* which is filled with prayerful meditations. Their progression shows that the more Augustine filled his thoughts with God, the more of God he understood. The more he understood, the more Christlike he became. Meditation renewed his mind and thereby helped renew his life. What meditation did for him, it can do for us.

JOURNALING: CREATING CHRONICLES

> It is hard for me to accept that the best I can do is probably not to give but to receive. . . .
>
> The more I think about the meaning of living and acting in the name of Christ, the more I realize that what I have to offer to others is not my intelligence, skill, power, influence, or connections, but my own human brokenness through which the love of God can manifest itself. . . .
>
> Every man or woman who lives the Christian life to the full cannot but exercise a deep influence on everyone he or she meets. What continues to fascinate me is that those whose whole mind and heart were directed to God had the greatest impact on other people, while those who tried very hard to be influential were quickly forgotten. . . .
>
> When I have no eyes for the small signs of God's presence—the smile of a baby, the carefree play of children, the words of encouragement and gestures of love offered by friends—I will always remain tempted to despair.[8]

These personal thoughts about life are excerpted from a journal kept by the late author, minister, and teacher Henri Nouwen, covering several months in his life from late 1981 to early 1982. It is, as he puts it,

> the personal report of my six-month sojourn in Bolivia and Peru. I wrote it in an attempt to capture the countless impressions, feelings, and ideas that filled my mind and heart day after day. It speaks about new places and people, about new insights and perspectives, and about new joys and anxieties. But the question that runs through all its pages and binds the many varied fragments together is: "Does God call me to live and work in Latin America in the years to come?"[9]

This journal (published under the title *¡Gracias!*) recounts Nouwen's experiences and then records his reflections on those experiences, especially in light of his commitment to Christ. His entries reveal a man vulnerable before God and his fellow human beings, a man growing deeper in his understanding of and appreciation for the Creator and Savior, a man in the process of searching for God's will.

This is what the love habit of journaling can bring. It opens doors to one's mind and heart as it encourages and accomplishes an ever-engaging conversation between creature and Creator, between the beloved and her Lover. Journaling is a form of listening—listening to one's God, oneself, and the other voices one hears. Journaling is also a vehicle for talking—to one's God, oneself, and the other voices seeking responses. Journaling is, in other words, a chronicling of conversation, especially that conversation between God and us. Gordon MacDonald says,

> The main value of a journal is as a tool for listening to the quiet Voice that comes out of the garden of the private world. Journal-keeping serves as a wonderful tool for withdrawing and communing with the Father.[10]

Through that oasis of words, we linger vulnerably in our Lover's presence, inviting him to wrap us in his arms, to enter and possess us more fully.

Jesus and Journaling

As beneficial as journaling is, I readily confess that you will not find a single instance of Jesus, Love Incarnate, practicing this discipline. In fact, as far as we know, the only time Christ wrote any words at all was when some religious leaders brought to him a woman accused of adultery, asking if they should follow the Mosaic Law and stone her for the offense. Before Jesus said a word, he "bent down and started to write on the ground with his finger." Then he stood up and said to them, " 'If any one of you is without sin, let him be the first to throw a stone at her.' Again he stooped down and wrote on the ground" (John 8:7–8). What he wrote in the dirt is not recorded in Holy Writ; what *is* recorded is that the crowd of accusers silently dispersed, one by one, until only Jesus and the woman remained.

Although our Savior wrote only on the ground, the words of his life caused a cataclysmic shift in history.

> He spoke such words of life as were never spoken before or since and produced effects which lie beyond the reach of orator or poet; without writing a single line, He set more pens in motion, and furnished themes for more sermons, orations, discussions, learned volumes, works of art, and songs of praise, than the whole army of great men of ancient and modern times.[11]

He is the fulfillment of the Old Testament, and the twenty-seven books of the New Testament would never have been written apart from his earthly life. His virtue, his authoritative teaching, his miracle-working power, his full submission to the heavenly Father, his love of all and compassion toward all . . . these and many other things about him ushered in the completion of God's written revelation to us. Jesus' followers took their Master's words and actions so seriously that they wrote them down, recording them, interpreting them, and applying them, all under the providential guidance of the Holy Spirit.

How did the disciples remember so much about what Jesus said and did? While scholars have largely answered that they memorized Jesus' words and remembered his deeds long before committing them to parchment, more and more scholars are recognizing the very real possibility that the disciples took written notes on what he said and did and on their experiences with him.

> Recent research has . . . pointed out that there is no need to think that the gospel traditions were only memorized by the disciples during their time with Jesus. Some of Jesus' teaching could well have been written down in brief, notebook-like memoranda for use during their mission. . . . Jewish children were taught to read and write, and each Palestinian community had a synagogue school where reading and writing was taught. . . . Absolute certainty about the extent to which such notes were used is of course impossible, but it is not at all improbable that during the ministry of Jesus the disciples used notes and written materials in conjunction with their preaching.
>
> Through memory and quite possibly through the use of notes, Jesus' teachings were received and retained by the disciples.[12]

The disciples' mental remembrances and written notes—dare we say their journal entries?—joined with the Spirit's work of teaching them "the meaning and significance [of Jesus'] words and deeds (John 14:26),"[13] resulting in the four gospels and the other New Testament books. These documents accurately record, teach, reflect on, interpret, and apply "the truths of the faith" (1 Tim. 4:6).

We have no record, then, that Jesus kept a journal, but it's likely that his disciples did. We are the indebted beneficiaries of their work.

Journaling Basics

A spiritual journal can contain all kinds of entries, such as

- records of daily or memorable events
- reactions

- conversations
- thoughts and feelings
- questions and doubts
- achievements and failures
- beliefs, both sure and unsure
- impressions, including what God seems to be saying
- prayers, as well as answers to prayers
- Bible verses
- study notes and meditations on Scripture
- notable quotes
- confessions
- misgivings
- thanksgivings
- dreams and ambitions
- concerns and anxieties
- plans for the future
- meditations on the past

The entries can be long or short, in longhand or shorthand, printed or handwritten or typed. As I see it, there are really only two requirements in journal-keeping.

First, *you must be honest and vulnerable.* Polishing your outside, while allowing your inside to fall apart from neglect, will do you no good. You must be devoted to going beyond the surface and delving into the disorder festering within. I agree with Elizabeth O'Connor, who writes,

> The keeping of a pilgrim journal requires a conscious, unswerving commitment to honesty with one's self . . . [which is] the first requirement for growth in self-understanding. . . . This we do by coming into possession of truth—by routing out lies and deceits. This takes a lot of courage, a lot of endurance, a commitment to press on when we want to shrink back. The goal is to make Jesus Christ the Lord of our life.[14]

In my journaling, honesty and vulnerability did not come easily—it's difficult to glimpse how ugly and foolish one can be. But until we see ourselves as we really are, we will not realize how far we have to go and how desperately we need our Lover's infinite help to get there. We cannot cure ourselves of deep-seated ills: We must have help, and we have this help in God, who has graciously supplied us with a vast array of healing aids—the church, Scripture, friends, family, the love habits, and his Spirit, to name but a few. He works through all he supplies to redeem and transform us from the inside out. Part of *our* cooperative labor in all this is to get at the truth about ourselves. This cannot be had apart from self-honesty—an honesty that will sometimes hurt and even turn our stomachs, as it will also at times lead us to laugh at our foolishness and praise God for evidence of his reforming work in our lives.

The second requirement for journaling is that *you must be ready to listen as well as to speak.* We are in a personal relationship with the living God, and that involves a two-way conversation. The Lord did not stop talking to his creatures when the New Testament was finished. We must be attentive to his many modes of communication if we are to *hear* him (not merely talk to him).

As I've made entries in my journal, I've heard God speak to me, and I've recorded his words there. They do not belong in the Bible because they are words for me, not for all believers.[15] They often direct or redirect me. Sometimes they comfort me; other times they discipline me. Frequently they remind me of what God has already revealed in his inspired Word. Whatever his words are and whatever they are meant to do, I've learned to write them in my journal, keeping a permanent record that I can return to time and again to rehear my Lover's words and revisit how I responded to him. The exchange provides a needed reminder of what I may still need to do.

To these two musts of journaling, I'm tempted to add a third: *Make regular entries,* weekly at least; daily would be best. Your frequency will largely depend on how you decide to use your journaling. I use my journal for many things, but most of all to pray and meditate. I find it easier to focus my mind when I write, so my prayers and meditations are usually best when I'm putting them to paper. Since I pray and meditate daily, my journaling is nearly daily as well.

Getting started with journal-keeping is fairly easy. The first thing you need is something to use as a journal. It can be a spiral notebook, a binder with notebook paper, a bound book with blank or lined pages, your desktop or laptop computer, or anything else that makes writing comfortable.

Once you've chosen your journal, decide how you want to set it up. For instance, my life is complicated enough without my journaling being a complex science, so I use a bound book with lined pages. When I make an entry, I start by writing down the day and date (e.g., Tuesday, 3–6–04), and underneath that heading is where I begin writing out my thoughts, feelings, recollections, meditations, prayers . . . whatever I wish to record for that day. This method gives me a good deal of flexibility; one day's entry may be no more than a sentence, while another day's may go on for several pages. The length doesn't matter because I have not imposed a structure that carries any preset limits. I write until I'm out of time or words; then, when I decide to make another entry, I add the appropriate heading and begin writing again. Simple and straightforward.

Other people like to divide their journal into sections: one for written prayers, another for recording favorite quotes or verses, another for listing prayer requests and answers, another for writing down the day's events, another for thoughts, impressions, feelings, and the like.

You may have a different approach in mind, or you might experiment with various setups. The goal is to make your journal user-friendly for you.

Once you're ready to start, I suggest making an entry that dedicates your journaling to the Lord, perhaps in the form of a prayer. When I began journaling many years ago, I wanted my mind and heart focused on God from the very start and for my efforts to be an offering to him. This is what I wrote:

> Father—
>
> I dedicate this journal to you, Lord, the Creator of language, the eternal Reason and Word. I want to know you, to enter into fellowship with you while I'm on earth in preparation for the intimacy I will enjoy with you in heaven. Please use my thoughts, words, and feelings to draw me closer to you, to increase my finite understanding of your infinite essence and mysterious ways. Only in knowing you will I come to know myself and to understand others. So I turn to you, the beginning and end of my search.

What you say or how you say it is not sacrosanct. What matters is that your words are genuine and come from your heart.

Moving Ahead

After you've chosen, structured, and dedicated your journal, what next? What should you write about? Because a journal is so personal, there really are no shoulds when it comes to subject matter: write whatever you like. With that in mind, I'll give some ideas for getting started.

One approach is to write a portion of Scripture, then spend the rest of your entry (maybe even your next several entries) interacting with that text. Wrestle with it, throw questions at it, draw out applications from it, turn your musings on it into prayers. Here's a journaling example of both applying and praying through a biblical passage:

> "Love is kind" (1 Cor. 13:4). Lord, often I am not kind. I am blunt and direct and speak without stopping to think how my words will affect the one to whom I am speaking. If only, if only, I could take the time to slip out of myself, to abandon my viewpoint and move over into the other person's position, how different my speech would be. Some things would go unsaid. Instead I would learn to trust God to work things out. Instead of opening my big mouth and feeling that if I don't set things right things won't be corrected, I would listen. How often I have trodden over sensitive hearts with words and tone that could be likened to heavy cobble-soled army boots. Lord, help me to temper honesty and directness with kindness.[16]

You could also record your thoughts on whatever else you're reading. While my formal degrees are in philosophy and theology, I read widely outside those subject areas. In my journal, I mention which books I'm reading (usually bouncing between three or four at any given time) and what I think about them. Are they helping me work through issues? What points are they developing that I find true, intriguing, or worth further investigation? What is being said that I believe is false? How is the author challenging my thinking?

Perhaps you don't read many books; maybe you spend more time watching movies, reading magazines or newspapers, listening to the radio, or researching online. No matter. When something strikes you, write about it in your journal. Don't let those opportunities for growth pass by without writing. Putting them down will help you remember them and thereby give them a chance to become a permanent part of who you are becoming.

There's also significant value in journaling as an outlet for expressing thoughts and feelings you may feel uncomfortable sharing with others. Your journal can become the place where you detail your self-doubts or struggles with family members or friends. You can verbalize your dissatisfactions with your marriage, children, or career. You can work through painful experiences or come to terms with lost opportunities and broken dreams. You can pour out your hurt, confusion, and frustration in imaginary letters you will never mail. In the process of bringing to light and objectifying what would otherwise remain hidden and subjective, you have eye-opening experiences that can bring clarity and healing in your life.

Madeleine L'Engle knows this to be true, calling the journaling experience her "free psychiatrist's couch" in *Walking on Water*. "If I can write things out I can see them," she says. "They are not trapped within my own subjectivity." She provides an example of how journaling helped her see through the pain of a situation and find resolution:

> Not long ago someone I love said something which wounded me grievously, and I was desolate that this person could possibly have made such a comment to me.
>
> So, in great pain, I crawled to my journal and wrote it all out in a great burst of self-pity. And when I had set it down, when I had it before me, I saw that something I myself had said had called forth the words which had hurt me so. It had, in fact, been my own fault. But I would never have seen it if I had not written it out.[17]

Journaling can also give you space to safely blow off steam. We all get angry and hurt, and at times all of us want to strike out at someone, whether with fists or words. A journal can be our medium to do so without inflicting emotional or physical damage on another person. Some of the psalmists used the written word to express their intense feelings about those they despised or hated. Here are choice selections from Psalm 109, written by David, whom God described as "a man after my own heart" (Acts 13:22):

Appoint an evil man to oppose him. . . .
When he is tried, let him be found guilty,
    and may his prayers condemn him.
May his days be few;
    may another take his place of leadership.
May his children be fatherless
    and his wife a widow.
May his children be wandering beggars;
    may they be driven from their ruined homes.
May a creditor seize all he has;
    may strangers plunder the fruits of his labor.
May no one extend kindness to him
    or take pity on his fatherless children. . . .
May their sins always remain before the LORD,

that he may cut off the memory of them from the earth. . . .
May this be the LORD'S payment to my accusers,
    to those who speak evil of me.
    —vv. 6–12, 15, 20

The eventual goal of such outbursts is to bring them under the scrutiny of God and allow him to help us resolve them in obedience to his will. He wants us to love even our enemies and try to be at peace with everyone.[18] This is hard work—in fact, it's impossible for us apart from the Spirit's ministry in our lives. Nevertheless, essential to the process of bringing our anger and hatred under control is giving them a safe place to vent. Our journals can serve that need.

You might also consider using your journal to brainstorm without fear of ridicule; you can articulate ideas, create new inventions, propose possible solutions to problems, consider the positives and negatives of future plans. As a writer with varied interests, I frequently use my journal to record thoughts about potential books or articles I'd like to write and see published. I outline ideas, sort through hesitations about pursuing them, and record stories I may want to use or feelings I may want to recall. Some ideas will never go beyond my journal, but many of those that find publishing homes were born there.

Another excellent benefit of journal-keeping is clarifying your own beliefs. Paul said that Christians should "take captive every thought to make it obedient to Christ" (2 Cor. 10:5); in a journal you can state your convictions, check them against Scripture and historic orthodoxy, and work through any discovered conflicts so that your thinking increasingly becomes Christlike.

Of course, self-discovery is one of the best results of journaling. The Bible calls on each of us to examine ourselves and our work so we might arrive at an accurate understanding of who we are, what we have accomplished, and whether we are standing firm in the faith.[19] In a journal you can take what's inside you and bring it into the open, where you can explore it and then seek to keep what is good and purge what is evil.

A word of caution: self-discovery will be messy and disturbing. You may find haunting memories you had long suppressed. There may resurface feelings of resentment you thought were history. You might glory in a job well done while simultaneously facing the reality of relationships damaged or health sacrificed in the process. *Don't let such prospects deter you from doing the spiritual spadework.* If you are in Christ, be encouraged by the fact that the Spirit is in you, striving to bring to completion the "good work" already initiated (Phil. 1:6). Good cannot coexist with bad without creating tension and division. God loves us so much that he wants to see us fully and completely whole. Achieving this will be painful and humbling, but whatever we suffer getting there will be trifling compared with all we will gain.[20]

Journaling can also be wonderful for prayer; there is perhaps no better cure for a wandering mind than the act of writing. My early years of praying were plagued with such a mental malady, but journaling has cured it. When I write my prayers, my mind, body, emotions, and will are engaged. I am fully present, more inclined to press my requests with good reasons, to confess my sins with contrition, and to praise the Lord with clearly articulated exultations. Some prayers are long, others short. In my journal are many of my prayers, as well as God's responses. I know he answers prayer—I have a written record to prove it. You can have one too by writing your prayers in your journal.

Finally, the ultimate purpose of spiritual journaling is to provide a chronicle of your walk with God. Human beings are forgetful creatures; we have trouble enough remembering things when times are good and easy. Add stress, pain, or upheaval to the scenario, and our ability to recollect crashes like a hard drive. God knows this—it's one reason he's given us a written revelation. He often called on the Bible's human authors to repeat certain events and their significance.

For example, you can't read through the Old Testament without repeatedly hearing about creation, the Abrahamic promise, the Exodus, the Mosaic Law, or Israel's complaining, idolatry, and construction under God. You can't get through the New Testament without reading reference after reference to Christ and the fullness of salvation available through him. God even gave us four diverse perspectives on Jesus' life (the Gospels), making it impossible for us to see the New Testament as anything less than a witness to the Son's incarnation for our redemption.

Some of Scripture's most significant words are *remember* and *do not forget*.[21] Even the church's rituals (such as water baptism and the Eucharist) recall the events that gave her life and make it possible for her to be an ongoing conduit of life to others.[22]

Through journaling you can record your witness of God's work in your life and in those around you. Creating a written account makes it easier for you to remember; if you ever forget, you can turn to your journal and rediscover what the Lord has done. This will help you avoid the kind of forgetfulness

James warns us about: "Anyone who listens to the word but does not do what it says is like a man who looks at his face in a mirror and, after looking at himself, goes away and immediately forgets what he looks like." Instead, you can become like "the man who looks intently into the perfect law that gives freedom, and continues to do this, not forgetting what he has heard, but doing it." When you do this, you will be "blessed" (1:23–25). Journaling will impress God's words upon you, helping you to see yourself both as you are and can become. Journaling can help you keep your "eyes on Jesus, the author and perfecter of our faith" (Heb. 12:2).

One Man's Witness

If you are still unsure about the value of journaling or feel intimidated by the prospect of carrying on a written interchange with God, consider what Gordon MacDonald says about his experience with this love habit. I quote him at length because he succinctly expresses the initial struggles he faced and the rewards he reaped.

> I became impressed by the fact that many, many godly men and women down through the centuries had kept journals, and I began to wonder if they had not put their fingers upon an aid to spiritual growth. To satisfy my curiosity, I decided to experiment, and began keeping one for myself.
>
> At first it was difficult. I felt self-conscious. I was worried that I would lose the journal or that someone might peek inside to see what I'd said. But slowly the self-consciousness began to fade, and I found myself sharing in the journal more and more of the thoughts that flooded my inner spirit. Into the journal went words describing my feelings, my fear and sense of weakness, my hopes, and my discoveries about where Christ was leading me. When I felt empty or defeated, I talked about that too in the journal.
>
> Slowly I began to realize that the journal was helping me come to grips with an enormous part of my inner person that I had never been fully honest about. No longer could fears and struggles remain inside without definition. They were surfaced and confronted. And I became aware, little by little, that God's Holy Spirit was directing many of the thoughts and insights as I wrote. On paper, the Lord and I were carrying on a personal communion. He was helping me, in the words of David, to "search my heart." He was prodding me to put words to my fears, shapes to my doubts. And when I was candid about it, then there would often come out of Scripture or from the meditations of my own heart,

the reassurances, the rebukes, and the admonishments that I so badly needed. But this began to happen only when the journal was employed. . . .

Today after twenty years of journal-keeping, I have acquired a habit. Hardly a morning passes that I do not open the journal and record the things I hear God saying through my reading, meditation, and daily experience. When the journal opens, so does the ear of my heart. If God is going to speak, I am ready to listen.[23]

MacDonald's experience is not one-of-a-kind. Believers such as Jim Elliot, John Wesley, George Whitefield, Blaise Pascal, David Brainerd, Francis Asbury, Frank Laubach, Reinhold Niebuhr, David Livingston, Thomas Merton, John Woolman, and Helmut Thielicke—to name but a handful—kept journals. All of them learned what MacDonald did. You have the same opportunity to grow your love relationship with God.

THE POWER OF THREE

Since "journaling is one of the most helpful exercises we can do to increase our capacity for meditation and prayer,"[24] I've provided an exercise that combines all three love habits. If you don't yet have a journal, use a notepad or computer or even some scraps of paper and try this exercise.

Begin with some moments given to prayer. Prepare your mind and heart for meditation and journaling by making the following prayer your own. (You can do this by simply praying the words as if they were yours.)

Grant to me, O Lord, to worship you
    in spirit and in truth;
    to submit all my nature to you,
that my conscience may be quickened by your holiness,
    my mind nourished by your truth,
    my imagination purified by your beauty.
Help me to open my heart to your love
and to surrender my will to your purpose.
    So may I lift up my heart to you
    in selfless adoration and love.
    Through Jesus Christ my Lord.[25]

One of the most fruitful subjects for meditation is, of course, God himself. Two attributes of God that have brought great comfort to believers are his omniscience (knowledge of all things) and omnipresence (presence to and among all things). Psalm 139 focuses on these truths in light of the experience of David, the greatest king of Israel. David's meditation could easily be yours or mine; it may even be the result of journaling. Bruce Demarest suggests that the entire "book of Psalms can be viewed as a collection of inspired journal entries."[26] If so, then Psalm 139 gives us a personal glimpse into David's private world with God.

Turn in your Bible to Psalm 139, write out the first eighteen verses, and pore over them. When David paints a picture, attempt to see it in your mind. When he conveys a feeling, try to feel it with him. When he poses a question, stop and ponder it before you read on and find his answer. When you hear his answer, place yourself in his position and consider how his answer applies to you. If his answer raises questions, reflect on those questions and try to think of possible answers. Write out everything that comes to your mind and speaks to your heart. Try not to let anything escape unrecorded. Feel free to turn your written meditations into written prayers. Permit the message of this ancient meditative song to vibrate deep within your soul, where it can become part of your life symphony.

When your meditations and journaling are done, end with prayer. Try using the last two verses of Psalm 139 as your closing petition. Speak them aloud or write them down. *God will always hear and answer his own words.*

10. Solitude and Silence:
alone in God's arms

"Be still, and know that I am God" (Ps. 46:10).
  Stillness.
  When kids are crying and demanding our attention?
  When we must drive talkative children to and from all their events?
  Stillness.
  When spouses hover and cling?
  When the tension at home grows thick?
  When family and friends can't take no for an answer?
  Stillness.
  When the phone won't stop ringing?
  When noise blares from radios and TVs, car horns and jackhammers?
  Stillness.
  When our employers heap greater responsibilities on us?
  When our employees fall ill and we're scrambling to pick up the slack?
  When there aren't enough volunteers, or when those we've relied on quit?
  Stillness.
  When we're forced to be aware of our surroundings in these violent times?

When our neighbors have suffered a break-in?

When a family member is dying and needs our constant care?

Stillness.

Is stillness even possible to achieve in our day? In fact, if we *could* find time to be still, would we *want* it?

I know a couple who have at least one television turned on whenever one or both of them are home. They're not always watching it—they simply like the constant sound. It makes them feel like someone is with them.

I know a woman who is always on the go. If she isn't with someone else, she's on the phone talking or preparing to meet someone. She can't stand to be alone or to be quiet, even for a short time. She's personable and fun, but she's also shallow. You can't be with her for long before you wonder if there's any depth beyond her many activities.

Some professionals I've worked with never travel alone, eat alone, or spend much time alone in their office; they seem to need an entourage around them. It's not that they must have staff constantly with them to do their job but that they derive a sense of self-importance from the attending parties. Their self-worth is tied up in having someone within earshot who will do their bidding, shower them with compliments, or cower before their insults. One way they show their desperate neediness is by avoiding solitude and stillness.

Jesus, on the other hand, didn't need constant noise for comfort. Nor did he fill his day with activities that would detract from the cultivation of his inner life. Nor did he derive his sense of worth from having twelve men as travel companions, as evidenced by the many times he withdrew from their company and even sent them journeying without him. Jesus loved people, loved spending time with them, teaching, healing, consoling, and guiding them. But he also loved to be by himself in "lonely places," to be still with his Father.

> Very early in the morning, while it was still dark, Jesus got up, left the house and went off to a *solitary* place, where he prayed. (Mark 1:35)
>
> [Jesus] was *alone* on land. (6:47)
>
> Jesus often withdrew to *lonely* places and prayed. (Luke 5:16)
>
> Jesus went out to a mountainside to pray, and spent the night praying to God. (6:12)
>
> After he [Jesus] had dismissed them, he went up on a mountainside by himself to pray. When evening came, he was there *alone*. (Matt. 14:23, all emphasis added)

Jesus sought solitude and stillness. Sure, he walked and talked with his followers day in and day out. Of course he welcomed children to his side, and yes, he spoke to crowds of thousands at a time. It's true he healed throngs of people most places he went; he also taught in the synagogues and attended feasts and festivals. Nevertheless, he also spent large portions of time apart from the multitudes, apart from the religious leaders, even apart from his disciples. Jesus looked for opportunities to be alone and to be still, and he wasn't shy about taking advantage of them.

When I first learned about Jesus' passion for solitude, I was drawn to him even more. I have always enjoyed alone-time, even as a child; I liked playing alone then, and I've liked working alone as an adult. When I'm alone, interruptions are minimal. My ability to concentrate is enhanced. My imagination can soar easily. I can get in touch with my state of mind and better grapple with my feelings. I can sort through problems and evaluate arguments with greater precision, and I can find more worthwhile solutions. Creativity flows naturally. I can recharge my batteries for social interaction. Most important, I can be still in the Lord's presence, communing with him more deeply and better hearing his voice. I love solitude. It brings me stillness.

Stillness is possible. It's even achievable. More than that, it's *necessary*. But stillness is not achievable apart from cultivating solitude and silence. The more these love habits form our lives, the more we will conform to Christ.

SOLITUDE: ALONE WITH GOD

The love habit of *solitude* is a voluntary and temporary withdrawal into privacy for spiritual purposes.[1] Such alone-time can be as short as minutes and as long as days or weeks, sometimes even months. Solitude can be away from people (outward solitude) or with people (inward solitude).

Jesus spent much time in *outward* solitude. Just before his ministry began, he spent forty days apart from all other humans. His companion was the Holy Spirit, who led him into the desert. The only other being with Jesus was Satan, his spiritual foe.[2] After Jesus had overcome his enemy's temptations, "angels came and attended him" (Matt. 4:11). Then, during his ministry, he "often withdrew to lonely places and prayed" (Luke 5:16).

Along with such times of outward solitude, Jesus likewise practiced *inward* solitude. Luke records that "once when Jesus was praying *in private* and his disciples were with him, he asked them, 'Who do the crowds say I am?'" (9:18, emphasis added). "In private" means he prayed inwardly, as if no one else was around. He practiced what he preached about prayer: "When you pray, go into your room, close the door and pray to your Father, who is unseen" (Matt. 6:6). Jesus retreated to the solitude of his heart, to the private room within, and there he prayed. His disciples were near enough that he could turn and ask them a question—a question that likely came to him during his inward solitude of prayer. This question eventually elicited the defining answer of his identity: that he was the "Christ of God" (Luke 9:20).

As much as Jesus spent time away from others, he knew that he was never alone. "The one who sent me is with me," Jesus said, adding, "he has not left me alone" (John 8:29). During the final Passover, he told his closest disciples they would soon leave him "all alone. Yet," he reminded, "I am not alone, for my Father is with me" (16:32). *Solitude meant intimacy, not isolation.*

Centuries earlier, David also expressed this truth. Regardless of where he went, God was always with him:

> Where can I go from your Spirit?
>   Where can I flee from your presence?
> If I go up to the heavens, you are there;
>   if I make my bed in the depths, you are there.
> If I rise on the wings of the dawn,
>   if I settle on the far side of the sea,
> even there your hand will guide me,
>   your right hand will hold me fast.
>   —Psalm 139:7–10

In both outward and inward solitude, we can count on God being with us. We are *never* alone; we *always* have at our side at least one companion, our Divine Lover. "'Immanuel'—which means, 'God with us'" (Matt. 1:23), is real.

Solitary Benefits

Perhaps the prospect of spending time alone, especially away from other people, seems scary. You may wonder, *What will I discover in the stillness of my own thoughts, in the quiet of my heart? Will I like what I find there?* You may already know what's there, and that's what frightens you. Could it be that this is why you work so hard to keep others around you? Is this why the many sounds and forms of distraction are so attractive?

Or maybe you equate solitude with boredom—excitement is activity, and sharing that activity with others is most exciting of all. How could there be enjoyment in doing anything alone? After all, one of the worst punishments for a criminal is being put into solitary confinement. Solitude is a form of retribution. Why would anyone want to commit himself to such pain?

If you harbor either of these perspectives on solitude, I'd like you to try on another pair of lenses. Put on the lens of love for a moment. Imagine the person you love the most. This is the person who brings a smile to your face whenever you think of him. (If the person is a female, substitute feminine pronouns.) In fact, not thinking of him is impossible—everywhere you turn, reminders of him pervade your world. Whenever you can, you want to be with him—talking on the phone, writing letters or emails, eating meals, watching movies, taking walks, playing games, sharing affection, reading aloud. You want to linger in his presence: What you do together is not nearly as important as just being together. And while you don't mind occasionally sharing him with others, for the most part you want him to yourself. It's those alone-times that are the most intimate, the most special, the most enjoyable. These are the times when you feel most secure. These are the times when you can genuinely be yourself, leaving pretense behind. With the one you love most, the masks can come off, because he loves you for you—the real you.

This is but a taste of what solitude with the Lord can be like. No one loves you more than God does. No one knows you better than he does. And although he knows your every secret sin, your every failing, your every fear, your every regret, he loves you infinitely more than the greatest human lover you can ever imagine. He readily forgives you for all and accepts you through all. You'll never have to look for him any further than your own mind and heart, for he is there: Immanuel is with you.

The fruit of the greatest love in existence is best tasted during the most intimate times, and those wonderful experiences of intimacy are ushered in by outward and inward solitude. There, with our Lover, we can talk one-on-one or rest silently in his presence. We can laugh and cry with him. We can share our hurts, whether through words or unspoken anguish. We can argue and wait for his omniscient response. We can meditate and pray and seek his direction. We can read his Word aloud or quietly. We can study his love letters or the natural art of his hands. In our alone-times with him, we can be active or inactive, talkative or attentive, playful or serious. *In solitude we can simply be in God's arms*—we don't have to do anything. We don't have to perform or achieve. There, in our Lover's embrace, we can rest, knowing we are accepted as we are. *This is the peace of stillness.*

I would be remiss, however, if I failed to tell you that solitude with God has a dangerous side. When you seek time alone with him, he gives you his all and expects you to give him yours. He wants your absolute devotion, and if you bring along any rivals, he will doggedly expose them for what they are. I acutely know this is true, for I've had rivals step between him and me. And I've tried to hold on to them while also holding on to God. But he would have none of it: I had to let go of my competing loves before I could receive all the love God wanted to give me.

One of these rivals was music. As I've mentioned, while I now teach and write, for about fourteen years I was a professional musician. In fact, I was a worshiper of music. I would not have said so then; if observers had put my dedication to music in these terms, I'd have told them they were out of their minds. "Of *course* music isn't my *god*," I would have said. "It's my life, my reason for being. That's true. My life is absorbed with music, but that's so I'll be the best musician I can possibly be." I proudly told people that I ate, slept, and drank music, and I wasn't exaggerating. From morning practice sessions (beginning sometimes as early as 3:00) to late-night band jobs, music and my passion to excel consumed my every waking moment. Music even dominated my dreams. Nothing else in life mattered as much as music did.

During the last half of this career, I performed as a converted Christian. I counted Jesus as my Savior, but he was not the only one I served: My allegiance was divided between him and my art. I didn't realize it then, but, it was true nonetheless. I had two masters, and one of them would have to go. "No one can serve two masters," Jesus said. "Either he will hate the one and love the other, or he will be devoted to the one and despise the other" (Matt. 6:24). Over time, the god eventually dethroned was music. My master-loves were reduced to One.

Strangely enough, I didn't languish in or agonize over the loss of my lesser god. By the time he died, I was consumed by another—the One who made music, the One who lifts all professions to plateaus they could never reach by acting as substitutes. The one true God had become my highest passion.

Music slowly came back to life, but this time not as my god. It returned more fully alive than before; however, this time it was *serving instead of subverting* the Lord. And, this time I understood the difference. Time spent alone with God helped me see that music was a rival love that had to take a lesser place in my life.

THE SOUNDS OF *SILENCE*

Along with solitude, we need *silence* to obtain stillness. In silence, more than in any other condition, we can sense Love's presence. Silence is . . .

not an absence but a presence; not emptiness but repletion. Silence is something more than just a pause; it is that enchanted place where space is cleared and time is stayed and the horizon itself expands. In silence, we often say, we can hear ourselves think. . . . In silence, we might better say, we can hear someone else think.

Or simply breathe. For silence is responsiveness, and in silence we can listen to something behind the clamor of the world. "A man who loves God, necessarily loves silence," wrote Thomas Merton. . . .

So it is that we might almost say silence is the tribute we pay to holiness; we slip off words when we enter a sacred space, just as we slip off shoes. A "moment of silence" is the highest honor we can pay someone; it is the point at which the mind stops and something else takes over (words run out when feelings rush in). A "vow of silence" is for holy men the highest devotional act. We hold our breath, we hold our words; we suspend our chattering selves and let ourselves "fall silent," and fall into the highest place of all. . . .

We babble with strangers; with intimates we can be silent. . . .

In love, we are speechless; in awe, we say, words fail us.[3]

There is no greater awe than being in God's presence: "Be still, and know that I am God." To this could rightly be added, "Be silent, for I, your God, am with you." There, in that stillness, in that quiet place, no matter how loudly the world's voices shout that love will shatter on the rocks of evil, we can hear Love say, "I will be exalted among the nations, I will be exalted in the earth" (Ps. 46:10). It is he who is "our refuge and strength, an ever-present help in trouble. Therefore we will not fear" (vv. 1–2).

It was only after the roar and destructive power of the wind, the earthquake, and the fire that God spoke to Elijah in a whisper, comforting his despairing servant with the knowledge that he was in control and that Elijah was not alone.[4] God came to his prophet, not out of the overwhelming sounds of power but in the soothing stillness of intimacy.

While he can come to us in any way he chooses, the record shows that God most often waits for us in the silent spaces of our lives. In Elijah's case, God created the space needed for the prophet to hear him. Through the love habit of silence, we can create the space in which we better hear from and simply rest with our Lover in gentle stillness.

The love habit of silence can involve getting away from the manmade noises that permeate our lives so that all we hear are the calming sounds of nature. However, silence is also about controlling our tongues—indeed, *stilling* our tongues—before our Lover, as Scripture directs: "Be silent before the Sovereign LORD" (Zeph. 1:7). The "LORD is in his holy temple; let all the earth be silent before him" (Hab. 2:20). "The LORD is good to those whose hope is in him, to the one who seeks him; it is good to wait quietly for the salvation of the LORD. . . . Let him sit alone in silence" (Lam. 3:25–26, 28).

Coming before God in quietness helps us to achieve stillness and to recognize anew that we are his beloved. Brennan Manning tells the story of a busy executive who went to a spiritual hermit and "complained about his frustration in prayer, his flawed virtue, and his failed relationships." The hermit listened to the executive, then fetched "a basin and a pitcher of water."

> "Now watch the water as I pour it into the basin," he said. The water splashed on the bottom and against the sides of the container. It was agitated and turbulent. At first the stirred-up water swirled around the inside of the basin; then it gradually began to settle, until finally the small fast ripples evolved into larger swells that oscillated back and forth. Eventually, the surface became so smooth that the visitor could see his face reflected in the placid water. "That is the way it is when you live constantly in the midst of others," said the hermit. "You do not see yourself as you really are because of all the confusion and disturbance. You fail to recognize the divine presence in your life and the consciousness of your belovedness slowly fades."[5]

Jesus knew the value of silence. During a time when he and his disciples faced so many demands that they couldn't even take a food break, Jesus told them, " 'Come with me by yourselves to a quiet place and get some rest.' So they went away by themselves in a boat to a solitary place" (Mark 6:31–32). Notice that Jesus saw the intricate connectedness between quiet, solitude, and rest: When he regularly went away to pray in solitude, he was seeking rest in silence as well. He not only used words to speak to his Father, he also rested quietly in the Father's presence. "Let him sit alone in silence" (Lam. 3:28), Jeremiah wrote centuries earlier, and Jesus did.

Imagine the Word of God incarnate sitting alone in God the Father's presence: at times praying, at other times remaining silent, controlling his tongue as he bends his ear to hear. Just as earthly fathers and sons do not have to dialogue to know they love each other, so it was between the heavenly Father and his only Son. *Being* together was enough. The Son knew he could trust his Father to speak when the time was right, so he waited patiently, relishing the intimacy of their love bond and the rest that silence fostered. *This is what trusting God brings.*

Silence before him shows we can trust being alone with him, trust him to understand what we do not say, and trust him to reveal himself to us in his way and in his time. Silence is "the ultimate province of trust"[6] between lovers. There the turbulence of life grows still, the agitated waters of demands and disappointments cease splashing about in our souls.

Loved ones who fidget during times of silence and persistently ask if something is wrong—when nothing really is—are insecure. They do not trust themselves or their lovers. They do not even trust love itself. For them, words are all-defining and harbors of safety; as long as words are flowing, these souls believe they can stave off loneliness. They see words as company, as love-giving, even as life-saving.

The Son of God knew better and rebuked the religious leaders of his day: "You diligently study the Scriptures because you think that by them you possess eternal life. These are the Scriptures that testify about me, yet you refuse to come to me to have life" (John 5:39–40). *The words themselves* cannot impart everlasting life, no matter how much they're studied. The highest life and greatest love and most intimate fellowship come from *God himself,* and his words reveal to us where these heavenly goods are found—in just one place, or, more accurately, in just one person: Jesus Christ, the incarnate Son of God. Look to him and you will find life and all its blessings. Turn away from him and you will find death and its attendant curses. *Christ* is the one and only way.

This is not to say, of course, that words lack power. Indeed, God spoke the universe into being; there is no power greater than that which creates something from nothing.[7] Still, notice *who* uttered the creative word: The words themselves take on the power and authority of *the one who speaks them.* A stranger who sings our praises may bring a smile to our face and a polite thank-you from our mouth. But when those same words come from someone we cherish, in whom our trust and honor reside—that's when we sit up and listen and feel humbled and deeply appreciative. Words matter, but the source of the words matters far more.

Our fallen world seems not to understand this. The other day while browsing the shelves of a large local store, I came across a host of books that, even in their titles, reveal how much intrinsic stock we put in words. Here are some that I found: *Word Power, Choose the Right Word, Verbal Advantage, How to Say It, Up Words for Down Days, 30 Days to a More Powerful Vocabulary, The 2,548 Best Things Anybody Ever Said.* I even came across one called *Depraved and Insulting English,* a primer for those who would like to learn how to disgust and belittle others.

In contrast, *agapē* informs us that who we are is revealed by what we say and don't say. Proverbs is filled with sayings wrapped around this insight.

> Wisdom is found on the lips of the discerning. (10:13)
> When words are many, sin is not absent, but he who holds his tongue is wise. (10:19).
> Reckless words pierce like a sword, but the tongue of the wise brings healing. (12:18)
> The heart of the righteous weighs its answers, but the mouth of the wicked gushes evil. (15:28)

Jesus reiterates what Proverbs teaches:

> Out of the overflow of the heart the mouth speaks. The good man brings good things out of the good stored up in him, and the evil man brings evil things out of the evil stored up in him. . . . By your words you will be acquitted, and by your words you will be condemned. (Matt. 12:34–35, 37)

The discipline of silence teaches us to be "quick to listen" and "slow to speak" (James 1:19). It helps us identify the time to talk and the "time to be silent" (Eccl. 3:7). It trains us to "keep a tight rein" on our tongues (James 1:26), moving us ever closer to being the person who is "never at fault in what he says," showing through his tongue control that he can "keep his whole body in check" (3:2).

The love habit of silence also reminds us that we are creatures, not the Creator. As Solomon wisely cautioned,

> Guard your steps when you go to the house of God. Go near to listen rather than to offer the sacrifice of fools, who do not know that they do wrong. Do not be quick with your mouth, do not be hasty in your heart to utter anything before God. God is in heaven and you are on earth, so let your words be few. (Eccl. 5:1–2)

Our love relationship with God is not between equals: *He* is infinitely great and holy. The difference between him and us is immeasurably greater than the difference between us and amoebas, for the first difference is one of infinity, while the second is merely finite. Therefore the *wise* person comes before the unlimited God in humble silence, quick to hear and slow to speak.

Also, in silence, we soon realize that whatever good we are or have ultimately has come from *Agapē* himself. Consequently, we owe him everything; he owes us nothing, yet he offers us the miraculous and gracious opportunity to "participate in the divine nature and escape the corruption in the world caused by evil desires" (2 Peter 1:4). We do not deserve such love, yet *Agapē* lavishes himself upon us.

I have learned these truths and more about the love habit of silence. As a teacher and writer, I work with words day in and day out. I read them and think them. I write them and meditate on them. I teach using them, and I am taught by them. I pray with them, and I often receive answers through them. I am even saved by the Word of all words—the One whom all words mirror and on whom all meaning depends. I see words, hear words, and touch words. Words guard me and haunt me, comfort me and scare me. They excite and sadden, inspire and deflate, empower and destroy. *Yet I've learned how powerful the absence of words can be.* In silence, I hear what whispers to me, what would normally elude me in the noise of the day. I've found that silence quiets me, and there I sense that I am beloved—beloved of God. Wrapped in his arms, I slip into the safety and peace only he can provide. There I find meaning and significance that runs deeper than words can adequately convey. His kisses come to me as all kisses do—in silence. His voice more clearly reaches me when my lips are closed and my ears are open. Love attends me most intimately in that place of quiet solitude. For these reasons and so many others, I have learned to love silence even more than I love words.

THE POWER OF PRACTICE

Since stillness requires silence and solitude, how do you find time to practice them in the daily hustle and bustle? After all, knowing what is best to do and desiring to do it are easier than actually making it part of your life. So how can you begin to incorporate silence and solitude? Here are some steps that I know are effective; I and many other Christians use them with success.

Snatching Stillness

One of the easiest ways to start is becoming alert to small opportunities to secure moments of solitude and silence. For example, when alone in your car, turn off the radio and cell phone. Enjoy the quiet freedom from being on call.

If you go for a walk, leave behind the iPod or Discman so you can take in your surroundings and be alone with God and your thoughts.

If you usually take a lunch break with co-workers, occasionally go to lunch by yourself. Maybe take food with you and drive to a park, or go to a restaurant where no one will likely know you.

When you find yourself alone at home, don't watch television or turn on the stereo or always do those chores clamoring for your attention. Take some time out for renewal. Be still. Rest. Listen for God and the natural sounds that whisper his reality.

Throughout each day, opportunities will arise for you to enter into at least brief periods of solitude and silence. Don't let them pass you by. Take advantage of them. These snatched times can bring stillness into the noise and demands of your days.

Cultivating Quiet Places

Snatching stillness will naturally lead you to want longer times of resting in God's arms; this will require finding one or more places that will provide you with such times. Many churches have rooms set aside for solitude and silence. Christians who live near the countryside, mountains, desert, or remote beaches have numerous options. If you live in a large metropolitan area or a crowded suburban development, then city parks, river walkways, and the like can provide places of relative quiet with few distractions.

One of my regular activities is to frequent coffeehouses or fast-food restaurants that have low-traffic, window-adjacent tables. I can sit there for a couple of hours and read, study, journal, pray, and simply be alone and quiet before God. I'm rarely interrupted, and my ability to concentrate has become so trained that I can almost always block out other customers and their conversations with ease.

Remember, you don't have to be physically alone to experience solitude or silence. If you doubt this, recall a time when you've been with other people and found your thoughts and emotions drifting elsewhere. You were alone inwardly; you were not with others in your mind and heart; within yourself you were in the company of one. The same experience can be achieved through the spiritual disciplines of solitude and silence: Without trying to find a lonely place to be by yourself, you can be in a busy public place and still be alone within. It may not be a restaurant or a coffeehouse. It could be a subway, airport, bus, park, zoo, or a host of other places. Try out different spots. Discover what kind of place you need to secure that stillness before God, then go to it when you can.

If you're in a life season where you simply cannot get away much (if at all), take a lesson from Susanna Wesley, the mother of John and Charles.

> [Susanna] had a very large family and for many years times of phys-
> ical isolation were scarce. It is well known that when she needed silence
> and solitude she would bring her apron up over her head and read her
> Bible and pray underneath it. Obviously that did not block out all noise,
> but it was a sign to her children that for those minutes she was not to
> be bothered and the older ones were to care for the younger.[8]

I too raised a large family—five children, to be exact. While they were growing up, I struggled over how to get alone-time with God. What I finally settled on was rising earlier in the morning than anyone else, or staying up later than my wife and children. Then I would sit at the kitchen table and enjoy quiet time with the Lord. When I was too tired for either of these options, I would steal away to my bedroom when everyone else was caught up in a program or movie. When that didn't work, I'd leave the house and go for neighborhood walks.

For a while I wrestled with guilt, thinking that when my children and wife were around I should be with them all the time. I eventually realized, however, that my energy level was often spent, and I felt out of touch with God. In that condition, I was of little use to my family; to give love, I had to receive love from the One who *is* love, which required spending quality and quantity time with him. So I worked through my false guilt and created new habits that greatly benefited me and my family; my times with God enhanced beyond measure the time I then gave to them. They got more of me—and a much better me—because I stopped neglecting my love relationship with the Lord.

You *can* find a place and time to be with God regularly, regardless of your situation. You may need to be creative and determined to overcome a number of obstacles, but the reward for your effort will pay off in dividends that will likely exceed your expectations.

Spiritual Retreats

I'm actually tempted to call these spiritual "treats" rather than retreats. Extended times of solitude and silence may be a one-day affair, or they could go for several days, even a week or more. They involve finding a place to be quiet and alone, or perhaps with other believers who are also remaining silent and respecting your need to still your tongue and be left alone. Country cottages, mountain cabins, monasteries, convents, retreat centers, beach houses, campsites, and out-of-the-way conference settings are ideal for an extended spiritual getaway. Other locations can work too: for example, a hotel room, the home of a family leaving for a vacation or mission trip, a vacant apartment or houseboat or trailer home available for temporary use.

Find somewhere that's away from your normal surroundings and from anyone close to you. Take your Bible and journal and perhaps a book or two covering any aspect of your relationship with God that needs deepening. Use this extended time of solitude to linger in his presence. Pray. Study. Meditate. Fast. Enter into long periods of silence. Seek God's will. Listen for his voice. Simply enjoy being his beloved. Let him refresh you.

When you emerge from such times, you'll find yourself renewed and ready again to give. "It is in deep solitude and silence," said Thomas Merton, "that I find the gentleness with which I can truly love my brother and my sister."[9] Give yourself this grace. Others will thank you for it.

11. Confession and Forgiveness:
Love's healing power

I once was a condemned man.

My crimes had brought me the death penalty. I was sitting on death row. I had created my own prison and earned my own sentence; I was a dead man walking, playing, working, sleeping, committing more and more offenses, doing what I wanted when I wanted. In the process, I was building my dungeon higher and stronger and adding to the already decisive evidence of my guilt.

At the time, though, I failed to understand my crimes' significance. I knew the sentence—at least what my parents, ministers, and Sunday school teachers had said about it. I knew they believed what God said in the Bible: "All have sinned" (Rom. 3:23), "sin is lawlessness" (1 John 3:4), and the "wages of sin is death" (Rom. 6:23). As far as the Judge was concerned, I was guilty before his bar of justice; my transgressions were so great that I was condemned.

But how could this be true? I had neither murdered anyone nor betrayed my country, nor done anything that deserved such a harsh sentence. Granted, I'd occasionally lied and lusted, stolen a few inexpensive items, betrayed my parents' trust, gotten in a few fistfights, said mean things, and pulled some dangerous and destructive pranks. But none of these wrongs deserved *death*. Besides, most were during my youth, when ignorant foolishness held more sway. I could accept justice being served with a slap on the wrist, a good lecture, perhaps even brief jail time, fines, or community service. But *death?*

Then I was told that the sentence came down from on high, not simply because of my bad deeds but also because of my family association. Because I was born human, I was a member of Adam's race; when Adam and Eve disobeyed God, they condemned themselves and every person who would follow, so Paul said, "Through one transgression there resulted condemnation to all men" (Rom. 5:18 NASB). God held me responsible not only for my sins but also for the sins of Adam, the first human. How unfair! How unjust! How could I be rightly sent to *my* death for *Adam's* crimes? And what did he do that was so bad anyway? The whole scenario seemed absurd.

Therefore, I rebelled against the ludicrous charge. If God was determined to judge me with severity and unfairness, then I would live as if he didn't exist. I would choose to ignore him and all who followed him. He could keep his crazy moral standard and judge away, but I would have none of it. I would live as I pleased, creating and living by my own standard. And so I lived—or so I thought.

In reality, every moral standard I set for myself I violated, and usually in short order. After every major offense (I ignored the many minor infractions), I tried modifying each standard, making it easier to keep, which only set me up for new failures. I also tried rationalizing away my wrongs so I could free myself from my own incrimination, but that only deepened my sense of helplessness and hopelessness. Out of sheer desperation I even tried to abandon all moral measure; this only highlighted my hypocrisy, for each time I heard myself condemn the actions of others, the pronouncement betrayed that I still held fast to certain convictions that stood in judgment over me. I could no more abandon morality than I could abandon reason—both were inextricably bound up in my humanity.

There was no escaping this prison of self-condemnation, and with each wrong thought or deed, my walls grew higher and thicker as my guilt drove me deeper into despair. The Judge was right: my sin was great and grave. I was a career criminal. I had long passed "three strikes and you're out." My failures were sure to keep multiplying, and I was unable to stop the spree. I deserved to die—in fact, my living was already a kind of death.

What could I do? Was there no hope? Could I return to the courtroom and throw myself on the mercy of the Judge? Would he remit my sentence and give me another chance? Could he give me the opportunity to rise above my criminal nature and live a better life?

I'm elated to report that the Judge did not wait for me to come to my senses and seek a rehearing; he had already meted out justice for my offenses and for every other member of the human family. God promised Adam and Eve that there would be a fight for their deliverance from sin and that he would win it through their very offspring.[1] He covered their guilt with the skin of animals, slain for their sakes.[2] Countless generations passed, waiting for the Promised One, all the while trusting that God would deliver them as he had so many others acquitted by faith.[3]

Finally, when the time in human history was right, God sent a second Adam.[4] This Adam was conceived in a young virgin and born a carpenter's son. He grew, worked, worshiped, learned, taught, preached, and delivered people from their lives of crime. Then he also was criminally charged, tried, condemned, and executed, even though he was unimpeachably innocent. Dead and buried, the Judge vindicated him, raising him bodily from the grave to his own right hand. Jesus of Nazareth, the foretold offspring of Adam, had come, and he lives on, having paid once and forever the high price for every offense. By choice he poured out the price, his own shed blood; he freely stood in our place, bore our sin, and let justice roll down on his head instead of ours.[5] Through him, we can stand before God completely forgiven. In addition, he is laboring within believers to make us sin-free zones—fully blameless, morally pure, undeniably Christlike in every way a human can be. And he will not stop until this work is done.

What motivated such a preposterous sacrifice for criminals? The Lawgiver himself had justly condemned us. The evidence was indisputable; the sentence was right; by every measure of justice, God would have been fully justified to execute us all, wiping us from the face of his earth with one sweep of his hand. Why did he not give us our deserved punishment? *Agapē*. The love that "is not easily angered," that "keeps no record of wrongs." The love that "always protects, always trusts, always hopes, always perseveres" (1 Cor. 13:5, 7). Love is the reason that the Judge gave us the opportunity for life instead of certain death: "God so loved the world that he gave his one and only Son . . . to save the world through him" (John 3:16–17). *Agapē*, our salvation and restoration, is at the heart of the love habits of *confession* and *forgiveness*.

No love relationship can long survive without confession and forgiveness. Whether intentionally or not, we often hurt one another, including those we hold most dear, through unkindness, insensitivity, neglect, harshness, hypocrisy, unfaithfulness, self-absorption, and a host of other sins. Whatever motivates us, and regardless of how we rationalize our actions, we end up wounding those we love. While our behavior can sometimes be misunderstood, our loved ones read us all too well, all too often.

They also sometimes hurt us. In fact, we pass along the pain to one another: We hurt our loved ones, they hurt us; we strike back with more hurt, they return a higher measure of hurt to us . . . and so goes the vicious cycle of pain.

Our only hope of breaking this malevolent spiral is the pervasive expression of *agapē* through the humble acts of confession and forgiveness. Each of us must admit the role we play in hurt's destructive downturn, and for each of us to receive and experience reconciliation, we must forgive our offenders and be forgiven by those we've offended. Without confession and forgiveness, relationships become encrusted with bitterness and hate, or, even worse, with indifference. In such parched ground, love withers and dies. Sin wounds— always. If those wounds are left to fester, sin ends in death—always.

The word *death* connotes the physical demise of a living thing. Funerals, wakes, caskets, eulogies, hearses, gravesites, and phrases such as "dead on arrival" and "rest in peace" come to our mind when "death" is uttered. In Scripture, however, *death* has a broader meaning: Death is the separation that tears asunder something designed to stay together.[6] For example, marriages are intended to be for the life of the partners, but divorce, desertion, or the death of one or both dissolves the marital bond.[7] Humans were created to live forever as soul/body unities, but the separation of the soul from the body at physical death destroys this union.[8]

Friendships are bonds of trust built on commonalities, but betrayal, hatred, and indifference can break these bonds and even turn friends into enemies.[9] In the broader realm of relationships, we can be separated from one another through abuse, adultery, deception, greed, lust, pride, envy, blame, and many other divisive weapons that can be wielded against others or turned against ourselves. If the resulting wounds are severe enough, separation occurs and death results.

The worst disunity of all is that which occurs between God and humans. If this persists to the moment of physical death, the disunity becomes permanent—the deceased person lives in everlasting separation from her Creator and Lover, forever "shut out from the presence of the Lord and from the majesty of his power" (2 Thess. 1:9). Conversely, for those who are truly in Christ, nothing "will be able to separate us from the love of God that is in Christ Jesus our Lord" (Rom. 8:39). In him are love and life incorruptible and immortal; death has no residence in Jesus.

In the biblical view, then, life is union and death is separation. Any created unity can be disunited, and it is this disuniting that brings death. Love and faith can overcome disunity, bring about reconciliation, and thereby give life; critical to this taking place are confession and forgiveness. Apart from these love habits, reunification is impossible. For us, only confession and forgiveness have any hope of healing relational wounds, especially those that have become dire or even terminal. These acts are so powerful that they can even resurrect dead relationships—if, that is, all parties involved want the miracle to happen and are willing to do their part to bring it about. Separation can be overcome—this is the promise of confession and forgiveness.

THE DARK SIDE

Confession and forgiveness are the loving lights that shine on the dark side of human existence while also reflecting what remains good. To grasp this, we must understand some basic facts about our condition.

The popular sentiment that "to err is human" is false, if by *err* one means "sin." Sin is an alien force, an invader, a parasite; God did not create it, and he did not make it part of our nature. When he created the first human beings, he declared them "very good" (Gen. 1:31)—*not* a mixed bag of good and evil. Sin entered human history later, through disobedience: Our first parents embraced sin when they chose to believe Satan over God, a creature over the Creator. Adam and Eve chose the illusion of independence over the reality of utter dependence, and in the process they chose against themselves.

God had warned them that disobedience would bring death. And it did—immediately. They suffered the death of *innocence* and experienced guilt and shame, which they tried to conceal with "fig leaves" (3:7). Their *intimacy* with God was shattered too, for when they heard him, "they hid from the LORD God among the trees of the garden" (v. 8). Their *joy* before God was likewise lost and replaced with fear; said Adam, "I was afraid because I was naked; so I hid" (v. 10). Their *marital harmony* and *sense of moral responsibility* also underwent corruption; the man blamed the woman for enticing him to eat from the forbidden tree, and he blamed God for giving her to him in the first place (v. 12); the woman, in turn, blamed the serpent for deceiving her (v. 13). And from that moment on their *days on earth* were numbered. Eventually the slow demise of their bodies would overtake them, and physical death would ensue.

Sin brought division—division between us and God, between you and me, between us and nature, even division within our souls and between our souls and bodies. Sin reigns in human experience, bringing death into every aspect of our lives. As a result of original sin and the sin we commit on our own, our daily living is marked by death.

That's the dark side of human existence. But it's not the only side.

Since sin is not a natural part of who we are, we will find restoration and completion by banishing the invader from our lives. Sin is the destroyer, eating away at our humanness and defacing the divine image. Sin is not us; we are sinners, yes, but sin is *un*human, *un*natural. *As created by God, we are good*. Paul said that "everything God created is good" (1 Tim. 4:4), not that everything *was* good but *now* is not—everything, at this moment, even after the Fall, is still good. Our humanness, as humanness, is good.

Sin, however, has tainted our humanness. If sin were blue, we would find ourselves tinged with blue inside and out. Sin is like a disease, inherited and fatal. Sin lessens and corrupts; sin eats away at our created goodness, distorting and demeaning what we are while barring us from the fullness that could be ours in every dimension of our lives. Peter Kreeft writes,

> [We are] ontologically good. God didn't make junk, and we still bear his image, however defaced. . . . But though ontologically we are very good, morally we are not. We are sinners. Our world is a battlefield strewn with broken treaties, broken families, broken promises, broken lives, and broken hearts. We are good stuff gone bad, a defaced masterpiece, a rebellious child. "We are not merely imperfect creatures who need to grow, we are rebels who need to lay down our arms" (C. S. Lewis).[10]

Sin, then, is an obscene distortion that deserves only to be shattered. By smashing it to pieces, we find wholeness, and wholeness is found not in we who are broken and sinful but in him, the Perfect One, broken for us. Christ "is the atoning sacrifice for our sins, and not only for ours but also for the sins of the whole world" (1 John 2:2). Through Jesus, we can have "forgiveness of sins" (Acts 13:38). He is the cure for our ills, the balm for our wounds. He is the reconciliation of our separation from God, from each other, from ourselves, and even from the rest of the natural order. He is the One who guarantees life after death and abundant life through this earthly journey marked by death. In him, our torn lives can be mended; even better, they can be made new.[11]

How? By a saving faith in Christ—a faith joined to genuine *confession* on the basis of what he has done for us. This is what brings our *forgiveness* from God, which in turn brings about our reconciliation to God and lays the foundation for our transformation in God.

THE CONFESSING LIFE

Confession is humbly acknowledging the truth about ourselves—telling it like it is. Confession is being honest with ourselves, with others, and with God. When we're truthful, we admit that we are creatures (not the Creator), and rebellious creatures at that. We have taken up arms against the Lord, striving to center our lives on ourselves rather than accept the reality of God as the Center of all life. Because of this, our confession must begin with the acknowledgment that God is God and we are not. That he is all-good and we are not. That we are lost without him and that he has provided for our rescue through the sacrifice of his Son. That death can be overcome only through the life that comes from Jesus.

Confessing Christ

Paul articulates these truths in his many letters, making clear that our confession begins with the gospel, the good news about Christ.

Contrary to popular opinion, the gospel is not about *how* we are saved—it's a set of historical *facts* about who Jesus is and what he has done for us. These facts are that Jesus is the eternal Son of God, "who as to his human nature was a descendant of David, and who through the Spirit of holiness was declared with power to be the Son of God by his resurrection from the dead: Jesus Christ our Lord" (Rom. 1:3–4); that "when the time had fully come, God sent his Son, born of a woman, born under law, to redeem those under law, that we might receive the full rights of sons" (Gal. 4:4–5).

> For what I received I passed on to you as of first importance: that Christ died for our sins according to the Scriptures, that he was buried, that he was raised on the third day according to the Scriptures, and that he appeared to Peter, and then to the Twelve. After that, he appeared to

more than five hundred of the brothers at the same time, most of whom are still living, though some have fallen asleep. Then he appeared to James, then to all the apostles, and last of all he appeared to me [Paul]. (1 Cor. 15:3–8)

The gospel is about Jesus from beginning to end—who he is and what he has done. It's about the One who came from heaven to earth; who took on a human nature, yet lived without sin; who obeyed the Father fully; who suffered in our place, taking upon himself the punishment we deserved; who died and was buried; who rose bodily from the dead, vindicated by God; who appeared alive to many human witnesses; who was and is and forever will be the promised Messiah, the Conqueror of sin and the devil, the embodied Messenger and Message of the love God is and pours out for all of us. That Jesus is the one true God is the gospel all must believe to be reconciled to God, for "it is the power of God for the salvation of everyone who believes" (Rom. 1:16). These facts have awesome power because they are the truth about him who is Truth.[12]

Thus, when we confess that the Jesus we believe in is the same Jesus that Paul and the other New Testament writers acknowledge and describe, we are making the true confession of the Christian faith. We are publicly proclaiming the One to whom we entrust our lives, with whom we have chosen to align ourselves: "In his confession a man indicates that he stands by the fact of Christ and submits his life to it."[13]

Confessing Sin

Along with confessing the truth about Christ, we must confess the truth about ourselves, which is that we have a serious problem we cannot fix. We are at odds with God. We have freely chosen to go our way rather than his. Even our very human nature is bent out of shape. We are sinful from conception: "Surely I was sinful at birth, sinful from the time my mother conceived me," lamented David (Ps. 51:5). All that we are, from top to bottom and from inside out, is corrupted. Nothing about us is as it should be: We do not think, feel, act, or react as we were created to. Nothing in creation does, except for the angels who refused to rebel against their Creator. Sin has wounded us all, and our acts of wrongdoing only make the damage more severe.

Since our rebellion is against God, when we sin, it is he—and he alone—who we sin against. After David committed adultery with Bathsheba and had her husband, Uriah, abandoned on the battlefield so he would die, Nathan the prophet confronted him, which brought David to his knees. He confessed,

"I have sinned against the LORD" (2 Sam. 12:13); he did not say, "I sinned against God and against Bathsheba and Uriah." Later when he wrote about this terrible time in his life, David said to the Lord, "Against you, you only, have I sinned and done what is evil in your sight" (Ps. 51:4).

In the past, I objected to taking David's statement in a straightforward way. After all, I reasoned, he committed adultery with Bathsheba and ensured that Uriah would be killed—certainly he sinned against them too. But I came to see that while David wronged these two people, his rebellion was not against them but against God. David struck Bathsheba and Uriah *because* he shook his fist at heaven; if he had not morally warred against *God,* he would not have hurt them. Lust, theft, deception, murder, envy, pride, arrogance, abuse of power—these evils and likely others were wrapped up in David's actions. All were committed against the Lord, for all violated his moral law. And, each sin was carried out against God in effigy, since Bathsheba and Uriah were divine image-bearers. Even worse, David—as God's anointed king *and* image-bearer—chose evil over good, thereby violating the Sovereign who had handpicked him to rule as his representative. In all of these ways, David "sinned against the LORD."

David's understanding of his sin exhibits a timeless truth about God and morality: *the Lord* (not people) is the standard for right and wrong; when we choose evil rather than good, we turn away from the standard and thereby sin. In the process, we and other people do get hurt, sometimes even suffering loss of life; nevertheless, it is against God alone that we sin.

Being held accountable to a standard, and to that which sets the standard, permeates the American judicial system. Suppose you burglarized a home and killed the owner in the process. After your arrest, you would appear before a judge to hear the charges against you. When they were read, you'd find that they're being brought by a much larger entity than the victim's family, whose names would not even be mentioned: the people of your state would be issuing the charges. Of course you'd know you stole from a particular family and killed one of its members—the state would know too. However, the state holds you accountable for violating the laws of the state; the citizens hold you responsible for violating the standards acknowledged by their elected representatives.

Likewise, when we defy God's commands, our lawbreaking will have harmed others, as well as ourselves, but we are held accountable to *him;* we violated the standard that flows from *his* perfect nature and, thus, sinned against *him*. Because he is the standard of right and wrong, he alone can rightfully and fairly judge our case. This he has done already: His verdict on us all is "guilty as charged."

Since we have broken God's laws, only he can forgive us. The first-century Jewish teachers knew this was true—that's why they reacted so severely when they heard that Jesus was forgiving sins. As far as they were concerned, he was blaspheming, for "who can forgive sins but God alone?" (Luke 5:21). But by forgiving the sins of a lame man, then healing him of his physical disability, Jesus showed them that he had the divine "authority on earth to forgive sins" (v. 24), which the Father confirmed through the miracle-working power of the Spirit. In other words, the teachers were technically right about forgiveness; what they did not understand was that Jesus was the Father's representative, carrying out his work, including the work of forgiveness.

When we wrong God, he must forgive us; otherwise we remain mired in our sin, bearing the righteous judgment that we are guilty. David knew this. After he confessed his sin against God, Nathan told him, "The LORD has taken away your sin" (2 Sam. 12:13). David understood that Nathan could not pardon him—only God could, and graciously did, through Nathan, his representative.

What is more, when we sin, we not only break the law of God, we also break our love bond with God. Death, which sin brings,

> involves breaking a relationship, all relationships. Death is not only a private biological event but the breaking of communion, of all communions. . . . The primary meaning of sin is not breaking divine law but breaking divine love, divine fidelity, divine relationship. Lawbreaking is a secondary, derived meaning.[14]

Therefore, when we confess our sin, we are, in effect, admitting to God that we are the reason for the estrangement between us; the bond of love has been broken, and we are to blame.

The love habit comes down to this: when we sin, our responsibility is to confess that we have wronged God, that we have broken the relationship, that we have violated his laws of love and goodness. And he *will* pardon our sin, as the beloved disciple reassured:

> If we confess our sins, he is faithful and just and will forgive us . . . and purify us. . . . My dear children, I write this to you so that you will

not sin. But if anybody does sin, we have one who speaks to the Father in our defense—Jesus Christ, the Righteous One. (1 John 1:9, 2:1)

When we confess our sin, our heavenly Defense Attorney goes to work pleading our case. With him fighting for us, who can stand against us? The Father always hears his Son, and the Son always speaks and does his Father's will. Talk about having the Judge's ear!

This reality is incomprehensibly wonderful, yet we should never have the impression that confession is a get-out-of-jail-free card. God is eager to forgive, but he does not save us from sin so we can go on sinning with impunity. The Holy Spirit is laboring to conform us to the image of our sinless Savior, and confession is one of the love habits we cultivate to cooperate with his work of purifying our lives. Once again, in his first epistle, John exhorts us to live in the light of our new life in Christ:

> This is the message we have heard from him and declare to you: God is light; in him there is no darkness at all. If we claim to have fellowship with him yet walk in the darkness, we lie and do not live by the truth. But if we walk in the light, as he is in the light, we have fellowship with one another, and the blood of Jesus, his Son, purifies us from all sin. (1:5–7)

John is emphatic: Sin is not to characterize the lives of believers. If we call ourselves Christians and keep living as if we are not—that is, if impurity reigns over our lives rather than righteousness and love—then we are not truly Christ-followers. Holiness and charity accompany saving faith;[15] the notion that a sin-riddled, loveless faith obtains everlasting life is biblically inconceivable. We also cannot earn our salvation, for we cannot de-corrupt ourselves.

When we trust Christ for salvation, we receive the Spirit, who begins repairing the damage sin has caused. This cannot go on without showing through our lives. Through the Spirit's transforming work, we will become more loving, honest, and vulnerable. We will reach beyond ourselves more as we think of serving our own interests less. We will not find the old sinful habits pleasurable but increasingly see them as they are—ugly, alienating, death-ridden. We will want more of God, and we will long for Christian companionship. We will want what's genuinely good and will regularly choose it as we more readily turn away from what seeks to remove goodness and wholeness from life. If we show no signs that the Spirit is at work purifying us, then he is not changing us but chastening us—not saving us from sin's power but convicting us of sin's penalty. True believers sin, but not habitually, as John plainly writes:

> In him [Christ] is no sin. No one who lives in him keeps on sinning. No one who continues to sin has either seen him or known him. Dear children, do not let anyone lead you astray. He who does what is right is righteous, just as he [Jesus] is righteous. He who does what is sinful is of the devil, because the devil has been sinning from the beginning. The reason the Son of God appeared was to destroy the devil's work. No one who is born of God will continue to sin, because God's seed remains in him; he cannot go on sinning, because he has been born of God. (1 John 3:6–9)

John gives three reasons why genuine Christians do not habitually sin.

First, they are in Christ; since he is sinless, they cannot also live in sin.

Second, Christ has defeated Satan, the father of sin. Therefore, anyone aligned with Christ is on the side of victory and does what is right; those who keep sinning show they have aligned themselves with Satan, the cosmic loser.

Third, born-again believers have the divine reemerging within them; becoming increasingly Christlike entails that they cannot go on living as if nothing is happening inside.

In short, true Christians will change for the better. More and more, goodness will mark their lives as evil is peeled away and purged. Confession plays an essential role in this purification process; when we yield to sin's enticements, confession is how we cooperate with the Spirit to beat sin back. Forgiveness is conditioned on our confession of sin—no confession, no forgiveness.

This process is *not* easy, and we *will* experience setbacks. The mere fact that confession is one of the spiritual disciplines—a love habit we must work at cultivating and maintaining—tells us that, on this side of heaven, our struggle with sin will not fully end. But God is committed to the task of making us perfect, holy and flawless through and through.

As the Spirit makes us more Christlike, sin will have less power in our lives; its corrupting influence will grow weaker and weaker as the Spirit straightens out our bent toward evil and orients us toward the Good. But he does not do his work apart from us. As he works *in* us, he works *with* us, and confession is one tool he provides to help us in our ongoing battle. Confession of sin is a means for pursuing purity.

Now let's consider what confession involves in our relationship to God. From Scripture and from subsequent reflections on its teaching, Christians have come to recognize four characteristics of confession.

(1) *We admit we have sinned.* We face the fact that we've been faithless in our love relationship with God. Self-justifications, rationalizations, excuses of all sorts and sizes are laid aside. We call our wrongdoing what it is—adultery with loves we've set against our Divine Lover.

(2) *We acknowledge our sin.* We come before God and name our sin as sin. Pointed specifics, not vague generalities, are the hallmarks of confession. "Lord, when I shouted at and berated my son this morning, I sinned against you and wounded him in the process." "Father, I know I lied in that meeting yesterday. I was trying to cover my tracks and save face, which were also acts of dishonesty."

(3) *We are sorrowful over our sin.* This should grieve us. It should lead us to abhor our sin, to regret deeply that we have offended the Lord and caused so much pain. In biblical times, people often expressed such sorrow with fasting, cries of lament, tearing their garments, or wearing sackcloth and pouring ashes over their heads. They took sin seriously. Today we may express remorse differently, but we dare not be flippant about our transgressions. When our sin puts a smile on our face, we have no sorrow.

(4) *We determine to avoid sin.* True confession creates in us a yearning for holy living. We want more of God. We want to eat and drink at his table. We want unbroken fellowship. We want our will to line up with his, his tastes to become ours, his goodness and love to permeate all we are and do.

Confession is how we learn to abandon our cravings for anything that falls short of the superabundance of Jesus Christ. Through confession, we turn away from the paltry offerings of sin and seek our satisfaction in the banquet hall of our King. Why should we, his sons and daughters, eat at the roach-infested, rundown motel at the edge of town when we can have our eternal fill of the finest delicacies in royal surroundings? We have tasted the best, and we must not settle for anything less. Confession brings us back to our Lover's home, which is where we belong.

FORGIVEN AND FORGIVING

The loving consequence of confession is *forgiveness.* When we confess Christ, thereby confessing our submission to him, and confess our sins against Christ, thereby confessing our redemptive need for him, we receive his forgiveness for our rebellion and are welcomed into his forever family.

These truths come out convincingly in what is known to us as the parable of the prodigal son, but would be better labeled the parable of the prodigal *sons*. Jesus first told this story, and I have chosen to retell it, bringing out cultural facts and word meanings that show its ongoing power and relevance.[16]

The Prodigal Sons

Two millennia ago there was a well-to-do, Middle Eastern Jewish family, a father and his two sons.

One day the younger son came to his father and demanded that he divide the inheritance between him and his older brother. Then, adding insult to injury, he pressured his father to grant him full disposition rights of his share so he could sell it.

His actions were an outrage, unthinkable and intolerable, tantamount to telling his still-healthy father that he wanted him to die. He had no legal right to make his demands, and there existed no custom to support him. Certainly fathers were allowed to divide their property between their children before death, especially when their health was badly failing; they would sometimes do this to avoid the eruption of disputes after they were gone. In such a case, though, fathers would retain disposition rights or in another way secure income from the property so they could meet their own needs for the remainder of their lifetime. Sons knew this—they would not think of violating their father's right to earn a living from the fruit of their toil. But for *this* son, whether his father lived or died or ate or starved made no difference. He wanted his inheritance and the ability to use it as he pleased—now. For all he cared, his father could sink into Sheol.

For this reprehensible act, the villagers would have expected the father to beat his son and throw him out of the house penniless, never permitting him to return. At the very least, they would have expected to see a verbal lashing and severe discipline. Indeed, it would have been within the father's rights to take similar action with his older son; after all, it was *his* duty to protest his brother's selfish offense and work to reconcile him with their father. Yet the older son just stood there, silent, as his brother insulted and deeply wounded their father. This told the father that his older son *also* wished him dead. How much this must have pained him! Imagine the depth of the spite and hatred he must have felt from both sons. How would he respond?

He startled everyone by doing as demanded: He divided his holdings between his sons and gave the younger the right to dispose of his share as he wished. The older son observed the transaction and accepted his share without even a hint of protest—he was every bit as disloyal. For his part, the father required nothing in return; his gentle treatment of his sons was in stark contrast to their coldhearted words and actions.

The younger son didn't dawdle—he went into the village and passed from buyer to buyer, selling off his inheritance for traveling currency. As word spread about this horror, his neighbors' anger intensified. He had to move quickly to escape the condemning looks and growing repulsion. Thus he bartered away within days what would have normally taken months to sell.

Then he left. His leaving was "a heartless rejection of the home in which [he] was born and nurtured and a break with the most precious tradition carefully upheld by the larger community of which he was a part."[17]

With his newfound wealth in tow, he traveled to a faraway land where Jews were few and Gentiles were plentiful. There he squandered his entire inheritance in wasteful living.

About that time a famine began ravishing the area; jobs became scarce, and money ran low. The young man became desperate and attached himself to a citizen of the land. During difficult times, the indigent frequently threw themselves upon the mercy of potential benefactors, and when a benefactor wanted to extricate himself, he would assign them tasks he believed they would refuse. This newfound savior was no exception: he told the begging Jew to go out to the fields and feed the pigs.

To Jews, pigs were unclean; no matter how destitute, the young man should have turned up his nose and walked away, but instead he accepted and became a swine herder. In fact, he was so famished that he longed to eat even the bitter berries off the shrub-like plants fed to the pigs—berries that lacked the nourishment to meet human needs. Much to his chagrin, he soon discovered that the food given him for his work was insufficient too. He could not stave off his hunger; he knew he was slowly starving.

As he considered his desperation, he finally realized he'd exhausted his resources. He would soon die if he didn't take a different course. While thinking about the home he'd left, he remarked to himself, "How many of my father's hired men have food to spare, and here I am starving to death!" (Luke 15:17).

So he concocted a plan: "I will set out and go back to my father and say to him: 'Father, I have sinned against heaven and against you. I am no longer worthy to be called your son; make me like one of your hired men'" (vv. 17–19). At least he still regarded himself as a human being and knew he was still his father's child, although he also knew that he had "lost the dignity of his sonship."[18] On the other hand, the facts and rationale for his plan showed that *he still wasn't ashamed over how he had treated his father.* His only sin, he thought, was squandering his inheritance—a sin for which he would ask forgiveness.

If his father went for the plan, the young man could save some face. He would be a hired servant—therefore a free man, not a slave—and have his own income, the means to live independently in the village. He would be able to maintain his pride and sense of self-sufficiency. With his earnings, he could also repay his father and thereby compensate for what he'd lost. Furthermore, since he would not be living in his father's house, he would not have to seek reconciliation with his brother. *His plan would allow him to work and buy his way out of the dilemma without restoring family relationships.*

The plan's worst glitch was the expected reaction of the townspeople and extended family. His relatives would likely cut him off completely, and the rest of the village would take out their pent-up hostilities on him for insulting his father, selling his inheritance, losing it to Gentiles, and humiliating himself and other Jews by herding pigs. He saw no way past this problem. The larger community would have to be faced and endured.

He set off toward home.

———

As he approached, his waiting father spotted him, and compassion welled up within him for his son. He knew the neighbors would badly treat his prodigal boy—certainly abusing him verbally and perhaps even physically—so he rushed through the village. Residents were stunned to see this nobleman in long-flowing robes running down the street. Men of such high standing *never* ran in public; they walked slowly, with pomp and dignity. Why would he humiliate himself so?

The answer was quickly apparent. In an act of incredible warmth and superlative love, he raced up to his wayward son, threw his arms around him, and kissed him repeatedly.

Others noted the scene and gazed in shock. This was the son who had despised his father, wished him dead. Yet the father embraced him as if he'd done no wrong. What other staggering, nonsensical gestures would they see?

The son began his prepared speech: "Father, I have sinned against heaven and against you. I am no longer worthy to be called your son" (v. 21).

But before he could finish, the father turned to his servants, who had finally caught up, and shouted with joy, "Quick! Bring the best robe and put it on him" (v. 22). This was his finest robe, reserved for feast days and great celebrations. By giving it to his son to wear, the father was assuring the community that he accepted his son without reservations and that they should do the same.

"Put a ring on his finger," he added (v. 22), indicating remarkable trust. Then he told his servants to put sandals on his son's feet—an irrefutable sign that they were to treat his son as a member of the family, not as a servant: He, like his father, was to be regarded as a master in the house. The overjoyed father likewise called for an all-out celebration: "Bring the fattened calf and kill it. Let's have a feast and celebrate. For this son of mine was dead and is alive again; he was lost and is found" (vv. 23–24).

So with the father, his beloved son, and their servants, the townspeople walked joyfully through the streets, spreading the news about the magnificent party that would soon take place at the nobleman's house.

The son never had a chance to finish his partial confession or carry out his plan; his father's profound outpouring of love led him to humbly accept forgiveness. *Agapē* won. The prodigal entered his father's house a cherished son, not a servant or hired hand. Freed from his past failures, he could join his father and make merry.

And a merry time it was! Devouring a fatted calf required more than a hundred ravenous appetites. Neighbors poured into the house; musicians began to play. People danced, sang, and clapped so loudly that the faraway field hands heard the commotion and came in.

The older son came too; he'd been in the fields directing the hired workers. As he approached, he noticed all the children outside, dancing, playing, singing along with the music. After being told what was going on, he went from curious to furious; he refused to go inside and join the revelry, even though custom clearly required his presence. He would be expected to mingle, to make sure everyone had enough food, to offer compliments, and to keep the servants at peak performance. But he would have none of it.

On the surface, he was "obedient, dutiful, law-abiding, hardworking.

People respected him, admired him, praised him, and likely considered him a model son." But when he witnessed the celebration his father was holding for his younger brother, he could not contain the resentful rage that had been simmering. "Suddenly, there becomes glaringly visible a resentful, proud, unkind, selfish person, one that had remained deeply hidden."[19] The father's joy became the catalyst that unmasked, for all to see, his older son's true character and loyalties.

When the great nobleman learned that his livid son was standing outside, he again humbled himself, came out, and pleaded with him in front of the children and gathering guests. But the son became hostile, choosing to embarrass his father by quarreling with him publicly.

"Look!" he indignantly blurted. "All these years I've been slaving for you and never disobeyed your orders."

Why is he referring to himself as if he were a servant or hired hand? the father wonders. *Doesn't he realize he's my very own son?*

"Yet you never gave me even a young goat so I could celebrate with my friends."

Why is he speaking so selfishly? He has the run of the house and access to all I have. Why is he acting as if he were a laborer haggling over wages?

"But when this son of yours who has squandered your property with prostitutes comes home, you kill the fattened calf for him!"

Now he publicly demeans his brother by this charge of carrying on with harlots. He's even distancing himself from our family—he calls his brother "this son of yours," and I am the father of them both. Why does he treat his own brother as if he's unrelated? And why is he treating me as if I'm no longer his father? Can't he see how much I love him? How can I help him see his brother as I do?

"My son," the father finally said, in an endearing tone of reconciliation, "you are always with me, and everything I have is yours. But we had to celebrate and be glad, because this brother of yours was dead and is alive again; he was lost and is found" (v. 32).

Once again he showed abiding love for his son, as well as the willingness to humble himself to make that love known.

The guests were stunned; twice in a single day they had witnessed this father's unexpected devotion. "What grace and mercy and love we have seen this day!"

This story is about God's love in the face of blatant, egregious sin. Both sons show that they wish their father dead. Both belittle and insult him. Both are self-centered and ungrateful. And yet their father responds with selfless love and bottomless compassion. The master of the house becomes a servant to his kids, humiliating himself before the entire community in order to win them. Although both ask to be treated as servants, their father treats them as sons.

Children can spurn fatherly love. Jesus tells us that, in the end, the younger son did not, but he leaves the issue open regarding the older son, not saying whether he accepted his father's overtures of love and grace. Nevertheless, we know that our heavenly Father's invitation is always there for all wayward prodigals.

God's arms are waiting to embrace us and bring us home as sons and daughters, loved and honored forever. We may be squandering our lives far from home, or we may be near the house living as servants in rebellion. To our Father, where we sin doesn't matter; what does is that we accept his humble, gracious invitation to enter his house forgiven and restored, to join the celebration already in progress. His home is filled with sinners—children who disobeyed him and lost their way. When they returned, confessing their sin and admitting their need, he rushed out to greet them, clothed them in his finest raiment, and escorted them home.

Notice, though, that *reconciliation is impossible apart from confession and forgiveness*. Broken relationships cannot be restored until the violator confesses his wrongdoing and the victim offers to forgive. God is eager and quick to forgive when we return to him and confess our sin, but we must turn from our faithless ways and start back toward home, with confession in our hearts and on our lips, so he can rush out to meet us. Love will not force itself on us. We must be willing to welcome love before it will wrap us in its arms.

The Forgiving Life

Confession is our part, and while forgiveness is God's, it's not *solely* his. Recall the disciples' prayer: "Forgive us our debts, as we also have forgiven our debtors" (Matt. 6:12). As God has forgiven, we are to become forgivers. Just as he pardons our sins against him, so we are to pardon offenses that hurt us. To those who've wounded us, we must channel the love our Father showers on us. Only his spiritual children can do this, because only they have the Spirit of Love active within them: "Once we are in God's house as sons and daughters of his household, we can be like him, love like him, be good like him, care like him."[20] Love makes it achievable.

Charles Swindoll illustrates this through the true story of a seminary student he calls Aaron. "Late one spring Aaron was praying about having a significant ministry the following summer. He asked God for a position to open up on some church staff or at a Christian organization. Nothing happened. Days turned into weeks, and Aaron finally faced reality—he needed *any* job he could find." This turned out to be "driving a bus in South Side Chicago," a rough and dangerous part of the city.

Aaron learned the route and soon was driving on his own. Not long after, a few gang members began hassling him. They would step into the bus, walk past him without paying the fare, ignore his warnings, and ride until they decided to get off, "all the while making insulting remarks to him and others on the bus." Finally, Aaron decided to take action.

> The next morning, after the gang got on as usual, Aaron saw a policeman on the next corner, so he pulled over and reported the offense. The officer told them to pay or get off. They paid . . . but, unfortunately, the policeman got off. And *they* stayed on. When the bus turned another corner or two, the gang assaulted the young driver.
>
> When Aaron came to, blood was all over his shirt, two teeth were missing, both eyes were swollen, his money was gone, and the bus was empty. Resentful thoughts swarmed through his mind. Confusion, anger, and disillusionment added fuel to the fire of his physical pain.

Determined to fight back, Aaron pressed charges against the gang members, and the police arrested them.

When all parties met in court, the scene was tense. The thugs glared at Aaron, and he stared back. Suddenly, though, Aaron was "seized" with a divine perspective. Bitterness gave way to compassion: "Under the Spirit's control he no longer hated them—he pitied them. They needed help, not more hate."

The trial proceeded, and the judge rendered his verdict: guilty. Then Aaron stood to his feet and asked the judge for permission to speak.

> "Your honor, I would like you to total up all the days of punishment against these men—all the time sentenced against them—and I request that you allow me to go to jail in their place." . . .
>
> As Aaron looked over at the gang members (whose mouths and eyes looked like saucers), he smiled and said quietly, "It's because I forgive you."
>
> The dumbfounded judge said rather firmly: "Young man, you're out of order. This sort of thing has never been done before!" To which Aaron

replied with insight: "Oh, yes, it has, your honor . . . yes, it has. It happened over nineteen centuries ago when a man from Galilee paid the penalty that all mankind deserved."

And then for the next three to four minutes, without interruption, he explained how Jesus Christ died on our behalf, thereby proving God's love and forgiveness.

Aaron was not granted his request, but the young man regularly visited the gang members in jail, led most of them to faith in Christ, and began a significant ministry to many others in South Side Chicago.[21]

God had shown Aaron his ministry, which began with an extraordinary—indeed, divinely motivated—act of loving forgiveness.

Our Father never asks us to do what he will not equip us to do; his forgiven children have the ability to forgive others because he has given us that capacity. His love enters us and expands our puny ability until we can love even our enemies. We can choose to guard our hearts against his work, but then we are choosing to love far less, perhaps in time to love not at all. We can have a shriveled existence, but why, and at what cost? Aaron could have chosen hatred over love and never discovered the ministry waiting for him. He instead followed Love's lead and in so doing found the capacity to forgive. He still received justice; he won a hearing before hate-filled men and led many of them to the Lover who heals hate; and he discovered a meaningful way to serve Christ. Love is always the best choice, and the forgiving life is love's way.

Forgiveness: What It Is and Isn't

What is forgiveness? At the very least, *forgiveness is a merciful and compassionate act of love that cancels the repayment obligation of the sinner*. God loved us so much that he sent his beloved Son to pay the high price for our sins. The cost was Jesus' blood, which covered all our sins "for all time" (Heb. 10:12). When by faith we accept his payment on our behalf, God cancels our moral debt.[22] PAID is written across our bill.

With our debt completely erased, God pardons us. Although we were guilty and deserved capital punishment, he hands us a full pardon while we're still in cells of our own making, imprisoned by our sin. All we have to do is accept his forgiveness:

Seek the LORD while he may be found; call on him while he is near. Let the wicked forsake his way and the evil man his thoughts. Let him turn to the LORD, and he will have mercy on him, and to our God, for he will freely pardon. (Isa. 55:6–7)

With our pardon in hand, we are set free to live life anew, released from bondage to evil and breathing the clean air of liberation. "It is for freedom that Christ has set us free" (Gal. 5:1).

And divine forgiveness does even more. Our Lord not only pays for our sins but also removes them from us, including their *ultimate* consequences. Salvation in Christ is full-blown; there are no half measures. It includes deliverance from the *penalty* of sin (death in all its forms), deliverance from the *power* of sin (the ability to lure us from the Source of love and life), and deliverance from the very *presence* of sin (heaven, eternal goodness to the fullest degree).[23]

None of us has yet known this absolute deliverance, and we won't until God recreates the world. This is where no evil will reside, where "nothing impure will ever enter," where no one "who does what is shameful or deceitful" will be found (Rev. 21:27). The entire recreated order will have the smell of only pristine freshness, the sights of only majestic beauty, the touch of only bountiful love, and the brilliant presence of the "Lord God Almighty and the Lamb" with all "those whose names are written in the Lamb's book of life" (vv. 22, 27). Here we will be imperishable, unable to ever experience death again. Here we will be incorruptible, unable to ever sin again.[24] Unity—the full realization of reconciliation and all its benefits—will be forever ours. In this new world, salvation in Christ will finally be complete.

Until then, God promises us that when we confess our sins, he hurls them away from us: "As far as the east is from the west, so far has he removed our transgressions from us" (Ps. 103:12). We may still suffer some of the fallout from our sins, but our sins themselves are banished, never to return again.

Because God is so gracious and loving in his forgiveness, he calls on us to do likewise. *Forgiven people must also be forgiving people.* When others hurt us, our Lover wants us to reach out to them as he has to us. His love was costly; so must ours be. His forgiveness was magnanimous; so should ours be. He gave us what we did not deserve and could never earn; we must do the same for others.

Just as forgiveness flows from God's nature, so it must flow from we who are being renewed into the image of Christ. Our old nature desired revenge and sulked in bitterness when wronged. Our new nature sets revenge and bitterness aside, meeting faults with the mindset of Christ, which so fully understood the bondage and blindness of sin that it could say before its wrongful accusers and brutal torturers, "Father, forgive them, for they do not know what they are doing" (Luke 23:34). Becoming Christlike involves learning to forgive as Christ forgave.

As for what forgiveness is not:

Forgiveness is not a feeling. Scripture nowhere suggests that forgiveness is inherently emotional. It may sometimes arise out of compassionate feelings, but compassion need not be felt before forgiveness is offered. Forgiveness is a deliberate, free act of the will to overcome hurt, bitterness, hate, and revenge with the virtue of love and all its goodness.

Forgiveness is not excusing evil. Indeed, forgiveness is predicated on the fact that actual evil occurred and that it cannot be excused. It must be faced and dealt with, and part of the response should be to forgive it.

Forgiveness is not an excuse for committing more evil. I've heard many people say we can keep on sinning because we can always ask God to forgive. Paul answered this mistaken view from the start: "Shall we go on sinning so that grace may increase? By no means! We died to sin; how can we live in it any longer?" (Rom. 6:1–2). We who are in Christ have been baptized into his death and raised with him so that "we too may live a new life" (v. 4). Our "old self was crucified with him so that . . . we should no longer be slaves to sin" (v. 6). Forgiveness, the beginning of our new life in Christ, should become the habitual rhythm of that new life. We are saved not to experience more death, which is what sin brings, but to overcome death by living as we were designed by our Lover.

Forgiveness is not condoning evil. Some people think offering forgiveness equals putting "It's okay" across the sin. Not true—evil is *never* okay, not condonable but only condemnable. "Woe to those who call evil good and good evil, who put darkness for light and light for darkness, who put bitter for sweet and sweet for bitter" (Isa. 5:20). Sin is sin and good is good; we are accountable for both. Even "forgiveness implies accountability. Forgiveness is aimed at sin . . . and sin is the kind of evil for which somebody is to blame."[25] Hence the need for wrongdoers to seek and receive forgiveness, and the need for victims to forgive those responsible.

Forgiveness is not forgetting that evil happened. In Hebrews God says, "I will forgive their wickedness and will remember their sins no more" (8:12). I've heard people conclude from this verse that when God forgives us, recollection of our sins completely drops from his memory; he cannot recall them; they are wiped from his mind. This interpretation contradicts divine omniscience—it's impossible for the all-knowing God not to know something: "Everything is uncovered and laid bare before the eyes of him to whom we must give account" (4:13). God does not cause himself to have amnesia over sins he's forgiven. He knows all things eternally, so he cannot *forget* anything.[26]

God remembering our sins no more, then, means that once he has forgiven them, he no longer counts them against us. Jesus has paid for our sins "once for all by his own blood, having obtained eternal redemption" (9:12). Therefore, where forgiveness has been granted based on his sacrifice, "there is no longer any sacrifice for sin" (10:18); payment has been made in full, complete and everlasting. The *debt*—not the *memory* of the debt—has been wiped away.

Consequently, when we forgive those who have wronged us, we are *not* required to forget what they did (though given enough time this may happen). We *are* required to treat their debt to us as fully paid—from this moment onward, they owe us nothing. Even so, society may rightly demand payment for criminal wrongdoing; that the personal debt is paid does not mean the social debt has been covered.

Forgiveness is not the negation of all consequences. When Aaron forgave the gang members who'd beaten him, they still went to prison to repay society. When we accept Christ's payment for our sins and therefore receive God's full forgiveness, we may still have to endure some consequences of our actions.

One consequence yet facing us is physical death: We are still mortal. Yes, Christ has conquered death, and death will not be able to separate us from God's love (Rom. 8:38–39), but we are still "destined to die once, and after that to face judgment" (Heb. 9:27). This judgment will be in front of Christ himself, where each of us will "receive what is due him for the things done while in the body, whether good or bad" (2 Cor. 5:10); we may reap rewards or "suffer loss" (1 Cor. 3:15), even though all our sins will have been forgiven.[27]

PRACTICING CONFESSION AND FORGIVENESS

Since the Christian life is a confessing and forgiving life, let's see how these love habits should show up in us.

When We Offend God

Since all sin is against God, we must first go to *him* when we sin. No matter who else is wronged or hurt, our debt of sin, requiring confession and forgiveness, is owed to him and him alone.

Are there sins you need to confess? If any come to mind, bring them to God in prayer, knowing that he is ready to rush to you, forgive you, and clothe you with the royal garments that show you are his beloved, forgiven child.

Or, more visually, you could jot down your sins on paper, and after you have confessed them and accepted God's forgiveness, take your list of sins, tear it into tiny pieces, and either throw them in the trash or set them ablaze. Let this act symbolize what God has done for you in response to your confession.

Then, go and enjoy your freedom to live in obedience to him. In the power of his Spirit, strive for the high call of holiness.

> As obedient children, do not conform to the evil desires you had when you lived in ignorance. But just as he who called you is holy, so be holy in all you do; for it is written: "Be holy, because I am holy" (1 Peter 1:14–16).

Also remember that if you sin again, confess it and move on. Don't let sin control or subvert you. With Christ as your Advocate, the Spirit as your Power, and the Father as your Lover, sin is completely outmatched. The victory is yours, as long as you persevere in the Light.

Confession, of course, is not only needed for outward offenses; as Jesus said, we can also sin in our hearts and minds.[28] Bitterness, lust, vengeance, heartlessness, envy, greed, neglect, betrayal—these are just a few of the condemnable acts we can commit without ever so much as raising our voices. Carrying them out inwardly is wickedness enough.

As you go through your days, pay close attention to the workings within you. When the unethical slips from fleeting to focusing, from innocent imaginings to flights of evil fancy, understand that you have inner sin needing divine forgiveness and purging. Get radical with it;[29] with the Spirit's assistance, do what it takes to rid its influence from your life.

You are in a spiritual war with evil. You can't make peace with sin, and you can't overcome its power on your own; you must stand fast and fight with spiritual weapons, which include the habits of love. The ultimate victory is yours in Christ, but the conflict will persist until he returns and forever vanquishes his enemies. In the meantime, he will protect you and fight alongside you, *and* the battles will be easier if you refuse to give sin even a toehold in your life.

When We Offend Others

When we commit offenses that have hurt others, what actions should we take? In Matthew 5:23–24, Jesus provided two steps to follow.

First, go to the offended person. If at all possible, arrange a face-to-face encounter. If the physical distance is too great, call the offended party by phone, or, if that's out of the question, write a letter or an email. Regardless, you must seek out that person in the brick-and-mortar world, not just through imagination or prayer.

Second, seek to be reconciled to the wronged person. This requires confession and contrition over the wrong done and requesting forgiveness. Through this process, the goal is to restore what was lost in the relationship, to heal the wounds inflicted.

In his book *Improving Your Serve,* Charles Swindoll mentions several problems we might face as we seek reconciliation, and he suggests ways to handle each.

> *"But what if he or she won't forgive [me]?"* . . . The important thing for each of us to remember is that you are responsible for *you* and I am responsible for *me*. With the right motive, in the right spirit, at the right time, out of obedience to God, we are to humble ourselves . . . and attempt to make things right. God will honor our efforts. The one offended may need time—first to get over the shock and next, to have God bring about a change in his or her heart. Healing sometimes takes time. . . .
>
> *"What if the situation only gets worse?"* . . . This can happen. You see, all the time the one offended has been blaming you . . . mentally sticking pins in your doll . . . thinking all kinds of bad things about you. When you go to make things right, you suddenly cause his internal scales to go out of balance. You take away the blame and all that's left is the person's guilt, which does a number on him, resulting in even worse feelings. But now it's no longer your fault. . . .
>
> *"What if it is impossible for me to reconcile because the offended person has died?"* . . . In such unique cases, I recommend that you share your burden of guilt with someone whom you can trust. A close friend, your mate, a counselor, or your pastor. Be specific and completely candid. Pray with that individual and confess openly the wrong and the guilt of your soul. In such cases . . . prayer and the presence of an under-

standing, affirming individual will provide the relief you need so desperately.[30]

When We Are Offended

Sometimes we're the wounded ones. If the offense is great enough, we feel "pain so deep and unfair" that we "cannot forget it."[31] It burns through us, scorching whatever it touches, making us even more sensitive to words and actions that barely brush against our wounds.

If injuries fester, hate sets in. We cannot "shake the memory"[32] of how much we've been hurt. Whenever the offender comes to mind, we cannot wish her well—we want to hurt her, to see her suffer, so she can feel our pain *and* have the terrible realization of how much damage she has done. By this point, hate has mushroomed into resentment and bitterness, which can easily give way to revenge. We have become chained to our own pain and even added torturous elements to it. As Lewis Smedes makes clear:

> Recall the pain of being wronged, the hurt of being stung, cheated, demeaned. Doesn't the memory of it fuel the fire of fury again, reheat the pain again, make it hurt again? Suppose you never forgive, suppose you feel the hurt each time your memory lights on the people who did you wrong. And suppose you have a compulsion to think of them constantly. You have become a prisoner of your past pain; you are locked into a torture chamber of your own making. Time should have left your pain behind; but you keep it alive to let it flay you over and over.
>
> Your own memory is a replay of your hurt—a videotape within your soul that plays unending reruns of your old rendezvous with pain. You cannot switch it off. . . . You are lashed again each time your memory spins the tape.[33]

What can we do about this? How can we find healing so that the anguish will be quenched and the hate will disappear?

> The only way to heal the pain that will not heal itself is to forgive the person who hurt you. Forgiving stops the reruns of pain. Forgiving heals your memory. . . . When you release the wrongdoer from the wrong, you cut a malignant tumor out of your inner life. You set a prisoner free, but you discover that the real prisoner was yourself.[34]

So how do we forgive our offenders? By going to the Wounded Healer. Only he can heal us; he knows exactly what to do, and he knows how deeply we hurt. After all, no one has ever been more ravaged by sin than he has. He even became "sin for us" as he hung on the cross (2 Cor. 5:21), so now it is "by his wounds we are healed" (Isa. 53:5). What Christ did *for* us, he can also do *within* us. He can bring us to where we can forgive from our hearts the wounds inflicted. This is Love's healing power; when it's unleashed, chains fall, walls crumble, and people are freed to risk loving again.

Here are some suggested steps for beginning this process.

First, write down the names of any individuals toward whom you harbor resentment, from recently or from a long time ago. Next to their names, note what they did and, as best you can, why you have not forgiven them.

Second, turn your thoughts toward our heavenly Father. Consider the high cost he paid to redeem you and how fully he has forgiven you. You may want to read Psalm 103:1–14 or Isaiah 53.

Third, return to your list and take each offense before the Lord in prayer. Confess your hatred and bitterness. Ask him to help you forgive. When Jesus talked about his followers forgiving others, he used a word for *forgiveness* that signifies hurling our resentment far away so it will no longer hold any influence over us.[35] It may take hours of prayer over days or even months before you can truly say that you have forgiven each person from your heart. You will know when forgiveness has begun "*when you recall those who hurt you and feel the power to wish them well.*"[36]

Some wounds run so deep that the idea of forgiveness seems like a cop-out. You can't imagine turning away from your anger and canceling the sentence of payment you've passed against your offender. The sin was too great, the pain too intense—he deserves to be punished. If anything, you want to pray for his demise, at least that he receive a just punishment for his crime.

Don't ignore these feelings. Like the pain that throbs around a fresh wound demanding medical attention, your inner hurt calls out for treatment too. It may need pastoral, psychological, or psychiatric care. It certainly needs to be tended by the Divine Physician, and, like any serious injury, it will need much care and plenty of time to heal.

First, however, know that your affliction requires attention, not revenge. History is replete with those who exacted retribution or brought the guilty to justice and still died with gaping internal wounds; because they never applied the balm of forgiveness to themselves, their bitterness plagued and eventually destroyed them. They discovered the truth of the Chinese proverb: "Whoever opts for revenge should dig two graves."[37]

Second, consider seeking help. A pastor or professional Christian counselor would be a good start.

Third, again, realize that forgiveness is often a lengthy process. While the "healing of forgiveness can *sometimes* occur in one immense rush of relief and compassion, [it] more often takes much longer."

> Forgiveness looms as a goal to be worked toward rather than a prize to be grasped; and it is something on which we may repeatedly lose or gain ground. It is possible to achieve a spiritual attitude resembling forgiveness toward someone and wake up the next week with the old hate burning as hotly as ever and the whole work needing to begin all over again. Wisdom may lie less in expecting forgiveness to occur as a spiritual drama in our own personal Damascus Road, and more in spending time in prayer over our hurt, in patiently pushing aside its incessant demand for attention, and in watching it shrink slowly and fitfully into remission.[38]

God has saved you to have life, not death. Forgiveness brings life back to you; hatred, bitterness, resentment, and revenge will only rob you of the life that could be yours right now. Choose life, and choose it daily, even moment by moment, until incessant hate has surrendered to effervescent love.

LINGERING ISSUES

Before we leave the love habits of confession and forgiveness, I want to address three issues that often leave Christians puzzled: Is it appropriate for us to forgive God? What if we cannot forgive ourselves? And must confession and forgiveness always lead to reconciliation?

Forgiving God?

I have read Christian writers and listened to Christian ministers talk about times believers may need to forgive God. These people have been deeply wounded; in many cases, they or their children have suffered terrible abuse of one or more kinds. Sometimes church leaders have even damaged them "in the name of God." Others may have lost loved ones to tragedy, or they may be victims of horrendous crimes. Perhaps they have endured lengthy times of poverty, or they have suffered from unjust criticism that irreparably tore their reputations to pieces and scattered them to the wind.

240 / *transforming* HABITS

Whatever the evil that befell them, they have blamed God for it: "He is sovereign, is he not? If he is, he could have protected me. He could have made my situation turn out much differently. The fact that he didn't confuses and angers me. It's unfair for him to treat me this way. It's just not right. He has wronged me and he is to blame, even if all he did was permit evil to hit me so hard." This is the basic reasoning that has compelled numerous leaders to urge those who feel and think this way to forgive God for what they've experienced.

I empathize with people who hurt so deeply that they blame God for their pain. I too have been wounded, sometimes by those closest to me, which is the worst source of pain. I know what it's like to be betrayed and berated. I've been maligned and misunderstood in devastating ways. At times I was so confused and upset over what I was enduring that I walked out into the middle of an empty field with stern words for God. I even yelled at him, demanding that he explain himself and right the wrongs being committed against me.

Nevertheless, the more I learned about who God is and how he works, the more I realized that my anger was misdirected. *God is not to blame for the evil that befalls us.* Indeed, he is actively working in the opposite direction of evil, seeking through everything to work "for the good" of his children (Rom. 8:28). Certainly, not everything that happens to us is good—evil is real and rampant—but God is so good and so powerful that he can bring good out of the worst travesties. Remember, it was he who used the horror of crucifixion to bring salvation to an undeserving world of rebels. Since he accomplished such great good through the death of his completely innocent Son, we can rest in the certain hope that he will bring good out of the evils perpetuated against us.

It is this conviction about and experience with the true God that has led me to direct blame to where it genuinely belongs. When evil is done, fallen angels, fallen humans, or a combination of both are responsible. And among the fallen, only humans can receive forgiveness, for only they have the ability to repent, to turn away from their sin and embrace the good.[39]

So is it ever appropriate to forgive God? No, not ever. He neither needs forgiveness nor seeks it from us. *We* need *his* forgiveness, and those who hurt us need our forgiveness too.

Forgiving Ourselves

Some people have hypersensitive souls, often damaged by abuse or tragedy. These people question almost everything they do; they find little or no value in themselves; they measure worth by performance, which never measures up. Consequently, they come to despise themselves, in myriad ways undermining their own lives. They sentence themselves to self-destruction, writing the verdict across their own hearts and sometimes carrying it out with brutal effectiveness.

If this describes you, even partially, you run the risk of turning the Bible's teaching on sin into added justification for your self-hatred. You need to come to know in your spirit how incredibly valuable you are in God's eyes. You are not a worthless worm or a useless cog; you are his adopted child, his precious jewel, his wondrous image-bearer. He has made you incomparably unique, so priceless that he paid the highest possible price to win you back.

I urge you to study and meditate on and pray over what Scripture and Christian theology teach about God's image and what it means for your life, especially for your self-perception and self-worth.[40] I ask you to approach the Lord and request that he daily show you how much he loves you. I also encourage you to seek the help of someone who is equipped to help you see your true value and show you practical ways to overcome the inner messages that seek to destroy you.

Also ponder this: If you are God's child, he has forgiven you in Christ. If, for whatever reason, you refuse to forgive yourself, you are continuing to pass a guilty sentence on one whom God has pardoned. Paul states this point clearly: "There is now no condemnation for those who are in Christ Jesus" (Rom. 8:1). Through him, you have been set free from prison; by not forgiving yourself, you erect a new prison of your own making and carry out punishment against yourself. None of this is God's doing—he has already forgiven you.

When we will not forgive what God has forgiven, we put ourselves in his place, which is not where we belong. C. S. Lewis said, "If God forgives us we must forgive ourselves. Otherwise it is almost like setting up ourselves as a higher tribunal than Him."[41]

We may *feel* unforgiven at times, but our confession before God brings his forgiveness—*without fail*. Believing this, we find peace.

Reconciliation Always?

Must confession and forgiveness always lead to reconciliation? While this is the goal and the hope, it is not always achievable. If either party is deceased, reconciliation is impossible, and if either refuses to restore the relationship, then broken it will stay. But there are also times when reconciliation is *inadvisable:* for instance, when one of the parties poses a physical threat or is an unrepentant abuser or holds power over you to the extent that you cannot deal with him and remain sane or safe. Some people we cannot or dare not trust, and if a relationship requires anything, it is trust.

With those who have wronged us and proven themselves untrustworthy, especially dangerously so, we may need to voice our forgiveness from a distance and indicate in strict but loving terms that reconciliation is not to be expected at this time. Trust must first be restored; the burden for this is on the offender, not on the forgiver. If the offender will not rise to the occasion, if he is determined to remain enslaved to his sin, then we should pray for him, asking God to help him and perhaps bring other helpful people into his life. But we need not reopen the relational door. We are not messiahs. God alone can save people from their sin; he has provided gifted people of various talent and expertise who can minister to those we cannot reach or dare not. "If it is possible, as far as it depends on you, live at peace with everyone" (Rom. 12:18); for those with whom peace is not possible, encourage others who can safely and skillfully reach out to them to do so as you seek their good through prayer.[42]

12. Service and Sacrifice: *for love of neighbor*

"I have set you an example that you should do as I have done for you," Jesus said (John 13:15).

"Great, Lord. What did you have in mind? Do you want me to heal the sick and raise the dead?"

"No, that's not what I meant."

"Well, then, how about telling great stories and preaching wonderful sermons? I can hold a crowd spellbound."

"I didn't mean that either."

"Okay, I get what you're after. You want me to criticize and expose corrupt government officials and religious leaders."

"You've missed my point again."

"Then tell me, Lord—what example did you set that I should follow? I'll do anything for you. Go on missionary treks to the earth's remote corners. Demonstrate on picket lines and do jail time in support of the defenseless. I'll run for political office to initiate social change. Tell everyone I meet about the good news of salvation. Give all I own to feed the poor. You name it, I'll do it."

"All right, then. Take a towel and a basin of water, and use them to clean the dirty, smelly feet of others."

"You're *kidding.* Where's the ministry value in *that?* What lasting good would it do? Their feet are just going to get dirty again. I'm interested in *souls,* not feet."

"I'm interested in whole persons. Why would I heal and resurrect bodies if *all* I cared about were souls? I want you to wash feet so you will learn the essence and attitudes of service."

"Isn't there another way?"

"There is always another way."

"Excellent, what is it?"

"The way of selfishness, pride, and rebellion."

"Sounds awful."

"Worse than awful. It's the road to hell."

This imaginary dialogue builds on a real event recorded in the gospel of John. The setting was Jesus' last Passover meal; he and his twelve disciples were together in a room, and all of them had dirty feet. With unpaved roads and open sandals, soiled feet were a common feature of the Holy Land. When guests arrived at a house, a servant commonly met them at the door, removed their sandals, and cleaned their feet; if the master could not afford a servant, then one of the early-arriving guests would accept the servant's role and wash the feet of the others. On *this* occasion, though, none of the Twelve chose to take on what they perceived as a demeaning task. So Jesus rose, took a basin and towel, stooped before each man, and washed and dried his feet. He "knew that the Father had put all things under his power, and that he had come from God and was returning to God" (John 13:3). *He was the King.* Yet he exercised his status as Ruler of all by kneeling before his creaturely subjects and humbly cleaning their soiled feet.

When he finished, he said,

> "You call me 'Teacher' and 'Lord,' and rightly so, for that is what I am. Now that I, your Lord and Teacher, have washed your feet, you also should wash one another's feet. I have set you an example that you should do as I have done for you. I tell you the truth, no servant is greater than his master, nor is a messenger greater than the one who sent him. Now that you know these things, you will be blessed if you do them" (John 13:13–17).

Jesus is our example; the example he gave us was *servanthood;* and the servanthood he showed us was the *ministry of the towel.* This means no act of service is too small, too dirty, too mundane, too menial, or too trivial. Whether in the spotlight or the shadows, in the pulpit or the pews, receiving accolades or being overlooked, if we are serving Christ's way, we are meeting needs for the sake of eternity, loving our neighbors while also loving God and ourselves.

SERVING LOVE'S WAY

Love gives, which is just another way of saying that love serves. Love never remains self-contained, self-focused. Love overflows its banks and waters everything within reach.

We see this in the sacrifices parents make for their children. Soon after mine adopted me as an infant and brought me home from the hospital, I started a pattern of behavior that would test any parent's love. Every hour on the hour, all day and all night, I woke up crying to be fed. My mother or father would prepare a bottle, and I would drink about one ounce of milk. Then I would stop, drift off to sleep, and restart the cycle the next hour. I also had a number of allergies and illnesses that interrupted my sleep and often altered what I could ingest. My parents took turns, 24/7, caring for their needy son.

One day, after I'd become an adult, I asked my mom if, during that rough first year, she ever regretted adopting me. "No, not once," she said. "We had waited so long for a child that when you came into our lives, we knew you were God's answer to our prayers. We loved you from the first day we saw you."

"I know that," I pressed. "But didn't you wish I would have slept through the night? Didn't you ever get frustrated or grow weary of taking care of me during that time? I think I would have."

"Well," she replied, "your father got to the point that he couldn't keep getting up during the night with you and still manage to stay awake in his classes at the university. So most of the time I got up with you and cared for you, with your dad relieving me as much as he could. But neither of us ever regretted in the least having you. You did not frustrate us or anger us. We knew you needed loving care, and we were delighted to be the ones to give you that care."

Only *agapē* gives like that. *Agapē* is the love that comprises Christian service.

Service-dominated love pervades the divine. In the Trinity, the Father lovingly offers himself to the Son and the Spirit, the Spirit lovingly serves the Father and the Son, and the Son lovingly gives his all to the Father and the Spirit. Mutual devotion defines their intimacy.

We also see the giving nature of love in the Trinity's act of creation. William Temple observed:

> The world is not necessary to God, but it results from his love. In making the world he brought into existence vast numbers of things, like electrons which always have to obey his law for them, and do so. But he made creatures—men and women—who could disobey his law for them, and often do so. He did this in order that among his creatures there might be some who answer his love with theirs by offering to him a free obedience.[1]

He had no need to create, but he did anyway because *love delights in giving*.

Even more amazing is that *before* God made anything, he *knew* his love would be spurned.

> God knew that I would be like Adam and Peter and Pilate, and even Judas. He knew that my sins would necessitate his crucifixion if his love was to be successful in winning my soul. In the act of creation he saw the cross. Yet, knowing the infinite price to himself, he still chose to create me. He loved me despite the nails I put into his own body. He prayed for *me* from the cross and said "Father, forgive them" (Luke 23:34), even as I crucified him. What crazy love is this? It is Love itself. It is the love of the author who chose to create a story with his own hellish agony in it, so he could create a story with my heavenly joy in it. Creation manifests absolute love.[2]

Love, and therefore service, are written into the very fabric of the universe. We cannot escape service any more than we can escape love. We can subvert service, using it primarily for selfish ends, but we cannot use it for selfish ends only—*every* person serves more than himself occasionally.[3] Love gives, and giving is the essence of service.

The ministry of the towel is the service of *agapē*. Unbelievers cannot give this kind of service, for *agapē* comes from God and wells up in those with whom his Spirit dwells. *Agapē* is the fruit of the Spirit; it does not result from the sole efforts of even the most determined person. Christian service, then, is service only believers can give, and because it's Spirit-inspired and *agapē*-motivated, it will be other-centered.

The greatest form of service we can offer is *sacrificial* service. When we serve others, we give out of the abundance Christ has given us. When we serve others sacrificially, we give at a higher cost to us, relinquishing something we hold dear for something far greater: the fulfillment of *agapē* for another. While service should be the normal way we live, *sacrificial* service should be what we are ready to give as our Lover or the circumstance calls for it.

For example, service is using a basin and towel to clean another's dirty feet; *sacrificial* service is what one woman did for Jesus. Humiliating herself before others, "she brought an alabaster jar of [very costly] perfume, and . . . began to wet his [Jesus'] feet with her tears. Then she wiped them with her hair, kissed them and poured perfume on them" (Luke 7:37–38).

Service would be teaching others how to conduct themselves ethically in the business world. *Sacrificial* service would be risking your reputation and livelihood to reveal unethical and illegal business practices at your company.

Service would be putting a comfortable percentage of your income into the offering plate. *Sacrificial* service would be donating beyond what you can afford, which is what a "poor widow" did in front of Jesus—she gave "all she had to live on" (Luke 21:3–4).

Service would be working alongside a friend to help him fix his car. *Sacrificial* service would be fixing the car at your expense without ever letting him know what you did.

Service would be providing an opportunity for your children to learn a team sport and its accompanying life lessons. *Sacrificial* service would be giving up your time to coach a youth team whether or not your children were on it.

When we turn our eyes to Jesus Christ, we see that his service was sacrificial from the start. As the Son of God, he was exalted above everything in creation, sovereign and limitless. Yet he freely and lovingly "laid . . . aside [his] equality with God . . . as He took on the nature of a slave and became like other men. Because He was recognized as a man, in reality as well as in outward form, He finally humiliated Himself in obedience so as to die, even to die on a cross."[4] For a season, the Son sacrificed the glory he had with the Father in heaven,[5] accepting human limitations so he could carry out Love's task among us. The task? "The Son of Man did not come to be served, but to serve, and to give his life as a ransom for many" (Matt. 20:28). "I am among you," he told his disciples, "as one who serves" (Luke 22:27). And he did—

fully, faithfully, humbly, and sacrificially.

Service need not be sacrificial to honor God. All service, when done in Christ and for Christ, is good: "It is the Lord Christ you are serving" (Col. 3:24). Nevertheless, the service that costs us something dear is that much more Christlike. Love can (and should, at times) be expensive. It was for Jesus, and it has been (and will be) for his followers.

Sacrificial Service Exemplified

If we are to serve as Jesus served, we must obey the commandment to love our neighbors as we love ourselves. But who is our neighbor? Whom should we love and therefore serve? When an expert in the Mosaic Law asked Jesus about this, he was answered with a story.[6] The parable of the Good Samaritan was shocking to first-century Jews, and as we probe into this simple-sounding narrative, we will see how much it shakes our world as well.[7]

The Opportunity

In Jesus' telling of an anonymous man traveling from Jerusalem to Jericho, his identity—name, family background, nationality, race, vocation, education, belief system—is left completely open. Moreover, Jesus says that thieves fell upon him and robbed him, stripped him of all his clothing, beat him until he was "half dead," then left him to die (Luke 10:30–31); these details ensure that he cannot be identified. In the Middle East, a person's ethnic and religious orientation can be quickly ascertained by his manner of dress or speech. Also, the words *half dead* mean "next to death" or "at the point of death." He was unconscious, unable to tell anyone who he was, reduced to desperate need.

Jesus does not specify some details that his hearers would have naturally supplied; for example, that the road between Jerusalem and Jericho was seventeen miles of danger, descending sharply and curving "through rugged, bleak, rocky terrain where robbers could easily hide"[8] and regularly did. However, while there were many concealed spots near the road, travelers from either direction could see fellow travelers quite far away. Remarks one man who has traveled this road, as well as many other Middle Eastern roads "by camel, by donkey, and on foot for twenty years":

> I know that the traveler is *extremely* interested in who else is on the road. His life may depend on it. A question put to a bystander at the edge of the last village just before the desert begins; a brief exchange with a traveler coming the other way; fresh tracks on the soft earth at

the edge of the road where men and animals prefer to walk; a glimpse in the clear desert air of a robed figure ahead; all these are potential sources of knowledge for the . . . traveler.[9]

Others, then, may have seen a scuffle in the distance and approached the area with heightened interest and caution.

Priestly Priorities

Continuing the story, Jesus says that the first passerby was a *priest* (v. 31). Priests served in the temple, offered sacrifices, and collected, distributed, and ate the edible tithes. They were also aristocrats, part of the upper class, so they did not walk between Jerusalem and Jericho (as the poor did) but rode on animals, such as donkeys.

Whether or not he saw his fellow traveler attacked, the priest certainly observed the beaten, motionless man as he approached. But he didn't help at all—didn't even come near. He was so intent on avoidance that he crossed to the opposite side of the road and continued riding along.

The priest could have tended to the victim's wounds and used his own mount to carry him to a safe place. Yet he refused, and Jesus doesn't say why. Perhaps the priest feared being ambushed by robbers. He also may have been protecting himself from defilement. According to the oral law of the time, the most unclean act was touching a corpse; contact with a non-Jew was second on the list. After all, the battered man could have been dead; the priest knew that touching a corpse would make him unclean and thereby prohibit him from carrying out his duties until he'd been ritually purified.[10] If it turned out that the man was not a Jew, whether dead or alive, the priest would have been regarded as unclean anyway. Whatever the motive, Jesus makes it clear that the priest failed to act out of love—he cared more for his personal safety and/ or status than for his fellow man.

Levite Takes Leave

The next passerby at the spot where the wounded, naked man lay was a *Levite* (v. 32). Levites assisted priests by taking care of the temple and performing a variety of other administrative tasks. The parable's wording indicates that the Levite not only saw the injured man but also came close before turning away and leaving him.

Once again, Jesus doesn't say why the Levite did not help. Perhaps he saw the higher-ranking priest pass by the victim, which may have led him to conclude that since the priest perceived no duty to assist, who was he to question a superior's judgment by helping the stranger himself? What if he offended the priest by appearing to challenge not only his interpretation and application of the law but also his compassion for others? Or he may likewise have feared being jumped by robbers or defiled by a dead man, though less fearful than the priest since he made the riskier move of getting close.

Regardless of the reasons, the Levite left the man for dead. Another opportunity to act lovingly was missed.

Samaritan Service

The third traveler to come down the road was a *Samaritan* (v. 33).

Jesus' listeners would have expected this passerby to be a Jewish layman. The story's progression would have seemed perfect: priest, assistant, layman, three "regressing" classes of people with ranked positions in the temple. If they were leaving Jerusalem after the daily sacrifices, representatives of all three strata would use the road out of town. Instead, Jesus rocked the world of his audience by introducing a Samaritan.

Jews *hated* Samaritans. The Mishnah, a collection of written laws considered by many Jews to be second in authority only to the Hebrew Scriptures, declares, "He that eats the bread of the Samaritans is like to one that eats the flesh of swine."[11] A contemporary scholar notes that the "Samaritans were publicly cursed in the synagogues; and a petition was daily offered up praying [to] God that the Samaritans might not be partakers of eternal life."[12]

The animosity between Jews and Samaritans was centuries old; they despised and often went out of their way to avoid one another. To Jews, Samaritans were heretics (among other things). Samaritans accepted the five books of Moses as authoritative but rejected the rest of the Hebrew canon. Samaritans also believed in worshiping one God, but they held that Shechem (rather than Jerusalem) was the true site of worship.

So along came a detested Samaritan, traveling through Jewish territory where doctrinal orthodoxy reigned. If he saw the priest and Levite on the road, he probably noticed how they crossed to the other side at a certain point. When he reached the same juncture, he approached the critically wounded stranger with tremendous compassion. If he feared for his safety and ritual purity, he did not let it deter him from rendering aid. He cleaned and softened the wounds with oil, disinfected them with wine, then bound them so they would stay clean and better heal (v. 34).

Oil and wine were standard first-aid remedies in the ancient world, and priests also used them in connection with sacrifices in temple rituals. The Samaritan used these elements in an act of *personal* sacrifice, giving of himself and his own resources. The priest and Levite were regularly reminded of the value of sacrifice since they frequently officiated at offerings in the temple; for whatever reason, though, they failed to make the connection between *ritual* sacrifice and *personal* sacrifice. In Jesus' story, the theologically orthodox are heretical in practice, while the theological heretic is orthodox in his behavior.

As if this were not enough, Jesus further inflames his Jewish hearers by adding that the Samaritan gave his own mount to the injured man and brought him to an inn, caring for him through the day and then paying the innkeeper to watch over him until he could return. The Samaritan's prescient settling of additional bills that might accumulate was important (vv. 34–35); stripped of his belongings, the stranger lacked the ability to pay, and if he could not pay, he would not be permitted to leave, perhaps even be arrested and thrown into debtors' prison.[13]

The Samaritan's actions were not only sacrificial but courageous. In Middle Eastern society, acts of blood-revenge were common. If family members believed a person had killed a loved one, they would seek to kill him; if they could not find him, they had the civil right to retaliate by killing members of his family, family relations (no matter how remote), and members of his tribe. By taking the wounded man to an inn, the Samaritan put his life in danger, running the grave risk that someone would recognize him and assume he was responsible for the injuries. Who else was there to blame?

> The group mind of Middle Eastern peasant society makes a totally illogical judgment at this point. The stranger who involves himself in an accident is often considered partially, if not totally, responsible for the accident. After all, why did he stop? Irrational minds seeking a focus for their retaliation do not make rational judgments, especially when the person involved is from a hated minority community. . . .
>
> An American cultural equivalent would be a Plains Indian in 1875 walking into Dodge City with a scalped cowboy on his horse, checking into a room over the local saloon, and staying the night to take care of him. Any Indian so brave would be fortunate to get out of the city alive *even* if he had saved the cowboy's life. So with the Samaritan in the parable, his act of kindness will have made *no* difference. Caution would lead him to leave the wounded man at the door of the inn and disappear. The man may still be unconscious, in which case the Samaritan

would be completely protected. Or the Samaritan could remain anonymous to the wounded man. But when he stays at the inn through the night to take care of the man, and promises to return, anonymity is not possible.

The courage of the Samaritan is demonstrated first when he stops in the desert (for the thieves are still in the area). But his real bravery is seen in this final act of compassion at the inn. The point is not his courage, but the price he is willing to pay to complete his act of compassion.[14]

The Real Question

The story now told, Jesus asked, "Which of these three do you think was a neighbor to the man who fell into the hands of robbers?" (v. 36). Notice that he did not re-pose the legal expert's original question (Who is my neighbor?), which he implicitly rejected. To Jesus, the true question was, *What kind of neighbor must I be?* The real issue concerns the one who should love and the extent to which that love should be shown. Once that's settled, the answer to the first query is simple: *Everyone* is my neighbor, including my enemies! Authentic neighbor-love has no limits—not race, nationality, worldview, social status, physical condition, or any other factor. The uncompromising standard of love is that we love whoever crosses our path. This requires that we become lovers ourselves.

The legal expert got the point but could not bring himself to say the word *Samaritan*. Instead, he answered that the real neighbor was "the one who had mercy" on the beaten man. Jesus then told him, "Go and do likewise" (v. 37). Imagine, a Jewish master of the Mosaic Law being commanded to follow the example of an unorthodox, despised Samaritan. Amazing. Boundary-shattering. And humanly impossible.

Only God can overcome our prejudices and help us love as we ought. We can never satisfy the high call of *agapē*, but the One who is *agapē* can. As we depend on him, he will perfect our love and love others through us.

> God is love. Whoever lives in love lives in God, and God in him. In this way, love is made complete among us. . . .
> We love because he first loved us. If anyone says, "I love God," yet hates his brother, he is a liar. For anyone who does not love his brother, whom he has seen, cannot love God, whom he has not seen. And he has given us this command: Whoever loves God must also love his brother. (1 John 4:16–17, 19–21)

For Christians, then, loving and serving others is not an option: It must become a way of life. And the others we are to lovingly serve are those with whom we come in contact. Jesus does not call us to explicitly love all of humanity; only God's love is that expansive and effective. Instead, we're told to love our neighbor—the ones close to us, the ones we, in our finiteness, can reach out and touch.

We must never forget, however, that this divine calling to love others is not achievable without the divine life inside us.[15] When *agapē* enters us, it overflows to our neighbors. We cannot contain God's love—we can hinder the flow, but we cannot halt it. *Agapē* always floods its banks.

SPHERES OF SERVICE

Since service is about loving our neighbor, we'll look at the spheres of service that clearly fall into this category. With each sphere, I'll suggest some practical steps you can take to make neighbor-love a reality.

Focus on Your Family

Our closest neighbors are those who live under our roof, or who brought us into the world in the first place, or who adopted us and gave us a home: *family*. Because they are the closest to us, they are sometimes the hardest to serve. We know their shortcomings all too well, and they know ours, uncomfortably so. We also tend to take them for granted, just as they often do us, which is all the more reason for us to begin with them. As much as it depends on us, we need to help build our families into genuine communities where grace and love abound. This requires our loving service to them.

If you are single or have no children, consider adapting the following ideas to fit your relationships with surviving family members; few of us have no blood family around whatsoever. If you have no living relations, though, you could skip this sphere of service and move to the next one.

If you're at home, take your journal and go into a family member's room. If you are away from your family and have pictures of them with you, pull them out and place them before you. What you're seeking is an object and/ or setting that will connect you in a concrete way to your family.

Next, look to the Lord to help you determine your family's needs, which will likely be multidimensional—spiritual, material, relational, psychological, medical, emotional, educational, vocational. Think about each member and list each one's needs. Think not just in terms of special or major needs but also in terms of the smaller, more routine needs. More time than you now have may be required to do this. Take all the time necessary, even if it means completing this step in chunks over the next several days.

With your list in hand, ask God to grant you wisdom and guidance on how those family needs can be met. Don't feel as if you must handle them on your own. The Lord is with you, and there are probably other people who can come alongside you to service certain needs more effectively.

Serving sometimes means standing aside and allowing others to meet the needs. My family knows that while I can fix small things around the house, major jobs require more expertise and skill, so I serve them by bringing in someone else to do the work I cannot. You may have a family member who needs counseling or vocational advice beyond your ability to supply. Be humble and caring enough to find others who can satisfy that need. If you can't think of someone, ask around. Keep God in the loop also. Several times he's brought people across my path without my mentioning the need to anyone but him.

Now begin serving. The best way to learn is to do. Start with something small, not an act that will make a big splash. You want to cultivate the discipline of true service, and for most of us that requires beginning with almost invisible tasks, ones that may go unnoticed for a while, certainly ones we do not announce or draw attention to.

If you need help coming up with ways to serve your family, here are some suggestions that perhaps will spark your own imagination.

- Make your family feel wanted with daily hugs and heartfelt praises.
- Let your spouse talk about her (or his) day at the office first, giving your full attention and support.
- Keep a supply of your family's favorite cold drinks in the refrigerator.
- Without fanfare or complaining, tackle some of those longstanding household tasks that have been frustrating your family.
- Encourage inquisitiveness in your family by providing understandable answers, informative books, and outings to places of interest.
- Pray with and in front of your family, setting an example

for what it means to depend on God.

- If you have a teenager harried by school, extracurricular activities, and/or a part-time job, give her a break from her household chores by doing them yourself for a week.

- Tuck notes of appreciation in lunch boxes and under pillows.

- Sit in silence with a hurting loved one who just can't talk about his sorrow right now. Let your presence, arms, and tears convey your love.

- If your wife has been cooped up with your younger children for several days, surprise her with a full day off. Take care of the kids, the meals, and the housework, and let her do what she wants for the entire day.

- Nurture the inner spirit of service through flash prayers. While with or thinking about your family, silently and briefly pray for them: "Lord, deepen your joy in my daughter"; "Father, show my wife your faithfulness"; "Holy Spirit, let your peace settle my husband's nerves." Your service will be hidden, but its fruit will soon flourish all around you.

- If travel or other circumstances frequently take you away from your family, then liberally use snail mail, email, and the telephone to stay in touch and express your devotion. Whenever possible, bring home specially tailored mementos for each family member.

- If you have family members unable to get out on their own, take them for car rides to beautiful settings or places that hold wonderful memories or carry the promise of fun.

- If you have a family member in prison, don't give up on him. Pray for him. Visit him. Write him. Discover which Christian ministries are active in the prison and seek to connect them to him. Prison need not be the end of the road; it can be the beginning of a new and better journey.[16]

God's Forever Family

"Therefore, as we have opportunity," Paul urges, "let us do good to all people, especially to those who belong to the family of believers" (Gal. 6:10). The closest family of believers to each of us is our local church. Here are some thoughts on how we can reach out to our brothers and sisters in Christ.

- Most important, discover your spiritual gift(s) and use it for the purpose God intended: to equip fellow believers for "works of service, so that the body of Christ may be built up until we all reach unity . . . and become mature, attaining to the whole measure of the fullness of Christ" (Eph. 4:12–13). The Spirit gives each Christian at least one spiritual gift to use "for the common good" of the church (1 Cor. 12:7). As Peter said, "Each one should use whatever gift he has received to serve others, faithfully administering God's grace in its various forms" (1 Peter 4:10). A spiritual gift is a "God-given ability for service."[17]

  The key passages that list the spiritual gifts and provide direction for their use are Romans 12:4–8, 1 Corinthians 12–14, and Ephesians 4:7–16. Read them, study them, discuss them with your church's leadership, and ask God to help you discover and use your spiritual gift(s).[18] God's people need you to exercise your gift in their midst.

- If you almost always agree to service requests, consider saying no more often. You may be undermining someone else's opportunity to serve, and you may be stretching yourself beyond your effectiveness.

- Show honor and gratitude to those in your church who serve faithfully, especially those who meet some of your needs. Your respect and words of encouragement will go a long way in uplifting the servants around you.

- Give regularly of your finances, and sometimes give sacrificially. God owns "everything under heaven" (Job 41:11), so what you have is under your stewardship, not your ownership. Give back to the One who possesses all: he will bless you far more than you can ever give to him.

Remember this: Whoever sows sparingly will also reap sparingly, and whoever sows generously will also reap generously. Each man should give what he has decided in his heart to give, not reluctantly or under compulsion, for God loves a cheerful giver. And God is able to make all grace abound to you, so that in all things at all times, having all that you need, you will abound in every good work. (2 Cor. 9:6–8)

- Contribute funds to your pastor's allotment for book purchases. If there is no such allotment, create one. His ongoing education is critical to your church's spiritual growth.

- Prevent gossiping from starting with you or being passed on through you.

- When missionaries come to your church, open your home to them and give them plenty of time and space to be still, rest, and reenergize. They need silence and solitude as much as anyone, perhaps more.

- Donate time and money to the missionaries your church sponsors. By helping them, you will be supporting their efforts to meet the needs of those they count as their neighbors.

- If you have a sound knowledge of a Bible book, a doctrinal teaching, an area of scriptural application, or anything else pertinent to Christian faith and practice, seek out opportunities to teach. Lead a small-group study or teach a Sunday school class. Don't keep what you know bottled up inside; get it out so other believers can benefit from what you've learned.

- Occasionally pay for a leader to have a night out or a weekend retreat. If he/she is married, cover the spouse's cost too. Show them how much you appreciate their sacrifices in service to you and the rest of the church.

- If you learn of a conflict brewing, especially one that you think could threaten the church's unity, pray and fast over the matter and find spiritually mature believers who will join with you, not to divide and conquer but to discuss the matter calmly and seek to resolve it wisely.

- Be especially sensitive to the weaknesses of fellow believers. Do not let your freedom in Christ "become a stumbling block to the weak" (1 Cor. 8:9). For instance, if you have no problem drinking alcohol in moderation but others do, refuse to drink when they're around. The same holds true with any activity that may distance those you know from Christ rather than draw them to him.

   On the other hand, loving service does not automatically yield to erroneous understanding. In contexts where Paul encouraged stronger Christians to look out for their weaker brethren, he also taught what all believers should embrace as truth: "nothing is unclean in itself" (Rom. 14:14 NASB), and "to the pure, all things are pure" (Titus 1:15 NASB). That is, weaker believers should not remain weak in their understanding but should learn that some of what they believe is amiss. Their conscience may be overly sensitive, their doctrinal beliefs sometimes false, and their ethical understanding occasionally ill-informed. Loving service involves teaching the truth, not simply capitulating to weak conditions. Most of all, we must speak the truth in love so everyone can grow strong in the faith.

- At the next potluck, don't just attend and eat. Stick around to help clean up: wash dishes, take out the garbage, wipe down tables, put up chairs, vacuum or mop the floor, clean the bathrooms. Do *whatever* is needed.

- If you are particularly skilled in a profession that could benefit your church, find a way to put it to use, even if infrequently. If you know computers well, perhaps you could create, help maintain, or enhance your church's Web site. If you're a police officer or security guard, you could be available to offer security at special events. Maybe you're especially skilled at developing leaders and leadership teams, or you're a master teacher, or you have proven experience and expertise in counseling. Whatever your proficiency, offer it, suggesting ways you can employ your talent to further your church's ministry.

Perhaps you believe you have very little to offer, or you've never served in your church before and are unsure where to begin. Or maybe there's something about you that embarrasses you, or that you think would seriously hinder your service. Before you pass judgment on yourself, consider the example of Jimmy Small:

> On Sundays his arrival was always unnoticed, for he would come long before anyone else. Yet he burrowed his old car into an obscure corner of the parking lot to leave the best places for others. He unlocked all the [church] doors, got the bulletins, and then waited outside. When you walked up he'd give you a bulletin and a big smile. But he couldn't talk. . . . Something had happened to his voice long ago. When I met him he was into his sixties and living alone. When he had car trouble, which was often, he never let anyone know and so would walk more than a mile to the church. . . .
>
> He had extensive arthritis, which stooped his shoulders and prevented him from turning his neck. It made hard work of always smiling, even though he couldn't speak a word. Everything about his life worked to keep him unheralded and in the background, even his name—Jimmy Small. Yet despite his drawbacks, setbacks, handicaps, and a plethora of potential excuses, he willingly served God. And he served in a disciplined way, which, in the sight of God, was neither small nor in vain.[19]

For Our Friends

It's easy to take our friends for granted; regardless of what we do or say, they tend to stick with us. What we have in common binds us together, and little seems able to break that bond. Nonetheless, our friends need our service too, and there are many ways we can reach out to them. For instance:

- If you learn that a friend is going through financial hardship, consider giving her an anonymous gift. Stick the funds in an envelope with only her name on the front (not in your handwriting!), then securely place the envelope somewhere she will surely find it but not conclude that you are the unnamed donor. Let your joy be found in her joy alone.

- If you are the one who talks most of the time, limit your next get-together to asking your friend questions and truly listening to his answers. Serve him by being "quick to listen, slow to speak" (James 1:19).

- Guard your friends' reputations. When rumors erupt and charges fly, give them the benefit of the doubt. Speak to them first; get their side of the story. And exhort those making accusations or spreading slander to hold their tongues and take up the issues with those directly involved.

- Pray for your friends. Regularly intercede on their behalf without any thought of gain for yourself.

- If some of your friends are non-Christians, show them the Lover of all through your loving words and actions.

- Serve your friends by allowing them to serve you too. Do not let pride prevent them from reaching out to you when you're in need. Giving to you can help them grow in service.

- Share your belongings with your friends, even those possessions you prize the most. Show them that your love for them does not stop with that favorite book, chair, tool, necklace, dress, coat, luggage, machine, etc.

- If a friend is sick, bring him food, clean his house, wash his car, drive him to and from the doctor's office, pick up (and even pay for) his medical prescription, change his bedding, read to him, pray with and for him, or simply sit in the same room with him. Do what you can to comfort and uplift him.

- On occasion—not just on birthdays and special holidays—give gifts of appreciation. These need not be expensive or elaborate; they can be as simple as a greeting card, a bouquet of flowers, a handwritten note, a small box of goodies, a memorable snapshot, or a magazine subscription. You will give the gift of encouragement when you give to say thank you for a friendship.

- If you have a friend who is the father or mother of young children and could use a night out, a day alone, or a weekend away, make arrangements to care for the kids so he or she can enjoy a needed break.

For Our Enemies' Sake

One of the toughest lessons in the parable of the Good Samaritan is that *loving service includes our enemies.* Jesus made this uncomfortably clear even when giving straightforward instruction:

> "Love your enemies, do good to those who hate you, bless those who curse you, pray for those who mistreat you. . . .
>
> "If you love those who love you, what credit is that to you? Even 'sinners' love those who love them. And if you do good to those who are good to you, what credit is that to you? Even 'sinners' do that. And if you lend to those from whom you expect repayment, what credit is that to you? Even 'sinners' lend to 'sinners,' expecting to be repaid in full. But love your enemies, do good to them, and lend to them without expecting to get anything back. Then your reward will be great, and you will be sons of the Most High, because he is kind to the ungrateful and wicked. Be merciful, just as your Father is merciful" (Luke 6:27–28, 32–36).

Neighbor-love must be shown toward those who mistreat us, and Jesus, in this passage, *implies* the answer to a common question: "If I love my enemies, how can I keep them from taking advantage of me?"

They may very well take advantage of you. You are free not to worry about that. Just love them. Leave the rest to My Father. He will take care of the situation and reward you.

Jesus is not talking about throwing caution to the wind. Some people are outright dangerous and destructive, and we should protect ourselves and our families from undue harm. At the same time, we can still find ways to show love to our enemies. *How* we do this will vary with the circumstances, but *that* we do it should remain a constant in our lives.

Consider, then, how you can show love to someone who has mistreated you. Begin the process by trying to see your enemy as God does, *as she is:* his scarred image-bearer with inherent value and worth.

She is a person for whom Christ died and rose from the dead. The gospel applies to her as much as to anyone.

She also is hurting. People who strike out at others are like wounded animals—they know they are in pain but resist attempts to relieve that pain. In fact, by fighting against those who wish to help, aching people bring even more pain on themselves. Her pain may be loneliness or emptiness. Perhaps she's struggling to make ends meet but her pride gets in the way of accepting assistance. Maybe she's afraid. Maybe she has been so scarred by others that she distrusts everyone.

Reflect deeply on her situation to see if you can arrive at some understanding of what may be causing her pain. More than likely, she is harming herself more with each sin she commits than she could ever harm you. Realizing this should make it easier for you to show her love.

Now commit her to prayer. Not only pray for her but pray for healing in your attitude toward her. Ask the Lord to help you see how you can be a Good Samaritan in her life.

Once you have in mind what you're going to do, go at it sensitively and caringly, and leave your expectations at home. Things may succeed or fall apart. You may melt a heart or encounter granite. Achieving certain results should not be your aim: Just love. Give the ministry of the towel—that's all you're after. The rest is up to God.

Servants at Work

The people with whom and for whom we work are also our neighbors. Scripture has much to say about work-service. Even in that worst of all work arrangements—slavery—we're called to give of ourselves as if the only one we're working for is Christ:

> Obey your earthly masters with respect and fear, and with sincerity of heart, just as you would obey Christ. . . . Serve wholeheartedly, as if you were serving the Lord, not men, because you know that the Lord will reward everyone for whatever good he does, whether he is slave or free. (Eph. 6:5, 7–8)

In this same context, the Lord gives masters the same obligation: "Do not threaten them, since you know that he who is both their Master and yours is in heaven, and there is no favoritism with him" (v. 9).

How can we lovingly serve those at work? Here are some ideas.

- Replace complaining with problem-solving. Complaining only creates more problems. Serving seeks resolution.
- Take some time to deal with the personal needs of others. This may require waiting until the end of the workday or meeting before the next day's work begins. It may also require hooking up the needy worker with someone who can better help. But don't act as if everything is all right when it isn't.

- Walk a fellow worker out to her car to provide an added sense of safety and security.

- If you're an employer or manager, do all you can to provide your employees with the pay that accurately reflects what their performance is worth.[20]

- Serve your customers well, which means treating them with honesty, integrity, faithfulness, and diligence.

- Create and maintain a working environment in which you and your fellow workers can thrive, not just survive.

- When you have a problem with a fellow worker, lovingly confront him and seek to work out a mutually agreeable solution.

- Speak of other workers more favorably than yourself. Love is not envious or boastful.

- Praise and honor those who do well. Don't take them for granted.

- Provide the education and training people need for excellence. Workers well equipped not only perform better but are more satisfied with their jobs.

- Treat all workers with dignity, including those being let go.

- Refuse to let office politics rule over you and adversely affect your attitude and performance. Remember, it is Christ whom you serve. Be faithful to him and his ways, and he will vindicate you and provide for you.

- If you are in a highly competitive environment, compete against yourself, not others. Try to beat your last performance with an even better one, not so you can embarrass or surpass someone else but so you can excel in service.

- Don't assume your way is the best way. Listen carefully to the ideas of others. Serve them by respecting their knowledge and experience and by encouraging them to contribute significantly to the organization's success.

Community of Strangers

The Samaritan loved a helpless stranger who could not repay his kindness. That's the kind of sacrificial service we will focus on now.

Needy people reside in each of our communities. We don't have to look to other cities or countries to find those who could use help, though there's nothing wrong with doing so.

More than likely, you've heard about people who need a neighbor's touch. They may live on your street, across town, or even farther away. Perhaps they are widows or orphans, unwed mothers or confused fathers. Maybe they are recovering from surgery and have no one to care for them once they leave the hospital. They might be homeless or in danger of losing their homes. Whatever their situation, they are hurting and hungry for love and support.

Come up with ways you can touch their lives. Think about what you have to give that will help. Move beyond the idea of simply mailing a check. Think instead in terms of your talents, time, spiritual gifts, emotional investment . . . those resources that involve sacrificial self-giving.

If you don't know of anyone who needs help, contact a local soup kitchen for the hungry, or a shelter for runaway kids or unwed mothers, or a safe house for abuse victims, or a hospital or prison. Many churches also have ministries to the needy; contact your church first to see what you can do to serve. Parachurch ministries and civic organizations are also good places to look; you'll have no trouble finding hurting people, as well as believers who need more help.

Another option is to start a ministry out of your own resources. During my musician days, I pulled together local professionals and encouraged their commitment to spending several hours a week giving private or group lessons to the poor. In many cases, the instruction was free; when we charged, our fees rarely rose higher than $10 for four lessons a month. Music stores sometimes supplied instruction books and used instruments at drastically reduced rates. At times we bought the music for our students and managed to find them free instruments. In our own small way, we gave young disadvantaged people hope and beauty in worlds they found usually bleak.

If you are homebound for some reason, pray for the needy. If you can, write letters of encouragement and hope, or use your phone or computer to reach out to the hurting. We can all find ways to love and serve, whatever our personal situation.

Finally, as you go about your daily business, keep your eyes and heart open. You may be traveling down a road someday and come across a suffering stranger. Don't pass by. Stop and help. Remember, the love habit of service is a lifestyle, not an event.

Let us, the followers of Love's way, make this prayer our request and ambition when it comes to service:

> Teach us, Lord,
> to serve You as You deserve,
> to give and not to count the cost,
> to fight and not to heed the wounds,
> to labour and not to ask for any reward
> save that of knowing that we do Your will.[21]

13. Evangelism and Apologetics: *for love of truth*

"Seeing your chapter title, I think you must be joking. How can you say evangelism and apologetics are, as you call them, 'habits of love'?" I can hear a fictitious objector saying, "I've perused a number of books on the spiritual disciplines, and I've never once run across apologetics in the list. As for evangelism, it's rarely mentioned at all, much less as a discipline."

"What you say is true," I would respond. "I too have found apologetics absent from lists of the spiritual disciplines, and evangelism I've found covered rarely. But what do you think this means?"

"I'm not sure. Maybe it means that evangelism and apologetics are reserved for specialists. They're spiritual gifts that only some Christians have."

"Well, I don't believe that's the case. Yes, evangelism is a gift of the Spirit,[1] but all Christians—whether or not they have the *gift*—are called to share the truth about Christ, which is what evangelism is about.[2] Apologetics is never listed as a spiritual gift, and all Christians are likewise told to be ready to engage: 'Always be prepared to give an answer to everyone who asks you to give the reason for the hope that you have' (1 Peter 3:15). Neither apologetics nor evangelism is the responsibility of a select few. All of us must evangelize—

share the good news about Jesus—and all of us must apologize for him."

"Whoa—apologize for Christ? I'm not going to tell people I'm sorry about Jesus. He hasn't embarrassed or shamed me. Why would I feel that way about him?"

"That's not what I mean. The concept of 'apologizing for Christ' is rooted in the Greek word *apología,* which means 'defense' or 'reply.'[3] When we apologize for Christ, we answer objections raised. We provide people with evidence that supports our claims about Jesus and what he has done in our lives. In the words of Jude 3, we 'contend earnestly for the faith which was once for all handed down to the saints.'"[4]

"Okay, I get it. But why, then, do so many writers on the spiritual disciplines leave out evangelism and apologetics? Can you explain that?"

"No, I really can't. I'd have to interview each author to discover that answer. But I can tell you this: We live in an era where, at least in the Western world, the social pressure against significant expression of religious devotion is substantial. Spiritual enthusiasts, especially Christians, are being pushed back to the private sphere, told to keep the elements of their faith boxed inside their homes and places of worship. Religious language and symbols are being increasingly banned from the public square under the guise of separation between church and state. Since evangelism and apologetics actively engage people in the public arena, they are coming under heightened criticism; practitioners are labeled as radical fundamentalists and bigoted elitists, treated as ignorant people who simply do not understand the intrinsic value of religious diversity. No one is allowed to say that one way is *the* way; 'truth is relative,' we're told, which means that no belief system has fully discovered or revealed the truth."[5]

"Good points. But what do they have to do with seeing evangelism and apologetics as spiritual disciplines?"

"You're right, I haven't made that clear yet. Maybe this will help: I'll show how Scripture teaches that all Christians are called to share and defend the faith. In other words, evangelism and apologetics are not options but necessities for all Christ-followers. In fact, they are activities—like all the other spiritual disciplines—that help us deepen our love relationship with God and our neighbors. So although they tend to get ignored in treatments on the spiritual disciplines, we must pay attention to them. We must cultivate them as love habits; when we do, they will help the Spirit nurture us in the faith and expand that faith to others who need to embrace it as their own. The world needs us to evangelize and apologize, even as it seeks to squelch our impact."

EVANGELISM: LOVE SPEAKS OUT

The last words a person utters on earth are usually important, revealing what he most values, what most concerns him.

Before Jesus left this earth, his disciples asked him, "Lord, are you at this time going to restore the kingdom to Israel?" He replied, "It is not for you to know the times or dates the Father has set by his own authority" (Acts 1:6–7). A clear answer. A definitive answer. An answer that should have halted all future speculations . . . but it did not. Books and articles, pamphlets and Web sites keep pouring forth, attempting to figure out when Jesus will return to reestablish his rule on earth and thereby "restore the kingdom to Israel." We never seem to learn.[6]

Still, these were not the final words of Jesus, not the ones he deemed most important. Following on the heels of his answer to the disciples' question was the following: "But you will receive power when the Holy Spirit comes on you; and you will be my witnesses in Jerusalem, and in all Judea and Samaria, and to the ends of the earth" (v. 8). With these words said, Jesus bodily ascended into heaven.

He wanted his disciples to focus not on his return but on the coming of his Spirit; the Spirit who empowered Christ would soon fill and empower his followers. What kind of empowerment? Not just power to live but also power to proclaim: "You will be my *witnesses*." This is the work of evangelism.

When Jesus spoke these last words, the disciples were on the Mount of Olives, a little more than a half mile from Jerusalem. From there they traveled to the ancient city, roomed and prayed together, and selected a man to take the place of the deceased Judas. They did not rush out to a foreign mission field to proclaim the gospel; rather, they stayed in their own neighborhood and waited for the Spirit, just as Jesus had instructed. The Spirit's entrance came with the power Jesus foretold:

> On the day of Pentecost, while "they were all with one accord in one place," the Holy Spirit descended on them [the disciples] as a mighty wind and baptized them with the fire of foreign tongues. Devout Jews from the world's nations heard their own languages come out of the mouths of the enraptured apostles. Amazement and perplexity gripped them. Some mocked the apostles, claiming they were overcome by the influence of "new wine." But Peter rose up and defended the strange happenings as the fulfillment of prophetic utterances that had long been embedded in the Hebrew Scriptures. Then he went on and explained

and defended the life, death, resurrection, and teaching of the Messiah of the New Covenant, the covenant He had enacted and secured by His sacrificial death and miraculous resurrection.

That day three thousand people repented of their sins, accepted Jesus as their Savior and Lord, and entered the ranks of the church.[7]

Love's Advance

The first part of Acts is a record of the Spirit empowering the church and the church cooperating with the Spirit to be Christ's witnesses where they already were, in Jerusalem (2:14–8:3). Then the fast-growing movement spread into Judea and Samaria (8:4–12:24), and eventually all the way to the imperial city of Rome—the Gentile crossroads to much of the then-known world (12:25–28:31). How far into the *rest* of the world did these early Christians get?

> We have good reason to believe, for example, that the Apostle Paul made it all the way to Spain planting churches throughout the Mediterranean area. Ancient writings, oral traditions, and other archaeological findings indicate that the Apostle Matthew took the gospel as far as Ethiopia; the Apostle Andrew to Scythia (which was north of the Black Sea); the Apostle Bartholomew to Arabia and India; the Apostle "Doubting" Thomas to India as well; Mark the evangelist (writer of the gospel that bears his name) to Egypt, where Eusebius says he became the first bishop of Alexandria; the Apostle James the Great may have gone as far as Spain; the Apostle Simon to Persia. And this is just a sampling of what Christians, laypeople and church leaders alike, did to spread the good news and establish the church to the "ends of the earth."[8]

In personal relationships, love always begins small—as small as two. A man and a woman meet and become friends. Their friendship brings in other friends they already have and may soon encompass even some of their friends' friends. As their bond develops, the man will introduce the woman to his family, and she will introduce him to hers. Friends of both families and extended family members may also become a part of the couple's circle, as may some colleagues of each. If they marry and have children, their children will lead them to still more people—their friends, other parents, teachers, coaches, extracurricular instructors, librarians, and carpool partners. If their kids grow up and marry, the couple's far-reaching network will expand still more. With the addition of each new person comes a new opportunity for love's extension to others.

As love draws more into its circle, the loved ones already there benefit. They share in the lives of love's new members, gaining from their expertise and experience. The older teach the younger the family's ways, often gradually clarifying to them what the family treasures are and why they're important. In turn, the younger may open to the older new perspectives, suggesting enhanced ways to do things or expanded ways to think about things. As family members learn from one another, both the family and its "neighbors" are enriched.

For love's advance to keep going, benefiting all it touches, each of us must choose to love those who enter our lives—these are our neighbors in our "Jerusalem." And the most loving thing a Christian can do is to tell a neighbor where the greatest love is found. This is what the apostles did; since then, the message of the sacrificial love of the Sacrificial Lamb has spread worldwide several times over. On every continent and in virtually every country and culture, members of the family of Christ live and love. And they love not only their own but those who could become their own.

There is no sign of love's expansion letting up. Love keeps spilling over into people's lives, regardless of any factor that tends to separate one person from the next. "God goes where he's wanted," says Philip Yancey,[9] and where God is wanted is everywhere in the world.

Love's Command

After the Father's Beloved commanded us to love one another, he linked it to how others would know they were encountering Christians: They "will know that you are my disciples, if you love [*agapē*] one another" (John 13:35). *Agapē* is our essential mark, informing all people that we are beloved children of the Lord. Take away *agapē*, and you lose the supernatural in personal relationships; without *agapē*, all that's left are the natural loves that have been corrupted by sin. Since *agapē* is divinely sourced and other-centered, loving fellow Christians *and* our neighbors is central to the command of love. "Love *one another*" covers the body of Christ, and "love your *neighbor*" (Matt. 22:39) covers everyone.

In addition to the reality that love must be passed on or it will atrophy, there's something more profound behind the command to love others: *agapē* seeks to replicate itself. Love reproduces. It strives to create its likeness. Love is never alone. Love bears children.

Eternal Love began this process at the initial moment of creating the universe—a universe designed with humans in mind, beings who would be made like the God who is *agapē*. He then gave these beings the power to procreate more divine image-bearers so *agapē*'s presence would "multiply, and fill the earth, and subdue it" (Gen. 1:28 NASB). Love was set to conquer all, to bring the entire earth under the loving care of his children.

Tragically, though, his children chose selfish love over selfless love. Because of this, they multiplied haters of Love rather than lovers of Love. These corrupted beings gradually turned a paradise into a wasteland.

Nevertheless, Love refused to withdraw into himself. Consistent with his nature, he kept reaching out his arms, offering his boundless love to his prodigals. Much to his joy, many accepted his gracious offer and began a spiritual life anew in their Lover's embrace.

However, it was not until the Lover of all sent his eternal Beloved into the world that his children encountered him among them once again, walking in his creation.[10] The Beloved revealed the Lover in a most personal and visible way; his life bore witness to Love's ongoing passion for restoring all who would return to the fullness of life. For those children who did answer Love's call to return, his Bond of Love changed them: They became reborn on the inside. Love spiritually replicated himself, creating new children, working to de-corrupt and purify them so they could bear his love in wonderful abundance.

Yet not all of Love's children wanted his Son in their midst. Those not yet spiritually "born again" (John 3:7) spurned Love's offer and torturously executed him. The Lover knew they would, so he prepared his embodied Beloved for this brutal death, also promising that he would rise from the tomb designed to contain him. *Love cannot be confined,* so Love's Son arose and presented himself alive to those children who had been reborn and had followed him. Then, after he returned to the side of the Lover who sent him, he sent his followers the Bond of Love, giving them the power they needed to be witnesses of the Beloved, just as the Beloved had been a witness of Love himself. Through these reborn followers and the Spirit who empowered them, *Agapē* would keep replicating himself in others until all who would return had done so. Then he would create a new paradise where they would forever thrive as they basked in Love's infinite self-giving.

This is the biblical story, God's work of renewal in human history. It requires that we who have been "born of the Spirit" (v. 8) be the Son's loving witnesses in a world racked by corruption. But what does it mean to be Christ's witness? Understanding this is critical to understanding the love habit of evangelism.

Love's Witnesses

In the New Testament, the concept of *witness* images a court of law, where people take the stand and attest to the occurrence of an event or the veracity of a discourse or the character of a person. These witnesses are sworn to tell the truth about what they saw, heard, touched, or in some other way experienced. They do not only *provide* evidence that something is either true or false, *they* are, in fact, evidence. Their character and knowledge are as much in evidence as their observation and testimony.[11]

When it comes to Jesus Christ, the impressive witnesses for who he is and what he did are numerous and varied.

Divine Witnesses

The greatest witnesses are God himself, Father and Spirit, both of whom are unchanging Truth and therefore incapable of lying.[12] They authenticated Jesus' identity at his baptism: the Spirit descended on him, and the Father declared him to be his beloved Son.[13] Jesus later said, "the Father who sent me has himself testified concerning me" (John 5:37), adding that the Spirit would come and keep attesting to his identity: "When the Counselor comes, whom I will send to you from the Father, the Spirit of truth who goes out from the Father, he will testify about me" (15:26).

The Divine-Human Witness

Jesus himself knew that he was "the light of the world" saying, "Whoever follows me will never walk in the darkness, but will have the light of life" (8:12). When some Pharisees challenged that he acted as his own witness (v. 13), he answered (vv. 14–17), "Even if I testify on my own behalf, my testimony is valid, for I know where I came from and where I am going." (Jesus knew his heavenly origin and destiny, while his critics did not.) He then appealed to the law, which held that the testimony of two or three witnesses was a legal requirement in court to "prevent false incrimination and uphold justice."[14] On this basis he said, "I am one who testifies for myself; my other witness is the Father, who sent me" (v. 18).

Scriptural Witness

Jesus also pointed people to the Scriptures as a witness to his identity. At the start of his ministry in Nazareth, he stood up in the synagogue, read from Isaiah, sat down, and told his audience, "Today this scripture is fulfilled in your hearing" (Luke 4:21). Later he told some of his Jewish critics, "The

Scriptures . . . testify about me" (John 5:39). After he rose from the dead, he met two of his disciples on a roadway and, "beginning with Moses and all the Prophets, he explained to them what was said in all the Scriptures concerning himself" (Luke 24:27).

God's Word testifies that the Son is the Bible's focus and fulfillment.

Works Witnesses

Jesus' acts likewise testified to his identity: "The very work that the Father has given me to finish, and which I am doing, testifies that the Father has sent me. . . . I have shown you many great miracles from the Father" (John 5:36; 10:32). Miracles verified his status as the God-man; when the Baptist's followers asked if Jesus was the promised Messiah, he answered them by pointing to his works: "Go back and report to John what you hear and see: The blind receive sight, the lame walk, those who have leprosy are cured, the deaf hear, the dead are raised, and the good news is preached to the poor" (Matt. 11:4–5).

By far, the greatest act of testimony to Jesus' identity was his bodily resurrection. Early in his ministry, some Jews demanded a "miraculous sign" to prove that he had the authority to act in God's name. "Jesus answered them, 'Destroy this temple, and I will raise it again in three days'" (John 2:18–19). They erroneously thought he had referred to the Jerusalem temple, but after he had risen from the dead, "his disciples recalled what he had said. Then they believed the Scripture and the words that Jesus had spoken" (v. 22): the temple in question was his body.

Conviction that God had vindicated the Son by raising him led Peter, at Pentecost, to proclaim the Resurrection and defend it as the fulfillment of biblical prophecy: "God has raised this Jesus to life, and we are all witnesses of the fact" (Acts 2:32). From this day forward, the Resurrection was the touchstone of the church's proclamation. As Paul states, the Son "as to his human nature was a descendant of David," but he was "declared with power to be the Son of God by his resurrection from the dead" (Rom. 1:3–4).

Unfriendly Witnesses

Some witnesses of Jesus were not friendly followers—some were even enemies.

A demon, speaking through a man that he possessed, said, "What do you want with us, Jesus of Nazareth? Have you come to destroy us? I know who you are—the Holy One of God!" (Mark 1:24). Another demon referred to Jesus as the "Son of the Most High God" (5:7).

Pontius Pilate, the Roman governor who interrogated Jesus and investigated the charges brought against him, found him innocent and determined that the "envy" of others was the motivating factor behind the accusations. Even Pilate's wife believed Jesus was "innocent" (Matt. 27:19; cf. Luke 23:13–15).

The Roman soldiers in charge of Jesus' crucifixion exclaimed after he died, "Surely he was the Son of God!" (Matt. 27:54).

In the first century, perhaps the most infamous human enemy was Saul of Tarsus, who relentlessly persecuted the followers of the Way, seeking them out, imprisoning them, interrogating them, and even sending them to their death. His zealous objective was to stamp out the church; however, when he had a personal encounter with the risen Jesus, Saul was radically changed. The persecutor of Christ became the proclaimer of Christ. Saul, feared enemy of the faith, became Paul, beloved advocate for the faith. God made him "his witness to all men of what you have seen and heard" (Acts 22:15).[15]

Friendly Witnesses

Surrounding Jesus was a host of friendly witnesses. His forerunner said of him, "Look, the Lamb of God, who takes away the sin of the world! . . . I testify that this is the Son of God" (John 1:29, 34). After hearing John's testimony about Jesus and following him for just a couple of days, Andrew sought out his brother, Peter, then said, "We have found the Messiah," and introduced Peter to Jesus (vv. 35–42). Philip, also after following Jesus, "found Nathanael and told him, 'We have found the one Moses wrote about in the Law, and about whom the prophets also wrote—Jesus of Nazareth, the son of Joseph'" (v. 45). Nathanael, after interacting with Jesus, declared, "Rabbi, you are the Son of God; you are the King of Israel" (v. 49). At the midpoint of his earthly ministry, Jesus asked his disciples who they thought he was; Peter said, "You are the Christ, the Son of the living God" (Matt. 16:16).[16]

Jesus' close followers understood who he was—they would later preach, defend, live out, and die for that message as Jesus began building his church through their pioneering efforts. They obeyed his command that they "must testify, for you have been with me from the beginning" (John 15:27). For the apostles, being Christ's witnesses was not optional, and they faithfully carried out his mandate.

We Are Witnesses

In this great tradition, we too are summoned to testify about Jesus of Nazareth. It's as much a command for us as it was for his earliest followers: the Great Commission appears in some form in all four gospels and the beginning of Acts.[17] Taken together, these texts make clear the nature of our *task,* by whose *authority* we are to act, what *power* will accompany us, the *extent* to which we must obey, the *promise* that will go with us, and the *response* we can expect.

First, our *task* is twofold: "Preach the good news" (Mark 16:15) and "make disciples" (Matt. 28:19). Preaching involves speaking in Christ's name about what Scripture teaches, especially about his suffering and resurrection, and the need for repentance and "forgiveness of sins" (Luke 24:47).

Making disciples requires going, baptizing, and teaching.[18] Our going can be to our family, to those who live near us or work with us, to those in our church, to others in our town . . . any and all neighbors and those we choose to make our neighbors. Our baptizing (by water) is to be in the name of the Trinity—Father, Son, and Spirit. And our teaching should encompass "everything" Jesus commanded, with the objective that we "obey" him (Matt. 28:20).

Second, our *authority* is Jesus. "All authority in heaven and on earth has been given to me," he told us (v. 18); when we testify about Christ and engage in making disciples, we represent him. The King has given us, his subjects, the right to act on his behalf. We have been granted the privilege of sharing the good news of his sacrificial love for all people.

Third, our *power* is the Holy Spirit, the One who enables us to be Christ's witnesses. Our testimony, no matter how faltering, is coupled with the enlightening work of the Spirit within us and the convicting impact of the Spirit upon unbelievers.[19] Therefore, we should not fear—love abides with us and empowers us, and "perfect love," the Spirit, "drives out fear" (1 John 4:18).

Fourth, the *extent* of accomplishment in our witnessing task is nothing short of the entire world: "You will be my witnesses . . . to the ends of the earth" (Acts 1:8). Of course, no one can do this alone; the apostles did not achieve this goal, and neither has any single missionary society, local church, or parachurch organization. We must work together in community, beginning with our closest neighbors. Individually, we must bear witness to Christ wherever we are, but it's only collectively that we can penetrate the rest of the world with the gospel.

Fifth, the *promise* is that our Lord will go wherever we go: "Surely I am with you always, to the very end of the age" (Matt. 28:20). Our Lover will not leave us to do the job by ourselves—he will remain "God with us."

Sixth, and finally, we can count on a mixed *response* to our testimony. Some will believe, while others will not: "Whoever believes and is baptized will be saved, but whoever does not believe will be condemned" (Mark 16:16). Love will not coerce conversion. Love proposes to all, and love weds everyone who says "I believe" and then demonstrates genuineness by seeking to keep their vows and deepen their relationship with Love. Those who refuse the proposal all the way to their grave are allowed to keep their guilt and condemnation. Love is a choice, and so is hell.

Evangelism Is . . .

Biblically speaking, then, *evangelism is the habit of testifying about God's salvation-love.* This love has been demonstrated in the life, ministry, death, and resurrection of his Son, and it continues to be demonstrated through the new life growing in the Son's witnesses. Salvation-love offers forgiveness of all moral debts, a forgiveness that cannot be earned but does involve an exchange. God promises that he will forgive the sins of the penitent, not of the unresponsive. We must ask for his forgiveness. We must put ourselves in his loving hands, throw ourselves on the mercy of our gracious Judge. When we do, he cancels the death sentence against us and gives us life anew, empowering us to live each day in loving submission to him. Forgiveness of sins is free to those who ask for it, but this is only the beginning of our restored relationship; God expects us to *keep* responding to him with more and more yeses and increasingly fewer nos. He comes to us not just as our Savior but also as our Lord. Through faith, we become part of the church, the bride of Christ, and our Groom rightfully requires our faithfulness. He has given us his all, and he commands us to give him ours. This exchange cannot be sidestepped, and it must be part of our evangelistic testimony.

So when we tell sinners about God's love for them as demonstrated through Jesus Christ and us, and when we encourage them to receive that love by faith, we must also tell them what they're asking for: a Lover who will expect their everything while he gives them his. The cost to them will be nothing short of the elimination or transformation of everything that stands in the way of perfect communion with Love. Our Lover is not content with partial anything.

> If anyone would come after me, he must deny himself and take up
> his cross and follow me. For whoever wants to save his life will lose it,

but whoever loses his life for me and for the gospel will save it. (Mark 8:34–35)

The way to the fullness of life and love is dying to anything and everything that opposes life and love. There is no other way.

APOLOGETICS: LOVE FIGHTS BACK

"All right, then," returns my fictitious objector. "I see what evangelism is and why it's a love habit. But how does apologetics fit with evangelism? I gather that you think they have an important relationship, since you're covering them in one chapter and have suggested in its title that they're both habits for the love of truth. What's their connection?"

"I'm glad you asked. Evangelism is speaking the truth about the Truth so others can see the Truth and embrace him. Witnesses should tell the truth and nothing but the truth, especially about him who *is* truth."

"Okay, I get that. What does it have to do with apologetics?"

"Well, apologetics *defends* the truth that evangelism *presents*. You see, witnesses will often have their testimony challenged."

"I've seen that happen. A witness takes the stand. One attorney asks her questions, soliciting the testimony he's seeking. After he sits down, another attorney rises and asks questions designed to put her on the defensive, to doubt what she saw or heard, and maybe even attempt to impugn her motives or character. His goal is to undermine her testimony."

"Yes. And when the witness is put in this kind of situation, she must offer the best defense she can muster. If she doesn't, she runs the very real risk of her testimony being discounted and therefore the truth of what she says being rejected as false."

"Are you saying that apologetics is defensive?"

"When it comes to evangelism, yes."

"So apologetics has other uses too?"

"It does. I'll show you what I mean."

Defending Love

Anyone who thinks love is wimpy has never been in love. Lovers support and defend each other.

Like most parents, mine worked hard to equip me in every way to handle life's attacks. When I was over my head, they would step in and fight for me or alongside me. I distinctly recall one of these occasions from when I was around nine or ten years old.

Our next-door neighbor swooped to our front door, and my mom invited her inside. Standing in the kitchen, the other mother (whom I'll call Ann) told my mom what her son (whom I'll call Richie) had said to her.

"Your son," Ann began in a tone that sounded like she was lecturing, "stood on the back fence and taunted my little Richie until he ran into our house in tears. I don't know all he said, but Richie told me that Billy was making fun of him. You need to talk to your son and punish him for what he did." She was visibly upset; I could see that in her scowling face and hands-on-hips stance. By now my mom had gotten to her feet and had set them firmly facing Ann.

"Ann," she said, calmly but firmly, "Billy did not tease Richie. He's been playing by himself in the backyard, and I've seen him through our sliding glass door. He has stayed to himself, minding his own business. Besides, Billy has a sweet spirit. He would not take it upon himself to hurt your boy. I don't know why Richie told you what he did, but Billy has done nothing wrong."

"You'll stick up for your son no matter what!" Ann accused, her scowl digging further into her face.

"No, that's not true," my mom answered. "Billy is not perfect, and when he's wrong, I talk to him about it and punish him if that's needed. But I know that he did not and would not do what Richie claims he did. I think you need to have a talk with your son and find out why he is lying to you."

Mom's voice had been steady and unruffled, but I could tell that it was being held in tight control, like a leopard inching her way, slow motion, toward the prey on which she planned to pounce.

Ann didn't take it well. She left in a huff, and it was a long while before I saw her in our home again.

After she left, my mom turned to me and asked, with probing firmness, "Did you get on our back fence and tease Richie in any way? Be honest with me."

"No, Mom, I didn't tease him. I did get on the fence, and I did see Richie in his backyard. But he was the one who told me to get off the fence, and he called me names too."

"Did you say anything back to him?"

"Nope, not a thing. I just got off the fence and went back to what I was doing."

During this whole exchange, my mom kept her eyes on mine; she had an uncanny ability to see into my soul. Almost always she could tell if I was lying, and I was telling the truth this time. She could tell.

"I knew you hadn't teased Richie. You wouldn't do something like that. That's not the kind of person you are."

My mom knew me inside and out. Like all kids, I got away with my share of shenanigans. But I swear she had eyes in the back of her head; she didn't even have to turn around to know what I was up to, good or bad.

Because she knew me so well, she could defend me before Ann. My character and its limits were all too familiar to her. She knew that while I might go wrong in some ways, hassling Richie would not have been one of them. And she was right.

As a child, my mother's intimate knowledge protected me from false charges and motivated me to respect and obey her much more than I likely would have. It was fabulous to be known and loved so well.

Likewise, when someone accused her of something, I knew immediately if the charge was true or false. I stood ready to defend her and always did, whether the accusation was true or not, and it almost always was false. Even on those rare occasions when the criticism had some teeth, I knew my mom so well that I could say why she likely said or did what she had, and therefore shed the light needed to significantly lessen the accusation's impact.

Love creates a bond between people that leads them to fight against whatever or whoever threatens to undermine or destroy that bond. This is as true in our love relationship with God as it is with fellow human beings. True love, wherever it exists, fights back, and in the trenches of that fight, the love bond is strengthened even more.

The Father equipped his Son with the Spirit and with godly parents so he could grow up into spiritual maturity. By the time Jesus was ready to start his ministry, he was ready to go one-on-one with the ultimate adversary. Jesus entered the wilderness "full of the Holy Spirit" (Luke 4:1)—in complete submission to the Father and drawing fully from the Spirit's infinite well of resources. As a result, he beat back Satan's assaults and left the wilderness completely victorious. In fact, he never lost against the devil, temptation, or anything else that tried to sever his bond of love with the Father.

Jesus also answered his human critics by words and deeds. To those who challenged his authority to forgive sins, he not only spoke forgiveness but proved his power by healing the physical condition of the man he forgave.[20] Against the Sadducees who disbelieved the resurrection from the dead, Jesus refuted their position with reason and exegesis[21] and later rose from the dead himself. In response to the Pharisees' misinterpretations and misapplications of the law, Jesus correctly interpreted it and wisely applied it while pointing out their errors.[22] The Gospels are replete with examples of our Lord teaching, defending, and living out the truth—all providing evidence that he was indeed all he claimed to be. He fought the good fight and he won it, amazing and often silencing his critics as well as winning many to his side.

The apostles followed their Master's example. As faithful witnesses, they presented the truth, lived the truth, and defended the truth. Matthew, the once-hated Jewish tax collector who left behind his livelihood to follow Christ, wrote to show how Jesus repeatedly fulfilled biblical prophecy, thereby proving to be the predicted Messiah. John, the closest of Jesus' disciples, wrapped his material around seven miracles so that his readers would have the needed evidence to "believe that Jesus is the Christ, the Son of God, and that by believing you may have life in his name" (John 20:31). Peter, the catcher of fish who became the Messiah's catcher of people, appealed to Jesus' miracles, bodily resurrection, and fulfillment of prophecy as divine vindications of his identity.[23]

Then there was Paul, formerly Saul. He became the early church's greatest evangelist, church planter, and apologist. Each time that he spoke as Christ's witness, proclaiming and defending the salvation message, he refused to use a canned approach—his presentations fit his audience. If they needed to hear about his past life in Judaism and the role he played persecuting the church, he shared that information, always adding, of course, the life-changing account of his encounter with the risen Christ and how he responded and was converted. If he was speaking to Jews who held the Hebrew Scriptures as authoritative, he habitually "reasoned with them from the Scriptures, explaining and proving that the Christ had to suffer and rise from the dead," declaring this Christ to be "Jesus" (Acts 17:2–3).

When Paul appeared before those who did not accept Scripture as their authority, he found common ground on which he could build his case. With the polytheistic and pantheistic philosophers of Athens, Paul started with an altar he had seen in their city, bearing the inscription TO AN UNKNOWN GOD. "Now what you worship as something unknown," he said, "I am going to proclaim to you" (v. 23). And that he did, beginning with the origin of the world and citing Greek poets (but not Scripture) along the way. No matter his approach, he witnessed the same results: some people believed the message and were saved, while others made no commitment to Christ, at least not at that time.[24]

What we see is that, for Jesus and his followers, witnessing involved more than proclaiming; it also involved *defending the proclamation*. Evangelism and apologetics worked side by side. When the message was challenged, a defense was made—sometimes evidence was provided along with the message even before criticisms arose. For instance, Jesus and his early followers sometimes performed miracles, authenticating their teaching and authority, only to address suspicions and accusations that followed afterward. Apologetics was not an afterthought; it was a vital part of the Christian mission from the very start.

The need to defend the faith has not waned. In our day, we're facing such philosophical assaults on Christianity as relativism, pluralism, nihilism, and postmodernism.[25] From the realm of science, naturalistic macroevolution poses a grave but declining threat.[26] On the worldview front, I believe pantheism, polytheism, and panentheism present the greatest challenges.[27] Atheism, long the tenacious opposition, appears to be losing ground, even though it must still be answered.[28] Islam and Mormonism are two of the world's fastest-growing religions. While Christians have more in common with Islam (which is theistic) than with Mormonism (which is polytheistic), both aggressively make converts and are hostile to orthodox Christianity.[29]

It's clear, therefore, that in our day we must prepare "to make a defense to everyone who asks" (1 Peter 3:15 NASB) and "contend earnestly for the faith" (Jude 3 NASB) that the church has presented and preserved for two thousand years. With Paul we, the lovers of truth, must seek to "demolish arguments and every pretension that sets itself up against the knowledge of God" (2 Cor. 10:5).

Of course, we cannot defend what we fail to understand. To effectively engage in apologetics, we must immerse ourselves in the truth so that it fills our minds and orders our wills. As we learn the truth, we must also teach it to fellow believers, sharing with family members what we have come to see.[30] This will enable more in the body of Christ to join with us in the apologetic task.

On the other hand, apologetics is not a love habit to be exercised solely with those who oppose the faith. Even in New Testament times, this discipline was also applied to shore up the faith of believers. Hebrews, for example, defends the absolute supremacy of Jesus Christ; its Christian readers were in danger of exalting others over him—including angels, Moses, Joshua, the Old Covenant, and the Aaronic priesthood.[31] Jude urged believers to defend the grace of God against false teachers who were claiming that faith in the gospel gave Christians license to sin. He refuted this subversive doctrine, thereby helping his readers better understand the truth and how to defend it. The more you know the evidence that supports the faith, the stronger your faith will become.

Apologetics Is . . .

Apologetics, then, is *the love habit of rationally and lovingly providing evidence for the truth of Christianity's essential beliefs and practices.* For unbelievers who challenge the faith, apologetics provides answers to objections. For fellow believers, apologetics shows them how to overcome challenges and contributes to their mind renewal by revealing the firm intellectual foundation upon which the faith stands. Christianity is reasonable, persuasive, and true. Apologetics demonstrates this, and evangelism proclaims it. The goal is to build vital roles for these two love habits in our lives.

LOVE THAT CONVINCES AND PERSUADES

Evangelism and apologetics both seek to persuade. Some of their methods may differ, but their aim is the same: to convince people of the truth and relevance of the Christian faith. For us to persuade others, we must first be persuaded. Not all Christians are.

I, for one, spent years struggling with doubts about the compatibility of the Christian God with the origin and prevalence of human suffering. You may have different issues that prevent you from being fully convinced that Christianity is true. Whatever they are, do not avoid them. Commit to tackling them. Make their resolution a part of your study, meditation, and journaling. Be relentless about this. There are answers—and good ones at that—but you must be willing to work at searching them out. God "rewards those who earnestly seek him" (Heb. 11:6). Seek truth, and you *will* find more of him. Learn more of him, and you will discover greater joy and inner serenity with far fewer doubts and much more certainty.

This focus turns the discipline of apologetics from defense to offense. You are preparing yourself for battle, preparation that includes dealing with your own questions and doubts. You are studying to answer faith challenges that well up within you, not just those posed by others.

I readily grant that finding good answers is easier said than done. With all the resources available—books, magazines, journals, study guides, cassettes, videos, Web sites, and more—where does one start looking? Here are two effective steps you can take.

First, *look for an introductory resource.* Every issue has its complexities, but until you learn the basics, you will not be prepared to move beyond them. Introductions are designed to cover a subject's key matters, and they usually mention other resources that can take you deeper into just about any facet of the subject. Not all introductions to a subject have the word *introduction* in their title. Many are simply written on a non-technical level for a wide audience and bear popular-sounding titles.

For instance, Lee Strobel's *The Case for Christ* and *The Case for Faith* are excellent introductions to some of the evidence for Christianity's truthfulness. One does not have to be a philosopher, historian, scientist, theologian, or psychologist to read these books, even though he interviews such professionals and draws compelling answers to numerous objections against the faith. The main thing is to find a resource you can reasonably grasp so you can understand the basics of the issue needing resolution.

For many people, one of the best resources will be an established course on Christian apologetics. You can usually find such courses at your local Bible college or seminary, as well as online. Good resources are available. You simply need to spend some time looking for them.

Second, *look for authoritative guides.* That is, seek out people who are respected in their field and know what they are talking about. At times I've waded through a fair amount of intellectual trash before I came across some real treasures. On this journey I've found people who are stellar guides and people who are lost in the caves of their own false assumptions and fallacies. I'm delighted to report that in virtually any area of study, you can find highly respected and brilliant Christians who show the way. Here is just a *small sampling* of those who have helped me through troubled waters. I've listed them next to *one* of their specialties, realizing that many are experts in two or more fields.

- *Bible:* Walter Kaiser, Jr., F. F. Bruce, N. T. Wright, Gleason L. Archer, Jr.

- *Theology:* Augustine, Thomas Aquinas, William G. T. Shedd, Robert L. Saucy

- *Philosophy:* J. P. Moreland, Jacques Maritain, Étienne Gilson, Richard L. Purtill

- *Apologetics:* Norman Geisler, Peter Kreeft, C. S. Lewis, Gary Habermas
- *Religions:* Walter Martin, Winfried Corduan, David Burnett, J. N. D. Anderson
- *Psychology:* Larry Crabb, Paul Vitz, Robert C. Roberts, C. Stephen Evans
- *History:* Jaroslav Pelikan, Mark Noll, Hugo Rahner, John D. Woodbridge
- *Science:* John Polkinghorne, William A. Dembski, Charles B. Thaxton, Michael Behe
- *Ethics:* Harold O. J. Brown, Paul Ramsey, Francis J. Beckwith, Scott B. Rae
- *Sociology:* Os Guinness, Richard John Neuhaus, Peter L. Berger
- *Literature:* Leland Ryken, Dorothy Sayers, Walker Percy, D. Bruce Lockerbie
- *Law:* Mary Ann Glendon, Hadley Arkes, J. Budziszewski, John Warwick Montgomery
- *Education:* Howard Hendricks, Frank E. Gaebelein, John Henry Newman, Mortimer Adler
- *Spirituality:* Dallas Willard, Richard Foster, Gordon MacDonald, Henri Nouwen

As you grow in your intellectual grasp of Christianity's truth, you will also be preparing to answer challenges to the faith. You will learn more about the various issues and ways of addressing them, especially when you learn from top-notch thinkers like those just listed. They know what's going on in the world, especially in their areas of expertise; they will tell you about the criticisms being leveled, and they will inform you of the viewpoints that seek to replace or seriously revise the Christian worldview. They will also walk you through their own answers to the criticisms and their own challenges to Christianity's rivals. The more you learn from thinkers like these, the more prepared you will be to defend the faith.

Through this approach, you will also see your own doubts and questions gradually drop away as they are answered. Questions I had years ago are gone, as are doubts that were connected to them. I still have questions—new ones—but none about the faith's essentials. I no longer doubt that Christian theism is the fully true worldview; I know this in the depth of my being. Rival views have some truth in them, but on the whole such models are false.

This level of conviction did not come to me immediately; it took years of patiently laboring through the issues. The work was sometimes difficult and tedious, but I would not trade one hour of it. Because I have become so convinced of Christianity's truthfulness, I confidently testify about it, proclaiming and defending it inside and outside the church. My life and the lives of those I touch will never be the same as a result. This can also be *your* experience, *your* joy.

Shine Your Light

One more thing: the more convinced you become of Christianity's truth, the more you will wrap your life around it. Persuaded witnesses not only speak out about the truth—they live it out too. We are beacons of the Light in a dark world, and the Light calls on each of us to "let your light shine before men, that they may see your good deeds and praise your Father in heaven" (Matt. 5:16). Notice Jesus said, "Let your light shine." Our choice is not *whether* we will be his witnesses; we already *are*. We are light-bearers just as surely as we are image-bearers. The question is, what kind of light-bearers will we be? Those in whom other people will see Jesus? Those who illuminate the way to him who is the Way? We will be this kind of light-bearer to the degree that our words about Christ match up with our actions under Christ.

All the love habits are God's means of transforming you into that kind of light. The more you become like him, the more your life will radiate him. Learning evangelistic or apologetic methods will not bring you such a life. Deepening your love relationship with God will.

If the prospect of sharing and defending your faith scares you, then take heart: you are not alone. Many Christians who came before you trembled over this, and I am no exception. In fact, I have felt sheer terror. But courage is forging through the fear, refusing to allow it to master you. Keep at the forefront of your mind and heart that the Fearless One is at work in you, and you will be able to overcome your fear.

Right after I became a believer in 1972, I was so excited about my new-found freedom in Christ that I spoke freely about him. Within a year or two, though, my enthusiasm was choked out by my nagging doubts about the faith's veracity. Intellectual struggles crushed my evangelistic zeal.

Thankfully, my discovery of the writings of R. C. Sproul, C. S. Lewis, John Warwick Montgomery, Francis Schaeffer, and other apologists started giving me solid answers to many of my most debilitating questions. My desire to speak out increased, and with it came more chances to let my light shine. It was about this time that I set myself up for a witnessing opportunity that kept me awake at night in fear and dread.

I was taking a course in political philosophy at the local university. My professor, Dr. Kessler, was an activist atheist, well-known on campus. I had great respect for him, even though our worldviews were polar opposites. He was bright and engaging, and I was rapidly learning in his course.

One of the assignments was to write and deliver a paper to the class on a topic pertaining to the course's subject matter. I chose biblical prophecy and how an understanding of it should affect our political philosophy. I ran it by Dr. Kessler, and he approved it. For the next six weeks, along with researching and writing, I read fourteen books on Christian apologetics, attempting to prepare for any objection I might have to answer.

The closer the day came for me to read my paper before the class, the more fearful I became. Restful sleep became elusive, and food held no flavor. I began questioning my own sanity. *Who do you think you are, believing you can speak for Christ in a philosophy class, of all places? You must be out of your mind.*

With terror rising to new heights, I asked friends and family to pray for me. I desperately needed God to settle me down. I was beginning to fear I'd stutter and stumble through my presentation. I didn't want that for me or for Christ.

When the hour finally arrived, my head was full of arguments and evidence for the faith, and my paper was as strong as I could possibly make it. I was as ready as I'd ever be, and my stomach was feeding on sheer adrenaline.

I do not recall much of what I said. But I do remember glancing at students' faces. They were riveted on my every word, eyes wide open.

When my presentation ended, they sat in silence. When Dr. Kessler dismissed us, he walked me out the door. He then turned to me and said, "You definitely got everyone's attention. I don't think they'll forget what you said. Remember, you're up to answer questions on your paper the next class session. Be ready."

"Oh, I will be, Dr. Kessler."

Two days later all of us arranged our desks in a large circle and sat facing each other. I was in the hot seat, and it didn't take long for things to heat up. Students started barraging me with questions, but not one inquiry had to do with my paper's topic. Their inquests were more typical: How do you know Jesus really lived? What evidence is there that he really rose from the dead? What makes you think the stories about him are more than sheer myth? If Jesus is the only way to God, then what chance do people have who have never heard about him? If God is all-good and he created all things, then where did evil come from? . . . All that time I'd spent studying those apologetics books paid off. I was able to answer every question, and my confidence rose as I did.

Seeing this kind of success did not sit well with Dr. Kessler. He finally broke into the middle of an answer and began throwing out one objection after another. "I think Christianity is an absurd religion," he said. "It's full of contradictions. Take the Trinity. The notion that God is three yet one is a logical absurdity. It makes no sense. The same is true about the Incarnation. How can the same being be infinite and finite at the same time? That's a contradiction if there ever was one. . . ." On and on he went.

As he talked, I sat there trying to figure out how to respond. I had not researched the logical issues he was raising, so I had no idea how to answer him.[32] What could I say? Silently, I asked for God's help. Then it came.

"Excuse me, Dr. Kessler," I quietly said.

"Yes, Mr. Watkins," he replied, politely yet firmly.

"I was just wondering: have you ever read the entire Bible?" I was barely looking at him.

"No, I haven't."

Looking at him a bit more directly, I asked, "Have you ever read just the New Testament or just the Old Testament?"

"No, I can't say that I have," he answered.

"Well, then, have you ever read an entire book in either Testament?" My voice was becoming bolder.

"No," he said flatly.

"How about a chapter anywhere in the Bible?"

"No."

"A verse, then? Just one verse?" I probed with a hint of incredulity.

"No, not even a verse." Now he was barely looking at me.

"Dr. Kessler, I don't understand. During this entire course, you have impressed upon us the importance of reading primary sources. It's not good enough, you've said, to read books on Marx, Marcuse, Lerner, or any other political philosopher. We must read and study the philosophers themselves, which is what we've done in this course. Until we do that, we have no room to critique them. I have seen the value of this approach firsthand, and I thank you for it."

"Yes, yes, okay, but what are you driving at?" He was growing impatient.

"What I'm driving at is this: You have raised some serious objections to Christianity, yet you haven't read Christianity's primary source—the Bible. You haven't even read just one verse out of it. Since you have not read this book, you have no business criticizing the faith that comes from it. You don't even know if your criticisms have any merit. How could you? Your criticisms are from secondhand sources at best. By your own admission, you have not derived a single criticism from Christianity's primary source document. So you have no room to criticize what you have not yet studied."

By this time, I was staring into his eyes, which were looking not at me but at the floor. Glancing around, I noticed that each student in the room had their eyes riveted on him. No one spoke a word. The room was as eerily still as the eye of a hurricane.

Just then the bell sounded, marking the end of class. Students slowly left their seats and filed out the door. Dr. Kessler left too, without saying a word to me or to anyone else.

————

The course soon came to an end, and Dr. Kessler awarded me an A for my work. Some months later, I went into the philosophy department office with a question for the secretary. When she asked my name, I heard a voice behind me: "You don't know Mr. Watkins? You should. Get to know him. He's one of the finest philosophy students we have." Turning around, I saw that the speaker was Dr. Kessler. He had a smile of respect on his face.

During the rest of my studies at the university, Dr. Kessler and I remained on excellent terms. He did not convert to Christianity, but he gained a new-found respect for Christians and for the faith they held fast. And he began reading and studying the Bible, even appreciating some of what he found there. Perhaps one day I'll see him again and be able to call him my brother in Christ.

Presenting and defending the truth does not guarantee conversions any more than your reading this book guarantees that you will develop and maintain the love habits called the spiritual disciplines. But *this* is certain: People cannot come to know Christ unless they are introduced to him. He has chosen you and me to carry on this task for the love of him, the love of neighbor, and the love of truth. If we love him, we will follow him in what he asks us to do.

Love that persuades flows from a persuasive life. A persuasive life flows from a person centered on the Center of all things. See him there. Live with him there. Draw your very life from him. And as you do, share and defend the truth you know, striving to continue learning it and growing up in it.

Our Lover will show himself through you so that more and more people will be attracted to him and his way. In you, they will meet him, and some will believe and be saved. Then they will join you as fellow children of God, your brothers and sisters in Christ. Together, you will experience and enjoy the fullness that only lovers can.

Endnotes

Chapter 2—The Supreme Source

1. The usual way John refers to himself in his gospel is as "the other disciple" or as the disciple "whom Jesus loved" (cf. 13:23; 19:26; 20:2; 21:7, 20, 24).
2. Walther Günther and Hans-Georg Link, "Love" in *The New International Dictionary of New Testament Theology*, Colin Brown, ed. (Grand Rapids: Zondervan, 1976), vol. 2, 539.
3. Ibid., 538.
4. Luke 12:4; John 15:14–15.
5. John 5:20; 16:27.
6. Günther and Link, 539.
7. Archibald Robertson and Alfred Plummer, *A Critical and Exegetical Commentary on the First Epistle of St. Paul to the Corinthians*, 2nd ed., in *The International Critical Commentary* (Edinburgh: T. & T. Clark, 1978), 292.
8. W. Phillip Keller, *A Layman Looks at the Love of God* (Minneapolis: Bethany House, 1984), 53.
9. Genesis 1:26–28. See also Henri Blocher, *In the Beginning: The Opening Chapters of Genesis* (Downers Grove, Ill.: InterVarsity, 1984), chapter 4.
10. For an overview of the growing scientific evidence that the universe is fine-tuned for human life, see Hugh Ross, "Big Bang Model Refined by Fire" in *Mere Creation: Science, Faith and Intelligent Design*, William A. Dembski, ed. (Downers Grove, Ill.: InterVarsity, 1998), chapter 15.
11. God does not *need* the admiration or applause of his creatures—*he* is the One who gives *us* all that's good. We need him, and, graciously, he gives us himself. We worship and praise him for this, not because he would be incomplete without it but because he is worthy of it.
12. Matthew 6:1–6.
13. Isaiah 14:13–14. A concise case for taking this passage as referring to Satan and not merely to a human ruler is found in C. Fred Dickason, *Angels, Elect and Evil* (Chicago: Moody, 1975), chapter 13.
14. Peter Kreeft, *Back to Virtue* (San Francisco: Ignatius, 1992), 100.
15. Job 11:7–11; Psalm 147:5; Romans 11:33.
16. Isaiah 43:10; 44:6–8; 45:5.
17. Galatians 4:3–7; Ephesians 2; Hebrews 2:14–17.
18. Lewis B. Smedes, *Love Within Limits: Realizing Selfless Love in a Selfish World* (Grand Rapids: Eerdmans, 1978), 36.
19. Luke 15:23–24.
20. Peter Kreeft, *Three Philosophies of Life* (San Francisco: Ignatius, 1989), 106.
21. Mark 1:11.
22. John 5:20.
23. Colossians 3:14; Galatians 5:22.

24. Citing Proverbs 3:11–12 in Hebrews 12:5–6, 10–11.

25. C. S. Lewis, *The Problem of Pain* (New York: Macmillan, 1962), 46.

26. Colossians 1:22; Jude 24.

27. Isaiah 5:20.

28. Revelation 20–22.

29. See C. K. Barrett, *The First Epistle to the Corinthians* (New York: Harper & Row, 1968), 304.

30. Matthew 5:45.

31. Luke 23:34.

32. D. Edmond Hiebert, *1 Peter* (Chicago: Moody, 1992), 272.

33. Smedes, *Love Within Limits,* 95.

34. Paul may even have a third meaning in mind for *stégei* in 1 Corinthians 13. The term can also mean "endures" or "perseveres"; it's used this way in 1 Thessalonians 3:1, 5. This latter interpretive option is more unlikely than the other two choices because Paul uses another word in 1 Corinthians 13:7 that means "endures." While he sometimes restates his point, there's no apparent reason for doing so here.

35. Smedes, op. cit., 106.

36. 1 Corinthians 6:3.

37. 1 Corinthians 15:50–54; 1 Thessalonians 5:23; Jude 24.

38. Romans 8:29; Colossians 3:9–10; 1 John 3:2–3.

39. Luke 6:12–16; Matthew 10:1; 11:2–5; John 17.

40. Matthew 26:69–75; 27:1–5; John 13:26–27; Luke 23:34, 39–43.

41. C. S. Lewis, *The Weight of Glory and Other Addresses* (Grand Rapids: Eerdmans, 1949), 15.

42. Luke 20; 22:1–6.

43. Charles Hodge, *A Commentary on 1 & 2 Corinthians* (Carlisle, Pa.: Banner of Truth Trust, reprint ed., 1983), 271.

44. Hebrews 4:15; 1 Peter 2:22; Matthew 3:17.

45. Job 1–2; Ephesians 6:11–13; 1 Peter 5:8–9; Revelation 12:7–17.

46. John 3:16–18; 15:1–9; Hebrews 10:26–31; 2 Peter 3:9.

47. Revelation 21:6–7.

48. Romans 8:29; 1 John 3:2.

49. These statements about God's love flow from the divine attribute of simplicity, which means that God is absolutely indivisible, uncomposed, without parts in his essence: All of God's attributes are one in him. Heinrich Heppe says,

> The divine attributes are not something different from the nature and existence of God, so that the latter may be thought of as distinct from the former; nor are they parts of the divine nature, so that their total makes up the unity of the divine nature; nor are they something accidental, so that God's nature would be thinkable without the attributes; in God's nature there is nothing which is not God Himself. . . . [E]very separate attribute of God is the identity of the whole divine being. (*Reformed Dogmatics,* G. T. Thomson, trans. [Grand Rapids: Baker, reprint, 1978], 57.)

50. Peter Kreeft, *The God Who Loves You* (Ann Arbor, Mich.: Servant, 1988), 64–65.

51. 1 Corinthians 13:1–3.

Chapter 3—The Way

1. See John 14–17.

2. Matthew 17:20.

3. Luke 2:52 in Charles B. Williams, *The New Testament in the Language of the People* (Chicago: Moody, 1966).
4. 1 Corinthians 3:9; 1 Thessalonians 3:2.
5. Hebrews 6:1 in Williams, op. cit.
6. Commentators and theologians disagree about the nature of this divinely bestowed reward. I am inclined to agree with those who see it as one of special service and privilege in the future kingdom life—eternity—planned for believers (see Matt. 25:14–23; 2 Cor. 5:10–11; Rev. 5:9–10; 7:14–17; 22:3, 12). I think it's a reward based on what we do with what we receive from God. If we draw on his resources and use them well, he will reward us. If we use his resources sparingly and poorly, he will not reward us even though he will save us (1 Cor. 3:10–15). *In my understanding, the reward is for service rendered, not for the gift of salvation.* Just as a reward can be gained, so it can be lost (Matt. 25:24–30; Col. 2:18; 2 John 8; Rev. 3:11). Paul did not want to be disqualified for his reward of service, which is why he trained vigorously and ran resolutely (1 Cor. 9:24–27).
7. Acts 9–28.
8. Philippians 3:12–14.
9. Jerry Bridges, *The Practice of Godliness* (Colorado Springs: NavPress, 1983), 263.
10. Matthew 1:18–23; Luke 1:26–38.
11. Luke 4:1–13.
12. Concerning the role of the Spirit in Jesus' human development, see the insightful work of New Testament scholar Gerald F. Hawthorne, *The Presence and the Power* (Dallas: Word, 1991).
13. J. Oswald Sanders, *In Pursuit of Maturity* (Grand Rapids: Zondervan, 1986), 168–69.
14. John 4:14; 6:35; 7:37–39; 10:10.
15. Paul's use of the word *body* (Greek: *sōma*) here does not refer to our whole selves. Rather, he uses the term to mean the physical part of our being, what we normally mean by "body." One indication of this occurs in Romans 12:2, where Paul refers to the mind (Greek: *nous*), using it to designate the mental or intellectual side of our self-expression as distinct from our body, which designates the physical side of our self-expression. If Paul had wanted to refer to our whole selves when urging us on to spiritual maturity, he could have easily substituted appropriate personal pronouns for *bodies* or *mind,* but he did not. For more on this interpretive issue, see Robert H. Gundry's landmark work *Sōma in Biblical Theology: With Emphasis on Pauline Anthropology* (Grand Rapids: Zondervan, 1987), 34–36, as well as John Murray's fine commentary *The Epistle to the Romans* in *New International Commentary on the New Testament* (Grand Rapids: Eerdmans, 1965), 110–16.
16. See Genesis 3; Isaiah 14:12–17; Ezekiel 28:11–19; 1 Timothy 3:6; Jude 6; 2 Peter 2:4; Revelation 12:3–4, 7–9.
17. 1 Corinthians 1:20; 2:6; 3:18–19.
18. J. P. Moreland, *Love Your God With All Your Mind: The Role of Reason in the Life of the Soul* (Colorado Springs: NavPress, 1997), 73.
19. 1 Corinthians 13; John 13:34–35.
20. In interest of space, there are some spiritual disciplines I will not address at this time; for example, fasting, fellowship, worship, and celebration. Nevertheless, all of them are love habits in the development of a personal love relationship. When we love someone, we can easily slip into festive joy (*celebration*) and sing her praises (*worship*). We want to spend a great deal of time with her, walking, talking, sharing, crying, upholding . . . just living life together (*fellowship* with God and with other believers). We also make sacrifices for those we love, including skipping meals so we can focus on more important things (*fasting*). No matter the spiritual discipline, the paradigm of love fits it.

Chapter 4—Simplicity: The God-Centered Life

1. Charles C. Ryrie, *Balancing the Christian Life* (Chicago: Moody, 1994), 9–10.
2. Kreeft, *The God Who Loves You*, 39.
3. See Blocher, *In the Beginning*, 106–07.
4. Francis J. Beckwith and Norman L. Geisler, *Politically Correct Death: Answering Arguments for Abortion Rights* (Grand Rapids: Baker, 1993), 42.
5. Owen Chadwick, *A History of Christianity* (New York: St. Martin's, 1995), 178.
6. John 14:23.
7. Matthew 12:50.
8. Romans 3:3–4.
9. Romans 8:1; Ephesians 2; Colossians 2:13–14; Titus 3:3–7.
10. Hebrews 4:1–13; Revelation 21–22.
11. John 14:12.
12. Kreeft, *Three Philosophies of Life*, 136.
13. C. S. Lewis, *Mere Christianity* (New York: Macmillan, 1952), 104.
14. Matthew 5:3, 5, 8–10.
15. Augustine, *Confessions: Books I-XIII*, F. J. Sheed, trans. (Indianapolis: Hackett, 1993), I.1.
16. Thomas R. Kelly, *A Testament of Devotion* (San Francisco: HarperCollins, 1992), 93.

Chapter 5—Submission: Freedom in Surrender

1. John 14:6.
2. Hawthorne, *The Presence and the Power*, 210.
3. For more on equality in the Trinity and the temporary submission of the incarnate Son, see the excellent essay by Gilbert Bilezikian, "Hermeneutical Bungee-Jumping: Subordination in the Godhead" in *Journal of the Evangelical Theological Society* 40:1 (March 1997), 57–68.
4. Mike Mason, *The Mystery of Marriage* (Sisters, Ore.: Multnomah, 1985), 154.
5. Cicero, *In Defense of Rabirius*, 5.16, as quoted by Michael P. Green, "The Meaning of Cross-Bearing" in *Bibliotheca Sacra* (April-May 1983), 132, no. 48.
6. Hans-Ruedi Weber, *The Cross: Tradition and Interpretation* (Grand Rapids: Eerdmans, 1978), 6.
7. Paul L. Maier, *In the Fullness of Time* (San Francisco: Harper, 1991), 165.
8. Weber, op. cit., 6.
9. Maier, op. cit., 165.
10. Weber, op. cit., 9.
11. E. Brandenburger, "Cross, Wood, Tree" in *The New International Dictionary of New Testament Theology*, vol. 1, 392.
12. Weber, *The Cross*, 6; Maier, *In the Fullness of Time*, 164.
13. Curtis C. Mitchell, *Praying Jesus' Way* (Old Tappan, N.J.: Revell, 1977), 65.
14. Michael Green's essay "The Meaning of Cross-Bearing" effectively challenges these misinterpretations of self-denial as well as several others.
15. Mark 8:36–37.
16. Napoleon Bonaparte, as cited in D. James Kennedy and Jerry Newcombe, *What If Jesus Had Never Been Born?* (Nashville: Thomas Nelson, 1994), 2–3.
17. William Lecky, as cited in Josh McDowell, *Evidence That Demands a Verdict* (Nashville: Thomas Nelson, 1979), vol. 1, 105.
18. Luke 23:39–43.
19. John 8:31–32, 36.
20. Mason, *The Mystery of Marriage*, 138.
21. Romans 2:10.
22. Ephesians 6:22–33; Titus 2:4–5; 1 Peter 3:1–7.

23. Hebrews 13:17.
24. John 16:11; Ephesians 2:1–2; 1 Peter 5:8–9; Jude 6; Revelation 12; 20:7–10.
25. Daniel 3.
26. Romans 1:3–4; 8:11; 1 Corinthians 6:14; 1 Timothy 3:16.

Chapter 6—Prayer: Connecting With God

1. God as our Groom (Ephesians 5:22–32; Revelation 19:7–9), Friend (Matthew 11:19; John 11:5; 15:13–15; James 2:23; Revelation 3:20), Father (Hosea 11:1–4; Matthew 12:50; Romans 8:14–17), Teacher (Matthew 7:24–29; John 13:13–14; 1 Corinthians 2:12–13), Master (Luke 5:1–11; 16:10–13), King (Psalm 103:19; Isaiah 44:6; John 18:37), High Priest (Hebrews 4:14–15; 7:23–8:6), Vindicator (Deuteronomy 32:36; Job 13:8; 42:7–9), Commander (Deuteronomy 5:32–33; John 12:49–50; 13:34), and Lover (Romans 5:6–10; 8:35–39; 1 John 4:7–19).
2. Psalm 139:1–4; Hebrews 4:13.
3. At the end of the disciples' prayer, most Bibles contain some variation of the words "For Yours is the kingdom and the power and the glory forever. Amen." (Matt. 6:13b NASB). But in those Bibles' marginal notes, they usually explain that this doxological ending is not in the earliest manuscript copies of Matthew, meaning that this ending was probably not part of the prayer that Jesus taught his disciples; hence the reason I've chosen to omit it from my discussion. See Colin Brown, "Prayer" in *The International Dictionary of New Testament Theology,* vol. 2, 869; D. A. Carson, "Matthew" in *The Expositor's Bible Commentary,* Frank E. Gaebelein, gen. ed. (Grand Rapids: Zondervan, 1978), vol. 8, 174.
4. Otfried Hofius, "Father" in *The New International Dictionary of New Testament Theology,* vol. 1, 614–15.
5. Romans 8:15.
6. Matthew 26:39, 42; Luke 23:34, 46; John 11:41; 17:1, 5, 11, 21, 24–25.
7. While *Yahweh* is first introduced as God's name in Exodus 3:14, it appears throughout Scripture. Translators routinely identify *Yahweh* for readers by stylizing it as "LORD" in almost all English renderings, while *Adonai* is stylized as "Lord."
8. See Willem Hendrik Grispen, *Exodus* in *Bible Student's Commentary,* Ed van der Maas, trans. (Grand Rapids: Zondervan, 1982), 55–56; Ronald Youngblood, "A New Occurrence of the Divine Name 'I AM'" in *Journal of the Evangelical Theological Society* 15:3 (Summer 1972): 144–52; Raymond Abba, "The Divine Name Yahweh" in *Journal of Biblical Literature* 80 (1961): 320–28; Charles R. Gianotti, "The Meaning of the Divine Name YHWH" in *Bibliotheca Sacra* (Jan.-Mar. 1985): 38–51; Étienne Gilson, *God and Philosophy* (New Haven: Yale University Press, 1941), chapter 2; Roland Kenneth Harrison, *Introduction to the Old Testament* (Grand Rapids: Eerdmans, 1969), 578–82; Joseph T. Lienhard, ed., *Exodus, Leviticus, Numbers, Deuteronomy* in *Ancient Christian Commentary on Scripture: Old Testament,* Thomas C. Oden, gen. ed. (Downers Grove, Ill.: InterVarsity, 2001), vol. 3, 19–23.
9. Exodus 12:12; Numbers 33:4. See John J. Davis, *Moses and the Gods of Egypt: Studies in Exodus* (Grand Rapids: Baker, 1986), 86–90.
10. George Eldon Ladd, *The Gospel of the Kingdom* (Grand Rapids: Eerdmans, 1990), reprint, 20.
11. Genesis 3; Isaiah 14:12–17; Ezekiel 28:11–19; Romans 5:12–14.
12. Ladd, op. cit., 110.
13. Matthew 12:22–28; John 11:25; Romans 6:20–23; 1 Corinthians 15:20–28; Colossians 1:21–22; 2:13–15; 2 Timothy 1:10; Hebrews 2:14–15.
14. Romans 6:15–22; Ephesians 5:18.
15. 1 Corinthians 15:24–25, 28.

16. Origen, as cited in *Matthew 1–13*, Manlio Simonetti, ed., *Ancient Christian Commentary on Scripture: New Testament*, vol. 1a, 133.
17. Matthew 10:1, 7–8; Luke 9:1–6.
18. Colossians 2:14; 1 John 1:9.
19. John 13:21–30.
20. Matthew 26:36–46; Mark 14:32–42; Luke 22:41–46.
21. Matthew 26:40–41, 43, 45, 56, 69–75; Mark 14:37–38, 40–41, 50–52, 66–72; Luke 22:45–46, 54–62.
22. Matthew 28; Mark 16; Luke 24; John 20–21; Acts.
23. John 20:19–23; 21:1–19; Acts 1:15–5:42; 10:1–12:17; 1 and 2 Peter.
24. Mark 1:35; 8:6; Luke 6:12; Matthew 14:23.
25. Luke 5:16.
26. 1 Kings 8:39; Psalm 139:4; Ezekiel 11:5; Matthew 6:8; Hebrews 4:13.
27. *The Oxford Book of Prayer,* George Appleton, gen. ed. (New York: Oxford University Press, 1985); Bob Benson and Michael W. Benson, *Disciplines for the Inner Life* (Nashville: Thomas Nelson, 1989), rev. ed.
28. I am indebted to James Bryan Smith's excellent work for the term "flash prayers." See *A Spiritual Formation Workbook: Small Group Resources for Nurturing Christian Growth* (San Francisco: Harper, 1993), 66.

Chapter 7—Guidance: Taking Our Lover's Hand

1. Mitchell, *Praying Jesus' Way,* 27–28.
2. Charles Hodge, *A Commentary on Romans* (London: The Banner of Truth Trust, 1864), rev. ed., 279.
3. Richard J. Foster, *Celebration of Discipline: The Path to Spiritual Growth* (San Francisco: Harper & Row, 1988), rev. ed., 33–34.
4. Foster, ibid., 42–43.
5. 1 Samuel 3:1–18.
6. Luke 4:1–13, 16–27; 6:1–5; 20:41–44; 24:25–27.
7. Matthew 5:17–18; John 10:35; 17:17; Hebrews 6:17–18.
8. Greek *anthrôpos,* "person."
9. Genesis 28:10–22.
10. Genesis 37–50.
11. Daniel 2.
12. Isaiah 6; Acts 10:1–11:18; 16:9–10.
13. Psalm 103:20; Daniel 10–12; Acts 7:53; Galatians 3:19; Hebrews 2:2.
14. Romans 1:18–2:16.
15. John of Damascus, *Orthodox Faith* 1.1, as quoted in Oden, ed., *Ancient Christian Commentary on Scripture: New Testament*, vol. 6, 40.
16. Patrick Glynn, *God: The Evidence* (Rocklin, Calif.: Prima, 1999), 22–23.
17. Kathleen Norris, *Dakota: A Spiritual Geography* (New York: Houghton-Mifflin, 1993), 202.
18. Romans 2:14–15.
19. See "Conscience" in *The New International Dictionary of New Testament Theology,* vol. 1, 348–53; Karl Rahner and Herbert Vorgrimler, "Conscience" in *Dictionary of Theology* (New York: Crossroad, 1981), 2nd ed., 89–90.
20. 1 Corinthians 8:7; Titus 1:15; Hebrews 10:22; 1 Timothy 4:2.
21. See Sanders, *In Pursuit of Maturity,* chapter 15.
22. Ignatius of Loyola, *Spiritual Exercises,* as quoted by Frank Rogers, Jr., "Discernment" in *Practicing Our Faith: A Way of Life for a Searching People,* Dorothy C. Bass, ed. (San Francisco: Jossey-Bass, 1997), 109.

23. For more on these issues and others, see my book *The New Absolutes* (Minneapolis: Bethany House, 1996).

24. 1 John 2:3–4, 22–23; 4:1–3, 19–21.

Chapter 8—Study: Depth Between Lovers

1. Foster, *Celebration of Discipline*, 63.
2. John 8:32.
3. Ephesians 5:11; 1 Timothy 4:1, 6; 1 Peter 5:8.
4. C. S. Lewis, *The Screwtape Letters* (New York: Macmillan, 1977), xiii-iv.
5. For an excellent introduction on the Bible (including its origin and inspiration), see Norman L. Geisler and William E. Nix, *A General Introduction to the Bible* (Chicago: Moody, 1986), rev. ed.
6. One of the finest introductions of this approach to Bible study is found in Howard G. Hendricks and William D. Hendricks, *Living by the Book* (Chicago: Moody, 1991).
7. Thomas J. Finley, "Dimensions of the Hebrew Word for 'Create'" in *Bibliotheca Sacra* (Oct.-Dec. 1991): 409–23, in which he says, "Several elements are common to the use of [*bārā*] in these passages. Most important, the performances [that is, God's activities] themselves are new or unprecedented. They are designed to convince the audience that God is the Performer. No human could ever do them" (422).
8. For more on the meaning of and relationship between *image* and *likeness*, see G. Charles Aalders, *Genesis*, 2 vols., William Heynen, trans., *Bible Student's Commentary* series (Grand Rapids: Zondervan, 1981), vol. 1, 71; Lawrence O. Richards, *Expository Dictionary of Bible Words* (Grand Rapids: Zondervan, 1985), 350–51; and Victor P. Hamilton, "*demut*" in *Theological Wordbook of the Old Testament*, R. Laird Harris et al., eds. (Chicago: Moody, 1980), vol. 1, 192.
9. Luke 24:45–49; John 20:19–31; Acts 2:22–36; 17:31–32; 1 Corinthians 15:1–28.
10. For some of the evidence that confirms this conclusion, see P. J. Wiseman, *Clues to Creation in Genesis*, Donald J. Wiseman, ed. (London: Marshall, Morgan & Scott, 1977).
11. Any good Bible commentary or lexicon explains this. For example, see Blocher, *In the Beginning*, 85, and Aalders, *Genesis*, vol. 1, 70–71.
12. For excellent treatments of human nature, including soul/body unity and image-bearing status, see J. P. Moreland and David M. Ciocchi, eds., *Christian Perspectives on Being Human* (Grand Rapids: Baker, 1993); Gundry, *Sōma in Biblical Theology*; and Ronald B. Allen, *The Majesty of Man: The Dignity of Being Human* (Sisters, Ore.: Multnomah, 1984).
13. The following list of questions was inspired by a similar list given in Hendricks and Hendricks, *Living by the Book*, 305–07.
14. Matthew 25:34–40; James 1:27; 2:15–16.
15. Romans 1:21–32.
16. Philippians 4:6–7; 1 Thessalonians 5:18; 1 Timothy 4:1–5.
17. Augustine, *Letter* 137, 3, as quoted in *Augustine Day by Day*, John E. Rotelle, ed. (New York: Catholic Book Pub., 1986), 18.

Chapter 9—Meditation and Journaling: Lingering in His Presence

1. Oswald Chambers, *The Moral Foundations of Life*, as quoted in *Oswald Chambers: The Best From All His Books, Volume II*, Harry Verploegh, ed. (Nashville: Oliver-Nelson, 1989), 193.
2. J. I. Packer, *Knowing God* (Downers Grove, Ill.: InterVarsity, 1973), 18–19.
3. John W. Wenham, *Christ and the Bible* (Downers Grove, Ill.: InterVarsity, 1973), 29.
4. Ibid., 18.
5. Luke 24:44–49; John 19:30.
6. Foster, *Celebration of Discipline*, 20.
7. 4:8–9, emphasis added, in Williams, *The New Testament in the Language of the People*.

8. Henri J. M. Nouwen, *¡Gracias!: A Latin American Journal* (San Francisco: Harper & Row, 1983), 16, 18, 58.
9. Ibid., xiii.
10. Gordon MacDonald, *Ordering Your Private World* (Chicago: Moody, 1984), 146.
11. Philip Schaff, as quoted in McDowell, *Evidence That Demands a Verdict*, vol. 1, 132.
12. Robert H. Stein, "An Early Recension of the Gospel Traditions?" in *Journal of the Evangelical Theological Society* (June 1987): 178–79. See also Donald Guthrie, *New Testament Introduction* (Downers Grove, Ill.: InterVarsity, 1970), rev. ed., 224–25.
13. Stein, ibid., 183.
14. Elizabeth O'Connor, *Letters to Scattered Pilgrims*, as quoted by Benson and Benson, *Disciplines for the Inner Life*, 133.
15. I believe, with the historic orthodox church, that the canon of Scripture is closed and that we have, in the sixty-six books of the Bible, all the writings God inspired and intended all his people to have, study, and apply (see Geisler and Nix, *A General Introduction to the Bible*, Part Two). Hence, what God tells you or me is private revelation meant for you or me, not public revelation meant for the rest of the church. Moreover, his private revelation will *never* contradict or oppose in any way his inspired written, public revelation; if it ever does, then it is not from him.
16. Source unnamed, as quoted by Ronald Klug, *How to Keep a Spiritual Journal* (Nashville: Thomas Nelson, 1982), 88. I altered the line breaks; all else is verbatim.
17. Madeleine L'Engle, *Walking on Water: Reflections on Faith and Art* (Wheaton, Ill.: Harold Shaw, 1980), 137.
18. Luke 6:27–36; Romans 12:18.
19. Romans 12:3, 16; 2 Corinthians 13:5; Galatians 6:3–4.
20. Romans 8:18–23; 2 Corinthians 4:16–18.
21. See Deuteronomy 8:11–20; 1 Chronicles 16:12–13; John 15:20–21; Ephesians 2:11–13.
22. See Matthew 28:19 and Romans 6:3–4 on baptism; Matthew 26:26–28 and 1 Corinthians 11:23–26 on the Lord's Supper.
23. MacDonald, *Ordering Your Private World*, 141–42.
24. Susan Annette Muto, *Pathways of Spiritual Living*, as quoted by Benson and Benson, *Disciplines for the Inner Life*, 132.
25. George Appleton, in *The Oxford Book of Prayer*, 8.18. I modified the prayer slightly by replacing the words *thee* and *thy* with *you* and *your*, respectively.
26. Bruce Demarest, *Satisfy Your Soul: Restoring the Heart of Christian Spirituality* (Colorado Springs: NavPress, 1999), 181.

Chapter 10—Solitude and Silence: Alone in God's Arms
1. This definition is based on one provided by Donald S. Whitney in *Spiritual Disciplines for the Christian Life* (Colorado Springs: NavPress, 1991), 176.
2. Matthew 4:1–11; Luke 4:1–13.
3. Pico Iyer, "The Eloquent Sounds of Silence" in *Time* (Jan. 25, 1993): 74.
4. 1 Kings 19:8–18.
5. Brennan Manning, *Abba's Child: The Cry of the Heart for Intimate Belonging* (Colorado Springs: NavPress, 1994), 55–56.
6. Iyer, "The Eloquent Sounds of Silence," 74.
7. Genesis 1; John 1:1–3; Colossians 1:16–17; Hebrews 1:3; 11:3.
8. Whitney, *Spiritual Disciplines for the Christian Life*, 189–90.
9. Thomas Merton, as cited in Norris, *Dakota*, 15.

Chapter 11—Confession and Forgiveness: Love's Healing Power
1. Genesis 3:15.
2. Genesis 3:21.

3. Hebrews 11.
4. See Romans 5; 1 Corinthians 15.
5. 2 Corinthians 5:21; Colossians 2:13–14; Hebrews 10:10–18; 1 Peter 2:24–25.
6. Robert L. Saucy states, "Scripture teaches that death occurs when something is *separated* from that which is its life" (Saucy, "Theology of Human Nature" in *Christian Perspectives on Being Human*, 46, emphasis added). See also the entries under the heading "Death, Kill, Sleep" in *The New International Dictionary of New Testament Theology*, vol. 1, 429–47.
7. Matthew 19:3–9; 1 Corinthians 7:8–40. See also Norman L. Geisler, *Christian Ethics* (Grand Rapids: Baker, 1989), chapter 15.
8. Psalm 104:29; Ecclesiastes 12:5–7. Citing Saucy again (op. cit., 39): "Scripture indicates that the being of man can be and is separated. This separation is seen particularly at the point of physical death which entered human existence as a result of sin (cf. Rom. 5:12). The separation of the person at death into the two original elements [of body and soul] is clearly explained by the writer of Ecclesiastes when he says, 'then the dust will return to the earth as it was, and the spirit will return to God who gave it'" (12:7 NASB).
9. Psalm 41:9; 55:12–14.
10. Peter Kreeft, *Making Sense Out of Suffering* (Ann Arbor, Mich.: Servant, 1986), 116. See also Augustine, *The Enchiridion on Faith, Hope, and Love*, J. F. Shaw, trans. (Chicago: Regnery Gateway, 1961), sec. 11–15, 26.
11. John 10:10; 1 Corinthians 15; 2 Corinthians 5:17–20; Colossians 3:9–11.
12. For an excellent discussion of the New Testament gospel, see N. T. Wright, *What Saint Paul Really Said* (Grand Rapids: Eerdmans, 1997), in which he demonstrates that for Paul, "the gospel" is not . . . a message about "how one gets saved," in an individual and a historical sense. . . . The gospel is not . . . a set of techniques for making people Christians. Nor is it a set of systematic theological reflections. . . . The gospel is the announcement that Jesus is Lord—Lord of the world, Lord of the cosmos, Lord of the earth (60, 153).
13. Dieter Fürst, "Confess" in *The New International Dictionary of New Testament Theology*, vol. 1, 347.
14. Kreeft, *Love Is Stronger Than Death*, 14.
15. 1 John 3:4–20; Galatians 5:6; James 2:14–26.
16. Luke 15:11–32. See Kenneth E. Bailey, *Poet and Peasant* (Grand Rapids: Eerdmans, 1976, combined edition of *Poet and Peasant* and *Through Peasant Eyes*), 158–206; Walter L. Liefeld, "Luke" in *The Expositor's Bible Commentary*, vol. 8, 983–85; and I. Howard Marshall, *Commentary on Luke*, New International Greek Testament Commentary series (Grand Rapids: Eerdmans, 1978), 604–13.
17. Henri Nouwen, *The Return of the Prodigal Son* (New York: Doubleday, 1992), 36.
18. Nouwen, ibid., 49.
19. Nouwen, ibid., 71.
20. Nouwen, ibid., 125.
21. Chuck Swindoll, "Where Is God in All of This?" in *Insights* (Winter '86), 16–18.
22. Colossians 2:13–14.
23. Paul's epistle to the Romans presents this comprehensive understanding of salvation. Salvation does not begin and end when we initially trust in Christ; its fullness includes every believer's *justification* (Rom. 1–4), *sanctification* (5–8, 12–15), and *glorification* (8:18–39), as well as the rest of creation's liberation "from its bondage to decay" (8:21).
24. 1 Corinthians 15:50–57.
25. Cornelius Plantinga, Jr., "Rehearsing Forgiveness" in *Christianity Today* (April 29, 1996), 32.
26. In fact, since God's all-embracing knowledge is timeless, if he literally forgot something,

his memory loss regarding it would have to be timeless as well. In other words, he would always not know some truth. But if he never knew a truth, then he could never forget it either. The notion that God can literally forget something he once knew to be true leads to the absurd notion that he could not have ever known what he supposedly once forever knew.

27. Numbers 14:19–38; 2 Samuel 12:1–23.

28. Matthew 5:21–22, 27–28.

29. Matthew 5:29–30.

30. Charles R. Swindoll, *Improving Your Serve: The Art of Unselfish Living* (Waco: Word, 1981), 60–62.

31. Lewis B. Smedes, *Forgive and Forget: Healing the Hurts We Don't Deserve* (San Francisco: Harper & Row, 1984), 2.

32. Ibid.

33. Ibid., 132–33.

34. Ibid., 133.

35. Allen C. Guelzo, "Fear of Forgiving" in *Christianity Today* (Feb. 8, 1993), 42–43.

36. Smedes, op. cit., 29.

37. As cited by Johann Christoph Arnold in *Why Forgive?* (Farmington, Pa.: Plough, 2000), 1.

38. Guelzo, "Fear of Forgiving," 45.

39. Concerning the final and already determined destiny of fallen angels, see Matthew 8:29; 25:41; Jude 6; Revelation 20:10. On the theological and philosophical conclusion that fallen angels are unable to repent and be saved, see Jacques Maritain, *The Sin of the Angel* (Westminster, Md.: Newman, 1959); Dickason, *Angels, Elect, and Evil*, 39–42; Thomas Aquinas, *Summa Theologica*, I.64.2.

40. Some resources that may help: Walter Trobisch, *Love Yourself* (Downers Grove, Ill.: InterVarsity, 1978); Earl D. Wilson, *The Discovered Self: The Search for Self-Acceptance* (Downers Grove, Ill.: InterVarsity, 1985); and two books by Dr. Paul Brand and Philip Yancey, *Fearfully and Wonderfully Made* and *In His Image* (Grand Rapids: Zondervan, 1980 and 1984 respectively).

41. C. S. Lewis, *Letters of C. S. Lewis*, as cited in *The Quotable Lewis*, Wayne Martindale and Jerry Root, eds. (Wheaton, Ill.: Tyndale, 1989), 221, n499.

42. Luke 6:27–28.

Chapter 12—Service and Sacrifice: For Love of Neighbor

1. William Temple, *Christianity and Social Order*, as cited in *Devotional Classics: Selected Readings for Individuals and Groups*, Richard J. Foster and James Bryan Smith, eds. (New York: HarperCollins, 1993), 253.

2. Kreeft, *The God Who Loves You*, 95.

3. Matthew 7:9–11.

4. Philippians 2:6–8 in Williams, *The New Testament in the Language of the People*.

5. John 17:1–5.

6. Recorded in Luke 10:30–37.

7. Many of the following insights (especially background material) come from three sources: Bailey, *Through Peasant Eyes*; Liefeld, "Luke" in *The Expositor's Bible Commentary*, vol. 8; and Marshall, *Commentary on Luke*. I am particularly indebted to Bailey's work.

8. Liefeld, ibid., 943.

9. Bailey, op. cit., 46.

10. Numbers 19:11–22.

11. Mishna *Shebiith* 8:10, as quoted in Bailey, op. cit., 48.

12. W. O. E. Oesterley, *The Gospel Parables in the Light of Their Jewish Background,* as quoted in Bailey, ibid., 48.
13. Matthew 18:23–35.
14. Bailey, op. cit., 52–53.
15. 1 John 4:16–17.
16. You can help this to happen, but you cannot make it happen. Service does not *guarantee* positive results.
17. Charles C. Ryrie, *The Holy Spirit* (Chicago: Moody, 1965), 83.
18. Some resources you may want to consult on spiritual gifts: Don and Katie Fortune, *Discover Your God-Given Gifts* (Grand Rapids: Revell, 1987); C. Peter Wagner, *Your Spiritual Gifts Can Help Your Church Grow* (Ventura, Calif.: Regal, 1997); D. Martyn Lloyd-Jones, *The Sovereign Spirit: Discerning His Gifts* (Wheaton, Ill.: Harold Shaw, 1986); Kenneth O. Gangel, *Unwrap Your Spiritual Gifts* (Wheaton, Ill.: Victor, 1983).
19. Whitney, *Spiritual Disciplines for the Christian Life,* 122.
20. 1 Timothy 5:18.
21. Ignatius of Loyola, "Dedication" in *The Living Testament: The Essential Writings of Christianity Since the Bible,* M. Basil Pennington, Alan Jones, and Mark Booth, eds. (San Francisco: Harper & Row, 1985), 224.

Chapter 13—Evangelism and Apologetics: For Love of Truth

1. Ephesians 4:11.
2. Just as all believers must have *faith,* even though not all believers have the spiritual *gift* of faith.
3. The noun *apología* appears eight times in the New Testament:

    [*Apología*] was often used of the argument for the defense in a court of law, and though [*apología*] has the idea of a judicial interrogation in which one is called to answer for the manner in which he has exercised his responsibility . . . [*apología*] can also mean an informal explanation or defense of one's position (see 1 Cor. 9:3; 2 Cor. 7:11), and [*apología*] would aptly describe giving an answer to the skeptical, abusive, or derisive inquiries of ill-disposed neighbors (Fritz Rienecker *A Linguistic Key to the Greek New Testament,* Cleon L. Rogers, Jr., ed. [Grand Rapids: Zondervan, 1980], 758).

4. NASB.
5. For support of these statements, see my book *The New Absolutes,* especially chapters 1–4.
6. See Richard Abanes, *End-Time Visions: The Road to Armageddon?* (Nashville: Broadman & Holman, 1998).
7. Keith A. Fournier, with William D. Watkins, *A House United? Evangelicals and Catholics Together* (Colorado Springs: NavPress, 1994), 160. See also Acts 2.
8. Ibid., 172–73.
9. Philip Yancey, as cited in Philip Jenkins, *The Next Christendom: The Coming of Global Christianity* (New York: Oxford University Press, 2002), 15.
10. Cf. Genesis 3:8; Matthew 1:23; John 1:14; 1 John 1:1–3.
11. See "Witness, Testimony" in *The New International Dictionary of New Testament Theology,* vol. 3, 1038–51.
12. John 1:14; Romans 3:4; Titus 1:2; Hebrews 6:18.
13. Mark 1:9–11.
14. J. Carl Laney, *John,* Moody Gospel Commentary, Paul Enns, gen. ed. (Chicago: Moody, 1992), 159. See John 8:17; cf. Deuteronomy 17:6; 19:15.
15. See also Acts 9:1–30; 22:1–21; 26:4–29.
16. Commenting on this passage in Matthew, biblical scholar D. A. Carson writes, "The 'you'

["Who do *you* say that I am?"] is emphatic and plural (v. 15). Therefore, at least in part, Peter serves as spokesman for the Twelve (as he often does: cf. 15:15–16; 19:25–28; 26:40; Mark 11:20–22; Luke 12:41; John 6:67–70; cf. Acts 2:37–38; 5:29)." (Carson, "Matthew" in *The Expositor's Bible Commentary,* vol. 8, 365).

17. Matthew 28:18–20; Mark 16:15–18; Luke 24:45–49; John 20:21–23; Acts 1:8.
18. In the Greek text of Matthew 28:19–20, "going . . . baptizing . . . teaching" are all participles, and the mood of the controlling verb, *make* disciples, is imperative. In other words, the force of the passage is that we *must* make disciples through these actions. See Carson, op. cit., 595.
19. Luke 24:48–49; John 14:26; 16:8–15; Acts 1:8.
20. Luke 5:17–26.
21. Matthew 22:23–34.
22. For instance, see Matthew 5:20–7:29; 9:9–13; 12:1–14.
23. Acts 2:22–36; 3:11–26.
24. Acts 17:4, 32–34.
25. For guidance on these issues, see Richard M. Weaver, *Ideas Have Consequences* (Chicago: University of Chicago Press, 1948); E. Michael Jones, *Degenerate Moderns: Modernity as Rationalized Misbehavior* (San Francisco: Ignatius, 1993); Stanley J. Grenz, *A Primer on Postmodernism* (Grand Rapids: Eerdmans, 1996); David S. Dockery, ed., *The Challenge of Postmodernism: An Evangelical Engagement* (Wheaton, Ill.: Victor, 1995); Francis J. Beckwith and Gregory Koukl, *Relativism: Feet Firmly Planted in Mid-Air* (Grand Rapids: Baker, 1998).
26. See Norman L. Geisler and J. Kerby Anderson, *Origin Science: A Proposal for the Creation-Evolution Controversy* (Grand Rapids: Baker, 1987); Michael Denton, *Evolution: A Theory in Crisis* (Chevy Chase, Md.: Adler & Adler, 1985); Michael J. Behe, *Darwin's Black Box: The Biochemical Challenge to Evolution* (New York: The Free Press, 1996); Phillip E. Johnson, *Darwin on Trial* (Downers Grove, Ill.: InterVarsity, 1993, 2nd ed.); J. P. Moreland, ed., *The Creation Hypothesis: Scientific Evidence for an Intelligent Designer* (Downers Grove, Ill.: InterVarsity, 1994); Dembski, ed., *Mere Creation.*
27. For explanations and critiques of these worldviews, see the book I coauthored with Norman L. Geisler, *Worlds Apart: A Handbook on World Views,* 2nd ed. (Eugene, Ore.: Wipf and Stock, 1989).
28. Along with the resources mentioned that challenge naturalism, the following demonstrate the continual fall of atheism: J. P. Moreland and Kai Nielsen, *Does God Exist? The Great Debate* (Nashville: Thomas Nelson, 1990); Paul C. Vitz, *Faith of the Fatherless: The Psychology of Atheism* (Dallas: Spence, 1999); Ralph McInerny, *Characters in Search of Their Author* (Notre Dame: University of Notre Dame Press, 2001); Glynn, *God;* David Ehrenfeld, *The Arrogance of Humanism* (New York: Oxford University, 1981); Geisler, *Is Man the Measure? An Evaluation of Contemporary Humanism* (Grand Rapids: Baker, 1983); and Robert Jastrow, *God and the Astronomers* (New York: W. W. Norton, 1978).
29. See Norman L. Geisler and Abdul Saleeb, *Answering Islam* (Grand Rapids: Baker, 1993); Francis J. Beckwith, et al., *The Counterfeit Gospel of Mormonism* (Eugene, Ore.: Harvest House, 1998).
30. 2 Timothy 2:2; 1 Timothy 4:6, 11, 13, 15–16.
31. See Ronald H. Nash, "The Notion of Mediator in Alexandrian Judaism and the Epistle to the Hebrews" in *Westminster Theological Journal* 40:1 (Fall 1977), 89–115.
32. I eventually did find answers to the logical issues Dr. Kessler raised. I put some of them into an essay I coauthored with Norman L. Geisler entitled "The Incarnation and Logic: Their Compatibility Defended" in *Trinity Journal* 6 (Autumn 1985), 185–97.